P9-BZD-295

The ADD/ADHD Checklist

SANDRA RIEF, M.A.

PRENTICE HALL
Paramus, New Jersey 07652

Library of Congress Cataloging-in-Publication Data

Rief, Sandra F.
   The ADD/ADHD checklist : an easy reference for parents & teachers
/ Sandra Rief.
      p. cm.
   ISBN 0-13-762395-X
   1. Attention-deficit-disordered children—Popular works.
2. Attention-deficit-disordered children—Education. 3. Attention-
deficit-disordered children—Behavior modification. I. Title.
RJ506.H9R54 1997   97-37991
618.92'8589—dc21   CIP

All rights reserved.

Printed in the United States of America

10 9 8 7 6 5 4 3 2 1

ISBN 0-13-762395-X

ATTENTION: CORPORATIONS AND SCHOOLS

Prentice Hall books are available at quantity discounts with bulk purchase for educational, business, or sales promotional use. For information, please write to: Prentice Hall, 240 Frisch Court, Paramus, NJ 07652. Please supply: title of book, ISBN, quantity, how the book will be used, and date needed.

PRENTICE HALL
Paramus, NJ 07652

A Simon & Schuster Company

On the World Wide Web at http://www.phdirect.com

Prentice Hall International (UK) Limited, *London*
Prentice Hall of Australia Pty. Limited, *Sydney*
Prentice Hall Canada Inc., *Toronto*
Prentice Hall Hispanoamericana, S.A., *Mexico*
Prentice Hall of India Private Limited, *New Delhi*
Prentice Hall of Japan, Inc., *Tokyo*
Simon & Schuster Asia Pte. Ltd., *Singapore*
Editora Prentice Hall do Brasil, Ltda., *Rio de Janeiro*

Dedication

This book is dedicated in loving memory of Benjamin—my precious son and inspiration.

Acknowledgments

My deepest thanks and appreciation to:

... all of the wonderful, dedicated educators I have had the honor of teaching with, sharing, and learning from over the past several years (especially my buddies at Benchley-Weinberger Elementary).

... my students (past, present, and future) whom it is my privilege and joy to teach. Some of my greatest pleasure comes from following "my kids" over the years and celebrating their successes and accomplishments!

... Itzik, Gil, Jackie, Ariel, Mom, all of my loving family and dear friends for their love, support, and encouragement.

... the special families who have shared with me their struggles and triumphs, and allowed me to be part of their lives.

... Sandra Wright, for her guidance and mentorship, and all she does for children.

... Susan Kolwicz, my editor, and Win Huppuch, my publisher, at Prentice Hall, for asking me to write this book and for being such a pleasure to work with.

About the Author

Sandra F. Rief, M.A., is the author of the best-selling book *How to Reach & Teach ADD/ADHD Children* (The Center, 1993), *Simply Phonics* (EBSCO Curriculum Materials, 1993), and co-author with Julie Heimburge of *How to Reach & Teach All Students in the Inclusive Classroom* (The Center, 1996). She is an award-winning teacher (1995 California Resource Specialist of the Year), and currently a special education teacher in the San Diego Unified School District. Sandra consults and speaks nationally and internationally on the topic of effective instruction, strategies, and school interventions for meeting the needs of students with learning and attention difficulties. She also developed and presented the videos *ADHD: Inclusive Instruction & Collaborative Practices* (National Professional Resources, 1995) and *How to Help Your Child Succeed in School* (Educational Resource Specialists, 1997).

Introduction

There are at least two million children and adolescents with attention deficit disorders in the United States. Every classroom teacher has at least one student with ADD/ADHD in his or her classroom, and needs to be aware and knowledgeable about the nature of the disorder, as well as the strategies effective in reaching and teaching these students.

Parents of children with ADD/ADHD also need to be well-informed and equipped with the skills and strategies that help in managing and coping with inattentive, hyperactive, and impulsive behaviors. It is often not easy to live with a child who has ADHD (either at home or school). Knowledge about the disorder is very important, because when we understand what ADHD is, and how it affects the child, it helps us become more tolerant and empathetic.

The purpose of this book is to help readers gain insight and better understanding of children and teenagers with ADD/ADHD, as well as the kind of support and intervention that is necessary for their success. This book is designed in a simple, concise, easy-to-read format of checklists that address a number of topics. There are sections with lists that provide basic information about ADD/ADHD, academic strategies for home and school, and other topics of importance for both parents and educators. One section of the book is written specifically for parents, because it addresses topics of interest that are relevant to meeting their child's needs at home. Another section is specifically for teachers—including checklists on topics that are of particular concern in the classroom. Suggested strategies in this section will help *all* students learn (not just those with attention deficit disorders). Although this book is primarily written for parents and teachers, many others interested in children with ADD/ADHD should find the information useful (i.e., physicians, mental health professionals, other school personnel, relatives).

I have had the privilege of teaching hundreds of children with attention deficit disorders and/or learning disabilities over the past 23 years. Some of my former students who had very significant to severe problems in elementary school are now doing extremely well—going to college and succeeding in their lives, in spite of the many challenges they and their families had to deal with over the years. In my teaching career I don't recall having ever met parents who don't want the best for their child, or who aren't interested in doing what they can to help their son or daughter.

It is always preferable to be able to identify children with ADD/ADHD or any special needs *early*—initiating interventions and supports at a young age in order to avoid some of the frustration, failure, and subsequent loss of self-esteem. However, it is NEVER too late to help a child. In many cases, the kind of help that makes a difference for a child does not take a huge effort on our part. Sometimes even small changes in the way we respond to our child/teen can lead to significant improvements. If I am able to convey any message throughout this book, I wish for it to be one of *hope and optimism.* When we work together—providing the necessary structure, guidance, encouragement, and support—each and every one of our children can succeed!

Sandra Rief

Contents

Section 1 **Checklists for Basic Information on ADD/ADHD** 1

Introduction   *1*

1. What Do We Mean by ADD/ADHD?   *3*

2. Definitions and Descriptions of ADHD   *4*

3. What We Do and Don't Know About ADHD   *5*

4. Characteristics of the Predominantly Hyperactive/Impulsive Type of ADHD   *9*

5. Characteristics of the Predominantly Inattentive Type of ADHD   *12*

6. Probable Causes of ADHD   *14*

7. ADHD "Look Alikes"   *16*

8. Critical Elements for School Success   *18*

9. Statistics to Consider Regarding Children/Adolescents with ADHD   *19*

10. Positive Traits Often Associated with ADHD   *21*

11. Making the Diagnosis: What Is a Comprehensive Evaluation for ADHD?   *22*

12. What Parents Should Expect from the School in the Diagnostic Process   *26*

13. A Comprehensive Treatment Program for ADHD   *28*

14. Questionnaires and Rating Scales for
Parents and Teachers   *30*

15. What Does It Take to Be an Effective School?   *32*

16. Most Commonly Prescribed Medications
in the Treatment of ADD/ADHD   *37*

17. If a Child/Teen Is Taking Medication   *40*

18. What Supports Do Teachers Need?   *44*

19. What Supports Do Parents Need?   *47*

Section 2 Checklists for Parents................50

Introduction   *50*

20. What Children and Teens with ADHD
Need at Home   *52*

21. Effective Behavioral Strategies for Parents   *54*

22. Preventing Behavior Problems in the Home   *57*

23. Preventing Behavioral Problems Outside
of the Home   *60*

24. Dealing with Hyperactive/Impulsive
Behavior at Home   *62*

25. Positive Incentives and Reinforcers
for Home   *65*

26. What Parents Can Do to Help Their
Children Get Organized   *68*

27. Homework Tips for Parents   *74*

28. Giving Directions—Tips for Parents   *79*

29. Environmental Modifications that
Make a Difference at Home   *81*

30. Pursuing an Evaluation for Your Child   *84*

31. Advocating for Your Child: Positive
Strategies for Parents   *86*

Section 3 Checklists for Teachers................90

Introduction   *90*

32. What Do Students with ADHD Need?   *92*

33. Effective Behavioral Strategies for Teachers   *94*

34. Preventing Behavioral Problems in the Classroom   *100*

35. Preventing Behavior Problems During Those "Challenging Times" of the School Day   *104*

36. Dealing with Hyperactive/Impulsive Behaviors at School   *107*

37. Positive Incentives and Reinforcers for School   *112*

38. What Teachers Can Do to Help Build Organizational and Study Skills   *115*

39. Homework Tips for Teachers   *120*

40. Getting Students' Attention   *123*

41. Focusing Students' Attention   *124*

42. Maintaining Students' Attention and Involvement   *126*

43. Keeping Students On-Task During Seat Work   *128*

44. Tips for Giving Directions in the Classroom   *129*

45. Helping Your Inattentive, Distractible Students   *131*

46. Environmental Modifications that Make a Difference in the Classroom   *134*

47. If You Suspect Your Student Has ADHD   *137*

48. Typical Teacher Referral Forms   *140*

49. A List of Don'ts for Teachers   *143*

50. Assessment/Testing: Modifications and Adaptations   *145*

51. Lesson Presentation: Strategies and Modifications   *149*

52. Adaptations/Modifications of Materials   *153*

Section 4 **Academic Strategies for Home and School**.......................158

Introduction   *158*

53. Common Reading Difficulties of Children/Teens with ADHD   *159*

54. Reading Strategies and Interventions for Home and School   *162*

55. Why Is Writing Such a Struggle?   *171*

56. Strategies to Help with Pre-writing   *173*

57. Multisensory Spelling Activities and Choices   *176*

58. Help with Editing Strategies and Other Tips   *180*

59. How to Help with Handwriting, Written Organization, and Legibility   *182*

60. Strategies for Bypassing Writing Difficulties   *185*

61. Math Difficulties and Interventions   *187*

Section 5 **Other Important Checklists for Parents and Teachers** 192

Introduction   *192*

62. The Necessity of a Team Approach   *194*

63. Accommodations for Memory Difficulties   *197*

64. Strategies for Aiding Memory Skills   *199*

65. Building Self-Esteem   *201*

66. Preschool/Kindergarten Issues and Strategies   *204*

67. Adolescent Issues and Strategies   *210*

68. Relaxation, Guided Imagery, and Visualization Techniques   *214*

69. Social-Skills Issues and Strategies   *218*

70. The Student Study Team (SST) Process *222*

71. What Is an IEP? *226*

72. What Is 504? *232*

73. Student Learning Style/Interest Interview *236*

74. Recommended Resources and Organizations *240*

✔ Checklists for Basic Information on ADD/ADHD

In the following 19 checklists readers are provided with the most current information regarding our understanding of ADD/ADHD at this time. Some of the lists will clarify what the "label" or diagnosis of ADD or ADHD actually means, with concise descriptions and definitions of the disorder.

There has been a tremendous amount of research in the field, and, consequently, a lot is now known about attention deficit disorders. There are also misconceptions, unsubstantiated claims, and much that is still unknown about ADHD. Some of the findings regarding probable causes, statistics, and other important information are shared in this section.

There are different types of attention deficit disorders, as well. Not everyone with ADHD is hyperactive. The characteristics of the predominantly inattentive type of ADHD, and the predominantly hyperactive/impulsive type of ADHD, are two of the checklists that follow.

The diagnosis of ADHD is very complex. To accurately diagnose the disorder requires a comprehensive evaluation. If someone displays the characteristics of hyperactivity, impulsivity or inattention, it could be for many reasons besides ADD/ADHD. There are a number of "look alikes" which must be considered and ruled out in the diagnostic process. Any evaluation for ADHD requires a considerable amount of input from the school, which is also described in this section.

Treatment for ADD/ADHD comes in many forms. There are a number of components to effective treatment and management of the disorder. Medication is only one of the interventions that has been found to be effective. This section includes checklists with information regarding what parents and school personnel should be aware of regarding medication and management, and what comprises a multimodal treatment plan for children and adolescents with ADHD.

1

The remaining checklists in this section include the factors and elements that are critical to the success of students with attention deficit disorders. There is so much that schools can do to enable these children and adolescents to achieve success. We will examine what it takes to be an effective school—one that reaches and teaches all of its students—including those with ADHD and other special needs. Individuals with ADD/ADHD have so much potential. They typically possess many strengths. One very important checklist (#10) focuses on the fact that there are many positive attributes associated with having ADHD. The last two lists in this section specify what supports both teachers and parents need in order to do our best in educating and parenting our children.

1. WHAT DO WE MEAN BY ADD/ADHD?

◆ ADD stands for **Attention Deficit Disorder.** It is the term that has been used for a number of years, and one that many people have heard of and associated with children/teens who have significant problems in the areas of attention, hyperactivity, and impulsivity.

◆ ADHD stands for **Attention Deficit Hyperactivity Disorder.** ADHD is now the official term that is being used to describe this disorder. In current books and articles you may see it written as *ADHD* or as *AD/HD*. It still means "Attention Deficit Hyperactivity Disorder" and includes all subtypes of the disorder: The **Predominantly Inattentive type** of ADHD (what I prefer to still call ADD), the **Predominantly Hyperactive and Impulsive type,** and the **Combined type.**

◆ For many the term ADD didn't quite fit the picture. The child's main difficulty wasn't the lack of attention, but the behaviors associated with hyperactivity and impulsivity. Now the term ADHD is misleading and confusing to some. There are children with ADD who *are not* hyperactive or impulsive. Realize that the newer term of ADHD (which could easily change again in a few years) includes the non-hyperactive/non-impulsive type under its umbrella name.

◆ The child with the *predominantly hyperactive and impulsive type* of ADHD has a much greater chance of being identified early and receiving a diagnosis and intervention, because the behaviors are often very disruptive and noticeable. These children get our attention! There has been much more research over the years about this type of ADHD; consequently, we know more about the most effective treatments for hyperactive/impulsive children and teens. *(See Checklist 4 on Characteristics of the Predominantly Hyperactive/Impulsive Type of ADHD.)*

◆ A child/teen with the *predominantly inattentive type* of ADHD (or ADD without hyperactivity/impulsivity) does not easily get our attention. The behaviors are not disruptive, so they can be overlooked or misinterpreted/misdiagnosed. Yet having this disorder can be very problematic for the child, resulting in significant academic issues and underachievement. *(See Checklist 5 on Characteristics of the Predominantly Inattentive Type of ADHD.)*

◆ For simplicity, and in my attempt to use the most current diagnostic label, I will usually be using the term ADHD (not ADD/ADHD). The term ADHD is meant inclusively—referring to all types of the disorder.

2. DEFINITIONS AND DESCRIPTIONS OF ADHD

The following are some descriptions of Attention Deficit Hyperactivity Disorder (ADHD) as defined by some of the leading experts and researchers in the field. As ADHD continues to be studied intensively, with more and more information learned each year, these descriptions are likely to be refined in the future.

♦ ADHD is a developmental disorder characterized by inappropriate degrees of inattention, overactivity, and impulsivity.

♦ ADHD is a neurological inefficiency in the area of the brain that controls impulses, aids in screening sensory input, and focuses attention.

♦ ADHD is a neurological disorder characterized by problems with sustaining attention and mental effort, excessive activity level, and inhibiting impulses.

♦ ADHD is a performance disorder—a problem of being able to produce or act upon what one knows.

♦ ADHD is a production disorder. It is not a problem of learning per se. A person with ADHD may know the information/material well; but it is a problem of being able to perform or output that information (especially written output), and do so with any consistency. These children are often described as "consistently inconsistent"—as some days they can perform a task well, and other days not at all.

♦ ADHD is a physiological disorder causing difficulty with inhibiting one's behavior and impulses, self-control, and goal-directed behavior.

♦ ADHD is a neurobiological disorder causing a high degree of variability and inconsistency in performance and output.

♦ ADHD is a developmental disorder resulting from underactivity in the attention/inhibitory center of the brain—the characteristics of which arise in early childhood and are relatively chronic in nature.

♦ With ADHD the attention center of the brain is not working well, which leads to problems in performance and production.

♦ ADHD is a disorder causing excessive activity level, excessive distractibility, and excessive responsiveness and emotional reactions.

3. What We Do and Don't Know About ADHD

We know the following:

♦ Approximately 2 million children in the United States have been diagnosed with ADHD.

♦ It is estimated that approximately 3–5% of the student population has ADHD.

♦ Many children with this disorder slip through the cracks. They have/had not been identified or provided with effective interventions.

♦ ADHD is diagnosed between 3 to 9 times more frequently in boys than girls. It is believed that many more girls actually have ADHD and aren't diagnosed because often they exhibit fewer of the disruptive behaviors associated with hyperactivity and impulsivity. Many girls have the predominantly inattentive type of the disorder and are likely not being identified and diagnosed.

♦ The challenging behaviors that are exhibited by children with ADHD stem from their physiological, neurobiological disorder. The inappropriate behaviors they may display are generally not willful or deliberate. Typically their behaviors and how they impact on others are not even within the child's awareness.

♦ Children with ADHD are more likely than their peers to be suspended or expelled from school, retained a grade or drop out of school, have trouble socially and emotionally, and experience rejection, ridicule, and punishment.

♦ In spite of difficulties, children/teens with ADHD may also have many strengths and high potential. They are often creative, intelligent, and gifted in certain areas (e.g., artistically, musically, athletically, verbally).

♦ ADHD is a lifelong disorder. It generally continues into adolescence, and up to 70% continue to exhibit symptoms into adulthood. However, the symptoms change as the person matures. Hyperactive behaviors of younger children (running around the classroom, falling out of chairs) are seen as fidgetiness, pacing, and less overt behaviors as adolescents/adults. Impulsivity seen in younger children looks different in teens and adults (i.e., changing plans and career path frequently, tendency to high-risk behavior).

◆ Many adolescents and adults are able to compensate for or by-pass many of the difficulties they had as children because they have jobs and lifestyles that allow them to do so. They use their areas of strength and interests, and rely on someone else in their life (e.g., secretary, spouse, assistant) to help with the tasks that are still areas of difficulty, such as organization skills.

◆ Children with ADHD do much better when they are provided with activities that are interesting, novel, and motivating.

◆ Children with ADHD do much better when they are able to work towards rewards that are more immediate. They are typically unable to maintain the effort when working for long-term goals and rewards. That is a characteristic of impulsivity.

◆ We know that ADHD is *not* a myth, *not* a result of poor parenting, and *not* a lack of caring, effort, and discipline.

◆ We know it is *not* laziness, willful behavior, or a character flaw.

◆ A very high percentage of children/teens/adults with ADHD have additional coexisting (comorbid) disorders.

◆ ADHD is one of the most common childhood disorders.

◆ There are degrees of ADHD ranging from mild to severe.

◆ ADHD isn't new. It has been around, recognized by clinical science, and documented in the literature since the turn of the 20th century, having been renamed several times (for example, minimal brain dysfunction and hyperkinetic disorder of childhood).

◆ ADHD has been the focus of a tremendous amount of study. There are literally thousands of studies and scientific articles published (nationally and internationally) on ADHD.

◆ ADHD is neurobiological in nature.

◆ There are different types of ADHD with a variety of characteristics. No one has all of the symptoms or displays the disorder in the exact same way.

◆ The prognosis for ADHD is alarming if not treated. Without interventions it can result in serious social, emotional, behavioral, and academic problems.

◆ When treated, the prognosis for ADHD is very positive and hopeful. With intervention, most children diagnosed and provided with the help they need will be able to successfully manage the disorder.

◆ There is no "quick-fix" for ADHD.

◆ There is no "cure" for ADHD.

◆ There are a number of other problems or disorders (i.e., learning, medical/health, social, emotional) that may cause symptoms that *look like* ADHD, but are not ADHD.

◆ ADHD causes problems with performance and work production.

◆ A number of factors can intensify the problems of someone with ADHD or lead to significant improvement (such as the structure in the environment, support systems available, level of stress).

◆ Stimulant medications that affect the neurotransmitters in the central nervous system are known to reduce the symptoms of ADHD.

◆ There are countless successful individuals with ADHD in every profession and walk of life.

◆ Children with ADHD can usually be taught effectively in general education classrooms (with proper teaching, management, supports, and assistive strategies).

◆ ADHD can be managed best by a multimodal treatment and a team approach.

◆ We know that it takes a team effort of parents, school personnel, and health/mental health care professionals to be most effective in helping children with ADHD.

◆ No single intervention will be effective for treating/managing ADHD. It takes vigilance, ongoing treatment/intervention plans, revision of plans, and going "back to the drawing board" frequently.

◆ We know a lot about which behavior management techniques and strategies are effective in the home and school for children with ADHD.

◆ We know a great deal about the classroom interventions, accommodations, and teaching strategies that are most helpful for students with ADHD.

◆ The teaching techniques and strategies that are necessary for the success of children with ADHD are good teaching practices and helpful for *all* students in the class.

◆ We know the specific parenting strategies that are most effective with children who have ADHD (e.g., positive behavioral management, structuring the environment).

◆ We know a lot about the medical intervention that is found to be effective in helping children/teens with ADHD. *(See Checklist 16 on Most Commonly Prescribed Medications in the Treatment of ADHD.)*

◆ We know many additional interventions that address social skills, anger control, relaxation strategies, organization/time management, learning styles, self esteem, and others that are helpful for individuals with ADHD.

◆ There are many resources available for helping children, teens, and adults with ADHD, as well as those living with and working with individuals with ADHD.

◆ We are learning more and more each day due to the efforts of the many researchers, practitioners (educators, mental health professionals, physicians) committed to improving the lives of individuals with ADHD.

What We Don't Know About ADHD

There is still a great deal we don't yet know about ADHD, including among other things:

✔ Other possible causes

✔ How to prevent or "cure" symptoms of ADHD

✔ An easy, conclusive diagnosis for ADHD

✔ What may prove to be the best, most effective treatments and strategies for helping individuals with ADHD

Hopefully, with all of the research and study taking place about attention deficit disorders, we will be learning more soon.

4. CHARACTERISTICS OF THE PREDOMINANTLY HYPERACTIVE/IMPULSIVE TYPE OF ADHD

Children and teens with ADHD have limited ability to inhibit their responses and control behavior. They will exhibit many of the following characteristics and symptoms (not all of them). Even though any one of these behaviors is normal in children at different ages to a certain degree, with ADHD the behaviors *far exceed* that which is normal developmentally (in frequency, level, and intensity).

Hyperactivity

✔ In constant motion—running and climbing excessively in situations where it is inappropriate

✔ Always on the go and highly energetic

✔ Can't sit still—jumping up and out of chair, falling out of chair, kneeling, standing up out of seat

✔ A high degree of unnecessary movement—pacing, tapping feet, drumming fingers

✔ Restlessness

✔ Always seem to need something in hands; finds/reaches for nearby objects to play with and/or put in mouth

✔ Fidgets with hands or feet

✔ Squirms in seat

✔ Makes inappropriate/odd noises

✔ Roams around the classroom; isn't where he or she is supposed to be

✔ Has difficulty playing quietly

✔ Has a hard time staying within own boundaries, and intrudes in other people's space

Impulsivity

✔ Talks excessively

✔ Blurts out verbally, often inappropriately

✔ Has great difficulty with raising hand and waiting to be called on

✔ Often interrupts or intrudes on others

✔ Can't wait for his or her turn in games and activities

✔ Can't keep hands/feet to self

✔ Can't wait or delay gratification—wants things now

✔ Knows the rules and consequences, but repeatedly makes the same errors/infractions of rules

✔ Gets in trouble because he or she can't "stop and think" before acting (responds first/thinks later)

✔ Has trouble standing in lines

✔ Doesn't think about consequences, so tends to be fearless

✔ Often engages in physically dangerous activities without considering the consequences (e.g., jumping from heights, riding bike into street without looking); hence, a high frequency of injuries

✔ Accident prone—breaks things

✔ Has difficulty inhibiting what he or she says; makes tactless comments—says whatever pops into head, talks back to authority figures

✔ Begins tasks without waiting for directions (doesn't listen to the full direction or take the time to read written directions)

✔ Hurries through tasks (particularly boring ones) to get finished, making numerous careless errors

✔ Does not take time to correct/edit work

✔ Often disrupts and bothers others

High Degree of Emotionality

✔ Easily angered; has a "short fuse"

✔ Moody

✔ Easily frustrated

✔ Gets upset and annoyed quickly

✔ Irritable

✔ Loses control easily

Other Common Characteristics

✔ Difficulty relating to others; gets along better with younger children

✔ Difficulty with transitions and changes in routine/activity

✔ Becomes overly stimulated

✔ Displays aggressive behavior

✔ Immature social skills

✔ Difficult to discipline

✔ Can't work for long-term goals or payoffs

✔ Low self-esteem

5. Characteristics of the Predominantly Inattentive Type of ADHD

This type of ADHD is what used to be called *ADD without hyperactivity* or "undifferentiated ADD." These are the children and teens who often "slip through the cracks" and are not so easily identified or understood. Since they don't exhibit the disruptive behaviors that get our attention, it is easy to overlook these students and misinterpret their behaviors and symptoms. It is normal to display any of the following behaviors at times, in different situations to a certain degree. With ADHD one has a history of showing many of these characteristics—far above the normal range developmentally—resulting in significant difficulty in performance (and many times achievement).

Inattentive Characteristics/Symptoms

- ✔ Easily distracted by extraneous stimuli
- ✔ Doesn't seem to listen when spoken to
- ✔ Difficulty following directions
- ✔ Difficulty focusing and sustaining attention (especially on work requiring mental effort)
- ✔ Difficulty concentrating and attending to task
- ✔ Often loses his or her place when reading
- ✔ Forgets what he or she is reading and needs to reread frequently
- ✔ Tunes out; may appear "spacey"
- ✔ Appears to be daydreaming (thoughts are elsewhere)
- ✔ Often confused
- ✔ Can't get started on tasks
- ✔ Fails to finish work; many incomplete assignments
- ✔ Difficulty working independently; needs high degree of focusing attention to task
- ✔ Gets bored easily
- ✔ Often sluggish or lethargic

✔ Doesn't pay attention to details and makes many careless errors (with math computation, spelling, written mechanics of capitalization and punctuation)

✔ Poor study skills

✔ Inconsistent performance—one day is able to perform a task, the next day cannot

✔ Disorganized; loses/can't find belongings (papers, pencils, books); desks, backpacks, lockers, and rooms may be a total disaster area

✔ Difficulty organizing and planning for tasks

✔ Little or no awareness of time

✔ Forgetful with difficulty remembering

NOTE:

It is believed that many girls who have been labeled "space cadets" may actually have this type of ADHD.

There is also a high frequency of coexisting learning disabilities with this type of ADHD.

Slow written output is very common with this type of ADHD.

Dr. Russell Barkley, one of the leading experts in the field, refers to this type of ADHD as being one involving slower "cognitive processing speed." It takes longer to "get it" regardless of how smart the person is.

Realize that children/teens diagnosed with ADHD Combined Type have a *significant number of both* the inattentive characteristics as well as the hyperactive/impulsive characteristics.

In addition, one may receive the diagnosis of the predominantly inattentive type of ADHD and still have *some* of the hyperactive/impulsive symptoms; or be diagnosed as having the predominantly hyperactive/impulsive type of ADHD yet still have *some* of the inattentive characteristics.

There is also a category used called Otherwise Specified ADHD. This is designated for the child who has prominent symptoms of inattention or hyperactivity/impulsivity that cause impairment, but the number of symptoms they exhibit are below the number required for the diagnosis (not meeting the diagnostic criteria).

6. Probable Causes of ADHD

ADHD has been researched extensively in the United States and a number of other countries. There have been literally thousands of well-designed and controlled scientific studies trying to determine the causes and most effective treatment for children, teens, and—more recently—adults with the disorder. Over the past few years there have been very exciting *international conferences* devoted to ADD/ADHD—bringing together leading researchers from around the world, and physicians, mental health professionals, educators, and parents sharing knowledge about their discoveries, and how to best treat and live with ADHD. To date, the causes of ADHD are not fully known or understood. However, based on the enormous amount of research, there is a lot of concensus of opinion about most PROBABLE CAUSES, which include the following.

◆ **Heredity:** This is the most common cause based on the evidence. ADHD is known to run in families as found by numerous studies (i.e., twin studies with identical and fraternal twins, adopted children, family studies). It is believed that what is inherited is a genetic predisposition to the disorder. A child with ADHD will frequently have a parent, sibling, grandparent, or other family member who had similar school histories and behaviors during their childhood.

◆ **Prenatal, during birth, or post-birth trauma/injury:** It has been found that trauma to the developing fetus during pregnancy or to the infant before, during, or after birth—which may cause brain injury or abnormal brain development—can be a cause of ADHD. This might include fetal exposure to alcohol and tobacco, early exposure to high levels of lead, or complications in the birthing process.

◆ **Certain medical conditions** such as hyperthyroidism have been found to cause symptoms of ADHD.

◆ **Certain illnesses,** such as encephalitis, that affect the brain may cause ADHD.

◆ It is believed that for those with ADHD there is a **deficiency or inefficiency of brain chemicals** (called neurotransmitters) in the part of the brain (frontal lobe) that is responsible for attention, inhibiting impulses and behavior, motor control, and handwriting.

◆ It has been found through brain imaging research that the **rate at which the brain of adults with ADHD metabolizes glucose** (the main source of energy) in the frontal lobe of the brain—the region responsible for attention, activity, and inhibition—is lower than the rate that adults without ADHD metabolize glucose.

◆ Clearly it has been found that ADHD appears to be **neurologically, biologically based.** There is very strong scientific evidence to support that ADHD may be due to imbalances in neurotransmitters and/or reduced metabolic rates in certain regions of the brain.

◆ It has been found that there is **less brain activity** taking place in the frontal regions of the ADHD brain (the areas known to be responsible for controlling activity level, impulsivity, attention). This underactivity has been found through studies revealing: less blood flow, lower rate of glucose metabolism (on PET scans), and lower electrical activity on EEGs, neuroimaging, and magnetic resonance imaging.

◆ In addition to the frontal regions, different locations in the brain and connections between these different brain sights are also believed to be affected when one has ADHD.

◆ There is also evidence of some **possible structural differences in the brains** of individuals with ADHD and those without.

◆ The reason that stimulant medications are found to be effective as part of the treatment for ADHD is that these medications are believed to stimulate the production of those neurotransmitters that those with ADHD are most likely lacking—therefore, helping to normalize the **brain chemistry.**

◆ It is also generally believed that **factors in the environment** (e.g., the amount of structure versus chaos, the effective management techniques being used, the types of supports in place) certainly affect the severity of the symptoms and behaviors displayed, and the risk for developing more significant problems in addition to the ADHD. However, these environmental factors are *not* found to be the *cause* of the ADHD.

◆ Research has not supported many of the other suggested causes that are popular in the media (i.e., due to diet, food additives, sugar). There are many theories about causes and appropriate treatments. It is suggested you be aware of scientific evidence as opposed to testimonial or hearsay evidence. There are some excellent resources on this topic, such as the outstanding book by Barbara D. Ingersoll, Ph.D., and Sam Goldstein, Ph.D., entitled *Attention Deficit Disorder and Learning Disabilities—Realities, Myths and Controversial Treatments* (New York: Doubleday, 1993).

7. ADHD "Look Alikes"

The diagnosis of ADHD is complex. There are a number of other medical, learning, psychiatric, and social problems that can cause inattentive, hyperactive, and impulsive behaviors. To make an accurate and complete diagnosis, these other possible causes which produce symptoms that "mimic" ADHD need to be considered and ruled out. It is also possible that ADHD is *only part* of the diagnostic picture, and that in addition to ADHD there are other coexisting disorders involved. This is, in fact, very common. There is a high rate of "comorbity" with ADHD—which means that all of the coexisting problems/disorders need to be identified in order to provide proper treatment.

The following can cause some of the symptoms that may look like ADD/ADHD:

✔ Learning disabilities

✔ Sensory impairments (hearing, vision, motor problems)

✔ Depression

✔ Substance abuse

✔ Oppositional Defiant Disorder (ODD)

✔ Conduct disorder

✔ Allergies

✔ Post-traumatic stress

✔ Mood or anxiety disorder

✔ Obsessive-Compulsive Disorder

✔ Sleep disorders

✔ Bipolar disorder

✔ Hyperthyroidism

✔ Rare genetic disorders (i.e., Fragile X syndrome)

✔ Seizure disorders

✔ Lead poisoning

✔ Hypoglycemia

✔ Fetal Alcohol Syndrome

✔ Chronic illness

✔ Speech and language disorders

✔ Tourette's Syndrome

✔ Pervasive Developmental Disorder

✔ Developmental delays

✔ Low intellectual ability

✔ Severe emotional disturbance

✔ Side effects of medications being taken (i.e., antiseizure medication, asthma medication)

✔ High-stress situations (i.e., physical/sexual abuse, divorce and custody battles, peer pressure and other peer/social issues, chaotic home life with inappropriate expectations placed on child) that the child/teen is living with—causing fear, stress, and anxiety

8. CRITICAL ELEMENTS FOR SCHOOL SUCCESS

✔ Teacher flexibility and willingness to accommodate

✔ Knowledge and understanding of ADHD

✔ Teacher tolerance and positive attitude

✔ Close home/school communication

✔ Clarity and structure

✔ Engaging teaching strategies (active learning and high student response opportunities)

✔ Concrete, multisensory, experiential learning

✔ Direct, focused instruction

✔ Variety, variety, variety

✔ Teamwork and collaboration

✔ Effective classroom management and positive discipline

✔ Administrative support

✔ Modifying assignments; cutting the written workload

✔ Limiting the amount of homework

✔ Help/training in organization and study skills

✔ Environmental modifications

✔ More time/more space

✔ Developing and bringing out student strengths

✔ Respecting learning styles/learning differences, privacy, confidentiality, and students' feelings

✔ Belief in the student—doing what it takes

9. STATISTICS TO CONSIDER REGARDING CHILDREN/ADOLESCENTS WITH ADHD

The fact that having ADHD places one at risk for developing academic, behavioral, and social difficulties becomes apparent when viewing the research and statistics—which are indeed alarming. The following statistics are direct quotes found in the texts listed after each.

◆ Up to 30–50% of children with ADHD may be retained in a grade at least once.

◆ As many as 35% of ADHD adolescents may fail to complete high school.

◆ More than 25% of ADHD adolescents are expelled from high school because of serious misconduct.

◆ Adolescents with a diagnosis of ADHD have nearly four times as many auto accidents and three times as many citations for speeding than young drivers without ADHD.

> From Russell Barkley's *Taking Charge of ADHD* (New York: Guilford Press, 1995, pp. 18–19)

◆ In research studies 20% to 60% of hyperactive teenagers are involved in antisocial behavior that results in referral to juvenile court. It is estimated that approximately 3% to 4% of the normal population of teenagers ends up in juvenile court.

◆ In other studies, 35% of hyperactive teenagers were suspended from school at least once as opposed to only 8% to 10% of the normal population.

◆ By high school, it is estimated that as many as 80% of hyperactive teenagers are behind at least one basic academic subject.

> From Sam Goldstein and Michael Goldstein's *Hyperactivity: Why Won't My Child Pay Attention?* (New York: John Wiley & Sons, Inc., 1992, p. 106)

◆ Barkley, DuPaul, and McMurray (1990) demonstrated that 65% of adolescents with ADHD also show indications of oppositional-defiant disorder.

◆ DuPaul and Stoner (1994) indicated that oppositional-defiant disorder/aggression was the most common disorder co-occurring with ADHD.

From William N. Bender's *Understanding ADHD* (Upper Saddle River, NJ: Prentice Hall, 1997, p. 16)

10. Positive Traits Often Associated with ADHD

✔ Energetic

✔ Highly verbal

✔ Spontaneous

✔ Creative

✔ Exciting

✔ Persistent

✔ Innovative

✔ Imaginative

✔ Risk-taker

✔ Tenacious

✔ Warm-hearted

✔ Ingenuity

✔ Compassionate

✔ Accepting and forgiving

✔ Inquisitive

✔ Resilient

✔ Fun to be around

✔ Sensitive to needs of others

✔ Resourceful

✔ Empathetic

✔ Good-hearted

✔ Gregarious

✔ Not boring

✔ Often high intelligence

✔ Humorous

✔ Outgoing

✔ Willing to take a chance and try new things

✔ Good at improvising

✔ Have an interesting perspective

✔ Are able to find novel solutions

✔ Inventive

✔ Observant

✔ Full of ideas and spunk

✔ Caring

✔ Helpful

✔ Can think on their feet

✔ Good in crisis situations

11.   MAKING THE DIAGNOSIS: WHAT IS A COMPREHENSIVE EVALUATION FOR ADHD?

The diagnosis of ADHD is a rather complex process. There is no single test for it, nor can any particular piece of information alone confirm or deny the existence of ADHD. It is highly recommended the child be evaluated by someone with a lot of expertise in attention deficit disorders who knows well how to evaluate and interpret all the information gathered from a number of sources.

◆ Part of the criteria for diagnosis is that the child meet the definition of Attention-Deficit Hyperactivity Disorder (ADHD) as described in DSMIV (the most current edition of the *Diagnostic and Statistical Manual* published by the American Psychiatric Association). This contains a list of nine specific characteristics associated with inattention and nine specific characteristics associated with hyperactivity/impulsivity. To consider diagnosis of ADHD the child must exhibit at least six of the nine characteristics of inattention, or at least six of the nine characteristics of hyperactivity/impulsivity. These behaviors must have been evident before age seven, and lasted for a period of time longer than six months. The behaviors of impulsivity, hyperactivity, and/or inattention must be found to exist to a degree that is "maladaptive and inconsistent with the child's developmental level." These symptoms must be pervasive (displayed in more than one setting), and serious enough to be affecting the successful functioning of the child at home and school. **Note:** Just meeting these criteria in DSMIV *does not* confirm a diagnosis of ADHD. It is just the beginning of the information-gathering process.

◆ **History:** An evaluation for ADHD will require taking a thorough history of the child's medical, developmental, school, and family history. The diagnostician will gather this information through interviewing the parents and asking them to fill out questionnaires regarding: *the child's medical history* (including pregnancy, delivery, birth history), *developmental history, family medical and social history,* and *school history.*

◆ **Other information gathered through interview and questionnaires** with parents and often the child regard the child's behaviors (past and present), emotional and social functioning, peer relationships, family relationships, discipline and behavior management used in the home, and interests. **Note:** A very critical part of the diagnosis is finding that the characteristics and symptoms associated with ADHD are not recent developments, but have existed over a period of time. The history will determine if this is the case. The family history may also indicate the possibility of a genetic link.

♦ **Behavior rating scales:** A variety of rating scales have been developed that are used as part of the diagnostic process. They are designed to assess the degree to which various behaviors exist. Typically, parents and teachers will be asked to fill out different rating scales (of which there are a number that are known to be quite useful and effective in evaluating the degree to which behaviors exhibited are considered a problem/concern). In addition to parents and teachers, other adults who work with the child frequently (i.e., school counselor, special education teacher) may be asked to fill out a rating scale. *(See Checklist 14 on Questionnaires and Rating Scales for Parents and Teachers.)*

♦ **Gathering current school information:** A very critical part of the diagnostic process is reviewing information that must be supplied by the school. Teachers must report through rating scales, questionnaires, narrative statements, phone interviews, or other measures precisely how he or she views the student's performance and school functioning. The teacher (and other appropriate school personnel) will need to share observations, work samples, and other evidence of academic, behavioral, and social/emotional issues. The teacher's observations and perceptions regarding the child's activity level compared to other students in the class is very important. So is the teacher's opinion regarding how well the child can: inhibit behavior, follow rules and directions, stay focused and on-task, initiate and follow through on assignments, exhibit self-control, and so on. *(See Checklist 12 on What Parents Should Expect from the School in the Diagnostic Process.)*

♦ **Review of school records:** School history of behaviors indicating ADHD will need to be obtained through past report cards (particularly citizenship grades, and teacher comments, as well as academic grades). Bus, office referrals, standardized school achievement tests, work samples, anecdotal records, etc., are all useful information. **Note:** A release of information must be signed by parents first before the school can share this confidential information.

◆ **Observations:** These observations of the child's functioning in various school settings can provide very helpful diagnostic information. How a child behaves and performs in an office visit is not at all indicative of how that same child performs and behaves in a classroom, playground, and lunchroom setting.

◆ **Assessment:** Part of the diagnostic process will require some specific assessment. This might include:

– *Academic achievement testing:* It is important to determine the child's strengths and weaknesses in academic skills. This can partly be determined through the student's grades/report cards, work samples, and informal screening measures. In cases where the student is performing well academically, that may be sufficient. Typically students with ADHD don't score well on group standardized achievement tests. That in itself can be important data. However, those tests administered at school each year generally do not accurately reflect the achievement or skill level of children with ADHD. Often an individualized achievement battery of tests will need to be administered to measure skills in reading, math, and written language. If the student is struggling or perhaps "underachieving" in specific academic areas, it will be important to do so.

– *Intelligence testing:* A thorough evaluation may involve some cognitive testing to determine the child's ability level and intellectual functioning. If the child is suspected to be quite bright, or to have less than average intelligence, this would be valuable information to know. In addition, if the child appears to have a possible learning disability, then a psychoeducational evaluation (including intelligence, academic, as well as "processing" tests should be administered as part of the assessment).

– *Physical exam:* An evaluation for ADHD needs to include a physical examination. Based on the child's physical exam, as well as medical history (through interview and questionnaire), a physician will try to find evidence of other possible causes for the symptoms, or additional issues that may need to be addressed (i.e., sleep disturbances, bedwetting, soiling, anxiety, depression, motor skill development). The physical may include a neurological screening and other screening devices. Most other medical tests (blood work, EEG, CT scans) are not done routinely in an evaluation for ADHD, unless indicated and requested by the physician. It is the physician's responsibility to determine the need for additional medical testing and to make decisions regarding appropriateness for medical treatment. **Note:** Although there are a number of other illnesses, conditions, and disorders that may mimic some of the symptoms of ADHD, this occurs rarely. Remember, there are no medical tests that indicate ADHD or that can either confirm it or rule it out. The physician must rely on all of the other data supplied (history, school performance/achievement, behavioral scales and observations, and other diagnostic assessment) to support a diagnosis.

 — *Performance tests:* Different tests are often used in a comprehensive evaluation that measure the child's ability to inhibit making impulsive responses and to sustain attention and focus on computerized tasks. Other measures of performance include tests that evaluate one's ability to organize, and pay attention to visual stimuli on paper-pencil tasks.

◆ **Note:** Whoever the parent chooses to conduct the evaluation for ADHD, it is important that this qualified professional has gathered sufficient data to be able to interpret and conclude:

 • how frequent and pervasive the symptoms are
 • the approximate onset of those symptoms
 • how significantly the symptoms/behaviors impact on the child's ability to function (the degree and severity)
 • what other possible factors may account for the symptoms or behaviors observed

◆ It is highly recommended to have your child diagnosed by professionals with a high degree of expertise and experience with ADHD. It is wise to do some investigating. Other parents of children with ADHD, the school nurse, psychologist, counselor, and parent support groups (i.e., local CH.A.D.D. chapters) are often good sources of referrals. A variety of physicians, child psychiatrists, neurologists, psychologists, and other mental health professionals in the community may evaluate your child for ADHD. A school-based evaluation can also be done to gather information towards making the diagnosis.

12. What Parents Should Expect from the School in the Diagnostic Process

Parents have a right to expect their school to be supportive and responsive in the diagnostic process. If parents choose to take their child for an evaluation outside of school, or even for a consultation with their child's physician, it is important that the school supply information that will shed some light on how the child is functioning in school.

◆ It will be necessary for parents **to sign a release of information form** that will enable the school personnel to communicate with other professionals outside of school, and provide documentation and data regarding your child. This might include phone conversations; making copies of some school records that indicate behavior, work production, academic skill, and performance; and any other assessment that has been done on the child (i.e., evaluations for learning problems, speech/language, motor skills). Copies of IEPs, referral forms, and report cards from the cumulative records are important sources of significant data indicating student needs.

◆ The classroom teacher should complete any rating scales or questionnaires provided. It is also very helpful for the teacher to write/type a paragraph or two indicating how he or she views the child in relation to other students in the classroom (i.e., behavior, performance, output). The teacher needs to identify concerns, the student's strengths, and describe the strategies/interventions that have been used to help the child (and to what degree of success). If the teacher or school has made efforts to support the student, and implemented various interventions, it is important to evaluate the effectiveness of those supports and interventions tried.

◆ Classroom observations by other school personnel is helpful data that a parent can expect. Sometimes observing the child in different settings of the school day provides significant information.

◆ The teacher should be able to supply work samples—originals or copies—with the date, and be willing to speak with whoever is conducting the evaluation about the child.

◆ The parent should expect that someone on the school site has at least some degree of expertise/knowledge about ADHD, and can provide information and resources (i.e., articles, books).

◆ If a school-based evaluation is to be done, the parent can expect that the school diagnostic team provide parents with paperwork that includes permission forms, statements of parent rights, a clear explanation of the process, and a team approach.

◆ No single person will be involved in the diagnostic process. Schools utilize a multidisciplinary assessment process, involving at least a few members of the team with different expertise/credentials. The school diagnostic team varies depending on the school district. Often it includes: a school psychologist, school nurse, special education teacher/resource specialist, and speech/language specialist. Other specialists and support personnel (i.e., guidance counselors, district counselors, social workers, adapted PE teachers, reading specialists) may be involved in the gathering of information—as well as the administrator and classroom teacher.

◆ Parents should expect the school to ask them to supply information regarding history, their perception of the child's development and performance, needs, etc. *(See Checklist 11 on Making the Diagnosis: What Is a Comprehensive Evaluation for ADHD?)* Parents will need to fill out rating scales, questionnaires, and probably be interviewed/verbally asked questions by members of the diagnostic team.

◆ Parents should expect that if the school conducts an evaluation, it be done in a timely manner and that all of the results/findings of the evaluation be shared with them. There will be a meeting set up once the evaluation is completed. In addition to having the results explained, parents will receive a copy of all reports.

◆ *See Checklist 70 on The Student Study Team Process . . . and Checklist 71 on What Is an IEP? for more information on assessment/pre-assessment procedures that are used in many schools.*

13.   A Comprehensive Treatment Program for ADHD

Once a child is identified and diagnosed with ADHD, there are many ways to help the child and the family. The most effective approach is a multifaceted treatment approach that might involve educational, behavioral, psychological, medical, and social/recreational interventions. This multimodal treatment program may include:

◆ Behavior modification and specific behavior-management strategies implemented at home and school

◆ Family counseling (because with an ADHD child in the house, the *entire* family is often affected)

◆ Parent counseling

◆ Individual counseling to learn coping techniques, problem-solving strategies, and how to deal with stress and self-esteem

◆ Psychotherapy

◆ Cognitive therapy to give the child the skills to regulate his or her own behavior as well as "stop-and-think" techniques

◆ Social skills training (sometimes available in school counseling groups)

◆ Numerous school interventions (environmental, academic, instructional, behavioral) to accommodate the child's needs

◆ Special school services and supports

◆ Teacher/school staff awareness training about ADHD

◆ Providing for a physical outlet (e.g., swimming, martial arts, gymnastics, track and field, dance, sports). **Note:** Team sports such as soccer or basketball are often better than team sports that require a lot of waiting for your chance to move and participate, like baseball. Activities such as martial arts (i.e., aikido) are often recommended because they increase the child's ability to focus and concentrate.

◆ Medical/pharmacological intervention: Medications (i.e., psycho-stimulants) have been found to be very effective in increasing children's ability to control impulsive/hyperactive behaviors as well as improve attention/focus.

◆ Involving the child/teen in activities that build upon his or her strengths and interests (i.e., arts/crafts, sports, scouts)

◆ Parent education/training is critical. It is very important for parents to learn as much as they can about ADHD in order to help their child and be an effective advocate. Parent support groups are excellent sources of training, assistance, and networking. Most communities also have parenting classes and workshops dealing with a variety of helpful management strategies. As parenting a child with ADHD is typically more challenging than parenting other children, it is often wise to seek out specialists who can train parents in effective behavior-management techniques/skills.

◆ When pursuing any treatment, it is a good idea to ask the school nurse and other parents of ADHD children (perhaps through an ADD support group) for references. Seek out doctors and therapists who are knowledgeable and experienced specifically with treating children with ADHD. Medical treatment is often extremely helpful and can make a major difference in treating children with ADHD. However, it is *never* to be used without the employment of behavioral, environmental, and other interventions at home and school.

◆ Ongoing teamwork and communication among parents, school personnel, physicians, and therapists/agencies is critical in any treatment plan.

◆ If a child displays the symptoms of possible ADD/ADHD, school interventions should be implemented at once—regardless of whether the child has been diagnosed with ADHD. School personnel may encourage the parents to pursue the evaluation for the purpose of determining how to best help and meet the needs of their child.

◆ All professionals working with the child/family need to have a knowledge-base about ADHD, and focus on the issues from a positive approach. Interventions should be designed to help the child recognize and draw upon his or her strengths, and build within the child a sense of control over his or her own behaviors. Parents should stay clear of professionals who tend to cast blame upon anyone (child, parents, school) or view ADHD from a negative perspective.

◆ Since ADHD often lasts throughout one's lifetime, a person may need some of the supports and interventions at different times in his or her life (assistance from educators, mental health professionals, physicians, tutors, coaches).

14. Questionnaires and Rating Scales for Parents and Teachers

There are a variety of different questionnaires and rating scales published and available for use in obtaining information from parents and teachers.

◆ Some of these scales/questionnaires include: School Situations Questionnaire; *Conners' Rating Scales—Revised (parent and teacher forms)*; ACTeRs (ADD-H Comprehensive Teacher's Rating Scale); *BASC;* Behavior Assessment System for Children—Teacher Rating Scales (BASC-TRS); Comprehensive Behavior Rating Scale for Children; *Child Behavior Checklist—Teacher's Report Form (TRF) and parent form (CBCL);* Devereux Behavior Rating Scale; Child Attention Profile; SNAP Rating Scale; *Brown Attention Deficit Disorder Questionnaire; and Home/School Situations Questionnaire.*

◆ In some of the questionnaires various situations in the home or school are described, and the parent/teacher rates if they see the child presenting difficulty in any of those situations and to what degree (mild to severe).

◆ Some of the rating scales describe behaviors for which the teacher or parent rates the frequency they observe the child exhibiting—from "never" to "almost always," or on a number scale (i.e., 1–5 or 0–4).

◆ The types of behaviors that parents are asked to rate and teachers asked to rank in comparison to other students in the class focus on existence or degree of:

✔ disruptive behavior

✔ demanding behavior

✔ excitability

✔ moodiness

✔ compliant, cooperative behavior

✔ oppositional behavior

✔ ability to interact and get along with other children

✔ ability to interact and get along with adults and authority figures

✔ ability to change activities and handle transitions/changes in routine

✔ ability to get started on tasks

✔ ability to complete work

✔ ability to follow directions

✔ organization skills

✔ distractibility

✔ independent work habits

✔ attention/on-task behavior

✔ talkativeness

✔ activity level

✔ fidgetiness

✔ ability to control emotions

✔ ability to display self control and inhibit behavior

✔ ability to concentrate and pay attention

✔ impulsive behavior

✔ ability to play quietly

◆ Teachers should be prepared to share with the evaluator information to questions they may be asked, such as the following:

✔ Describe the child's strengths.

✔ Describe the concerns/child's difficulties.

✔ Describe the current educational functioning levels and performance.

✔ Has the child had any testing or school assessments?

✔ Does the child receive any special education services?

✔ What services are available at the school?

✔ Has the child ever repeated a grade?

15. What Does It Take to Be an Effective School?

✔ Strong support systems within the school, and sufficient allocation of support service personnel—counseling, health services, special education to meet the needs of the school site

✔ Dedicated educators who love children

✔ Setting and maintaining high expectations for educators and students

✔ Commitment to collaborative school/community approach

✔ Challenging, motivating, and integrated curriculum

✔ Many engaging, fun activities for students

✔ Incentives, rewards, and positive attention/recognition

✔ An emphasis on cooperation, communication, and bringing out/recognizing the strengths of everyone

✔ Close home/school communication and parental involvement

✔ Attention to individual learning styles and multiple intelligences

✔ A learning environment that is positive, child-centered, nurturing, and success-oriented

✔ Schoolwide implementation of organization/study-skills programs

✔ Schoolwide expectations and rules/procedures that are well-defined, practiced, and reinforced by all staff members

✔ Schoolwide implementation of behavioral interventions

✔ A school environment and physical campus that is student oriented and reflects student interests, ownership, and pride (e.g., student-made murals, art work, and projects displayed for all to see)

✔ Recognition of individual talents and abilities of students and staff

✔ Commitment to inclusive practices—allowing and encouraging the participation of ALL students in school activities and mainstreaming whenever feasible

Teachers Who:

✔ Are flexible, enthusiastic, and positive role models

✔ Provide nurturing and encouragement to students

✔ Are willing to grow, extend themselves, and aren't afraid of change

✔ Are committed to meeting the individual academic and emotional needs of their students

✔ Motivate and inspire their students to be the best that they can be

✔ Believe in and are committed to learning-style differences

✔ Are creative, challenging, and maintain high expectations of all students

✔ Make strong efforts to meet the needs of each of their students

✔ Accept each child and appreciate his or her uniqueness

✔ Have knowledge and training in ADHD, Learning Disabilities, and other needs of students in inclusive classrooms

✔ Are well trained in effective, up-to-date teaching practices and strategies

✔ Are willing and committed to collaboration and teamwork

✔ Provide adaptations and accommodations that will allow students with special needs and varying developmental levels to achieve success

✔ Are willing to devote the extra time and effort needed to implement interventions and modifications

✔ Encourage and welcome parents and volunteers in the classroom

✔ Display positive attitudes

✔ Teach relevant, motivating lessons, activities, and curriculum that taps the interests and strengths of all students

✔ Provide balance, options, variety, and choices

✔ Utilize a variety of teaching strategies and delivery systems to address the range of learning styles in the classroom

✔ Make learning fun

✔ Reflect enthusiasm for learning

✔ Provide frequent monitoring of student work and feedback to students and parents

✔ Focus their classroom management on problem prevention

✔ Model respect and appreciation for diversity (ethnicity, cultural, learning styles, etc.)

✔ Incorporate a lot of variety in instructional strategies and techniques

✔ Are attuned to learning styles, multiple intelligences, and developmental levels of students

✔ Provide for a great deal of active/hands-on learning and participation of all students

A Support Team* That:

✔ Is proactive, prioritizing early identification and interventions for children

✔ Works cooperatively with teachers and parents

✔ Is knowledgeable and well-versed in Learning Disabilities and ADD/ADHD, and their appropriate interventions

✔ Views itself as a resource for parents as well as staff; involved with parent education and staff development/teacher training

✔ Is visible and accessible to children, parents, and staff

✔ Interfaces with social workers, counselors, and physicians who may be involved in the child's care

✔ Makes referrals to appropriate social agencies or educational resources

✔ Makes observations in the classroom to facilitate assessment and educational interventions

✔ Prepares substantial documentation for outside agencies involved in ADHD assessment or counseling

✔ Is responsive to requests for student testing/evaluation

*This "team" consists of the school nurse, resource specialist/special education teacher, counselor, school psychologist, speech/language therapist, social worker, adapted P.E. specialist, etc.

Administrators Who:

✔ Are encouragers and motivators

✔ Are positive role models, inspiring staff to high performance and excellence

✔ Provide support to teachers

✔ Enable their teachers to build skills, stay updated in current teaching practices/strategies, and grow professionally and personally

✔ Make the effort to know the students, welcoming them personally with a smile and pleasant greeting, interacting and showing a personal interest

✔ Are open, accessible, and interested in what school staff, parents, students, and the community have to say

✔ Involve themselves in Student Study Teams, and actively participate in positive interventions for students

✔ Strongly support the collaborative effort, finding creative ways to enable staff to find the time and means to collaborate effectively

✔ Respond sensitively to students' individual needs and placement

✔ Place students' needs as top priority

✔ Maintain expectation from all on campus (students, full staff, parents) that we respect one another in words, actions, and body language

Parents Who:

✔ Are actively involved in the education of their children

✔ Communicate regularly with teachers

✔ Support the school through active involvement and volunteerism

✔ Take advantage of educational opportunities to increase their knowledge, awareness, and skills

✔ Attend school functions and activities

✔ Are committed to a team effort on behalf of their child

School Aides, Office Staff, and Other School Personnel Who:

✔ Are caring, nurturing, positive, and supportive

✔ Are helpful, respectful, and welcoming to parents and families

✔ Give of themselves to the school, supporting teachers and students

✔ Maintain confidentiality and professionalism

16. MOST COMMONLY PRESCRIBED MEDICATIONS IN THE TREATMENT OF ADD/ADHD

There are two main categories of medications typically used in the treatment of ADD/ADHD.

Stimulant Medications

These are the most commonly prescribed medications for ADHD, and generally the first choice of physicians in treating children with ADHD. Stimulant medications have been used for children and studied for around 50 years. It is suspected that these stimulant medications increase the production of neurotransmitters in the brain to a more normalized level—enabling the child to better focus attention, and regulate his or her activity level and impulsive behaviors. These medications include methylphenidate (Ritalin®), dextroamphetamine (Dexedrine®), and pemoline (Cylert®).

◆ Ritalin® and Dexedrine® come in short- and long-acting forms. The short-acting form of the medication starts to work about 30 minutes from the time it is taken, metabolizes quickly, and is effective for approximately 3–5 hours.

◆ Children on this medication often require an additional dosage to be administered at school. (Sometimes a third small dose is administered to enable the child to function more successfully in the late afternoon/evening hours.)

◆ A long-acting, sustained release form of the medication is sometimes prescribed. It takes longer for the effect to kick in and it lasts for at least 6–8 hours. Although the benefit is that a midday dose is not necessary to be taken at school, it is reported by many that the sustained-release form of the medication may not have quite the same effectiveness as the short-acting form.

◆ Cylert *may be* used if Ritalin or Dexedrine is not successful for a child. It is usually taken in the morning—once a day—and lasts all day. Cylert, however, requires careful monitoring of liver functioning through blood tests. According to the manufacturer's label warning: "Because of its association with life-threatening hepatic failure, Cylert should not ordinarily be considered as first line drug therapy for ADHD."

◆ Adderall® is a new stimulant medication on the market, which is administered once or twice a day.

◆ *Benefits of stimulant medications:* For approximately 70–80% of children treated with stimulant medication, symptoms improve to various degrees. In many cases the improvement seen in school is dramatic. The medication can have a positive effect on: ability to control impulses and emotions, attention and focus, ability to inhibit behaviors, ability to regulate activity level, organization, ability to initiate and complete tasks, interactions with others, ability to slow down and think before acting, and ability to sustain the mental effort and increase work production.

◆ *Side effects:* There are some possible side effects that may occur with stimulant medications for ADHD. Stomachaches, headaches, irritability, and sensitivity to criticism are common when beginning treatment with Ritalin. Loss of appetite, weight loss, and difficulty falling asleep are other side effects of stimulants. Sometimes the medication is changed if these symptoms continue, but often the symptoms diminish with time. Mood swings or irritability as the medication wears off (commonly called the rebound) can also occur. Usually the rebound effect can be altered by the physician adjusting the dosage or the times the medication is given. A very small number of children develop tics (involuntary muscle movements) in the form of facial grimaces, sniffing, coughing, snorting, or other vocal sounds on stimulant medication. In most cases these tics do not continue if the medication is stopped.

Tricyclic Antidepressants

This group of medications is also believed to work by acting on neurotransmitters in the brain. These medications are often prescribed for a child who cannot tolerate or is not responding to a stimulant medication, or given to children who are showing signs of clinical depression as well as ADD/ADHD. This category includes these more commonly used medications: imipramine (Tofranil®), desiprimine (Norpramine®), and amytriptyline (Elavil®). The tricyclic antidepressants take some time to build up in the bloodstream and reach a therapeutic level.

◆ *Benefits:* These medications also reduce the symptoms of hyperactivity and impulsivity. They help with mood swings, emotionality, anxiety and depression, as well as sleep disturbances.

◆ *Side effects of antidepressants:* Common side effects are dry mouth and constipation. Other possible side effects are dizziness, confusion, increase in blood pressure, and rapid or irregular heart rate.

◆ There are less commonly used medications for treating ADHD. These include: clonidine (Catapres®), buproprion (Wellbutrin®), nortriptyline (Pamelor®), fluoxetine (Prozac®), and others.

◆ Clonidine (Catapres®) is helpful in controlling oppositional behavior, severe hyperactivity, and aggressiveness.

◆ Sometimes the child is best treated with a combination of medications. Remember, there is always a trial period that requires very close observation as to the time of day, specific behavioral improvement or lack of, that needs to be reported to the physician. This feedback is very important as the physician tries to balance the medication(s) and determine the proper prescription, dose, and/or combination.

◆ Teachers will need to closely monitor and communicate their observations with the parent, school nurse, or physician. Teachers must also report observed possible side effects of the medication. **Note:** Medication in the treatment of ADHD is not meant to sedate the child or make the child lethargic. If a child is over-medicated, this may be observed. If so, report your observations at once.

◆ *See Checklist 17 on If A Child/Teen Is Taking Medication for advice and recommendations to parents and schools.*

Note:

It is advised that parents communicate closely with their child's physician and have their questions answered regarding the medication, possible side effects, precisely how/when it is to be administered, and how its effects will be monitored.

Close communication is necesssary between the parent and teacher regarding the timing of medication given at school.

17. If a Child/Teen Is Taking Medication

What Teachers Need to Know

Parents do not easily make the decision to put their child on medication. Typically, parents agonize over the decision and frequently avoid the medical route for years. No parent wants to have their child take a "drug." They often are fearful and feel guilty. Avoid being judgmental and sharing your personal philosophy about the rights and/or wrongs of medication with parents. It is between the parents and the physician to decide whether the child receives medical treatment. The school's role is to support any child taking medication. School personnel need to be aware of and sensitive to the issues involved with medicating children and fully cooperate as appropriate. Teachers in particular need to be involved with: close observation of the child; communication with parents, doctor, and school nurse; and making sure the child is receiving the medication as prescribed on time.

♦ Generally it is the school nurse who acts as the liaison between the parent and teacher in helping to manage the medication at school. Coordination and communication between all parties involved is essential for optimal results. Through frequent classroom observation and discussions with teachers, the nurse can keep the physician and parents informed of progress or lack thereof.

♦ You are an integral part of the therapeutic team because of your unique ability to observe the child's behavior and ability to attend while on (or off) medication. These observations (by behavior scales, collection of work samples, responses to behavior management) help the physician to regulate the dosage and/or determine if the medication is effective. You should feel free to contact the parent, physician, and school nurse with input, observations, and any concerns you might have. In fact, most physicians provide behavioral observation scales for teachers to fill out at various intervals.

♦ It is also important for you to understand that medication, dosages, and times are often changed or adjusted until the right "recipe" or combination is found for the child. Because children metabolize medication at different rates, many experience some side effects, or become tolerant to medication. It is common for these adjustments to become necessary. You will need to observe and communicate if the child is having recurring academic, social, or behavioral problems at certain times of the day.

◆ Children receiving medication for ADD/ADHD often are prescribed a dosage to be taken during school hours. It is important that medication be given on time. Generally, that means it is administered during the lunch period or right after lunch. With Ritalin, for example, the peak action is approximately two hours after the child has received it; the effects dissipate in about four hours. Many children experience aggressive, emotional, or impulsive behavior when the medication's effects wear off. When the next prescribed dose is not given on time or is given late, these children are found crying, fighting, or otherwise "in trouble" on the playground or cafeteria. When the child returns to the classroom, he or she is not ready or able to focus on the lesson and is often disruptive. Realize that it takes approximately 30 minutes for the next school dose of medication to take effect. Careful timing to avoid this rebound irritability effect will help considerably.

◆ Many children/teens have a hard time remembering to go to the office at the designated time for medication because of the very nature of ADHD. It becomes the responsibility of the teacher, school nurse, counselor, and/or office staff to help with the administration of medication. Ways to remind the student (or alert you that the student needs to take midday dose) may include:

- a beeper watch/watch alarm for the student (or you)
- "coded" verbal reminders over the intercom
- private signals from you to the student
- scheduling a natural transition of activities at that time and setting a clock radio or other signal to indicate that time of day
- a sticker chart kept where the medication is dispensed, rewarding the child for remembering
- color-coded cards given to the child by you or attached to his or her desk
- self-stick notes placed near your schedule or in plan book reminding you to quietly direct the student to leave the room for medication

◆ It is very important to provide these reminders to students discreetly—without breaking confidentiality or discussing medication in front of other students. Pairing the medication time with a daily activity is also a good technique because it helps establish a consistent schedule.

◆ In the nurse's absence, the office staff should be provided with a list of children who take medication, sending for the child if he or she does not come in to receive it.

◆ It is important for you to know that the medication does not control the child. The medication helps to filter out distractions, allowing the child to focus on the task at hand. It diminishes impulsivity, letting the child make better choices. Medication therapy is most effective when combined with educational strategies specific to the child with ADHD, behavioral modification techniques, parental awareness and training, counseling, and management of the child's environment.*

> *The above information is advice from Sandra Wright, school nurse, as summarized from Section 20 on "Medication and School Management" in *How to Reach and Teach ADD/ADHD Children* by Sandra Rief (West Nyack, NY: The Center for Applied Research in Education, 1993).

◆ You will need to monitor and observe students on medication carefully, and report changes in academic performance, work production, ability to stay on task, behavior, peer relationships, as well as any possible side effects the child may be experiencing.

◆ Schools will need to keep medication in a locked place, in clearly labeled prescription bottles/containers, maintaining careful records of the dosage, time of dispensing, and person administering the medication.

◆ School personnel working with/observing the child will be asked for feedback on medication effects, which can be done through specific checklists/rating scales, narrative reports, phone calls, or progress notes.

◆ Parents should be reminded in advance if the school supply of medication is running out so they have plenty of time to renew the prescription and deliver to school.

What Parents Need to Know

◆ If your child is on medication it is very important that you take responsibility for making sure he or she receives it as prescribed in the morning—on time and consistently.

◆ You will need to supervise that your child takes the medication and *not* make it your son or daughter's responsibility to remember to do so.

◆ Close monitoring and management of the medication is very important. If it is administered haphazardly and inconsistently, your child is better off without it.

◆ Be aware of the possible side effects. Realize that appetite is one of those side effects, so make sure to discuss with the doctor and plan your child's meal times (i.e., breakfast) accordingly.

◆ Be responsive to calls from the school regarding medication. Be sure the school has the permission forms and filled prescriptions they need on hand.

◆ Communicate with the school nurse and teachers. Your purpose for treating your child with medication is optimal school performance and success. This requires teamwork and close communication among the home, school, and physician.

◆ Be sure to take your child for all of the follow-up visits that are scheduled with his or her doctor. These are necessary for monitoring the medication's effectiveness.

◆ Educate yourself about the medication treatment/intervention. Talk to your physician and ask all the questions you need. There are excellent books and other resources available on medication treatments for ADHD. Check your local bookstore or library for books on ADD/ADHD. *(See Checklist 74 on Recommended Resources and Organizations at the end of this book for some suggestions.)*

◆ Be aware that when a child is started on medication therapy, there is always a trial period when the physician is trying to determine the appropriate medication and dosage. Some are fortunate to find immediate improvement with their medication. Others will take longer until an effective medication and dosage are determined. Some will not benefit at all, and some cannot tolerate any medication. However, in at least 70% of children (most estimates are higher), medication is found to be very effective.

18. What Supports Do Teachers Need?

Parents and administrators need to realize that you frequently have several students in need of extra assistance and support in your classrooms. Some require academic/instructional interventions and modifications; others need individualized behavioral plans and supports. There are students in the classroom who are English language learners (and are not proficient yet in the English language). Other students are experiencing social/emotional problems due to situations in their personal lives. In any "inclusive" classroom that has students of various skill and developmental levels, you are responsible for making adaptations that will reach those students who are having more difficulty learning, as well as extend the learning opportunities/curriculum for those students who are gifted or high achievers. It is not by any means an easy job to be an effective teacher. The following are some of the supports you need in order to meet the needs of students, including those with ADHD.

◆ You must have training about the special needs of your student population. Since every classroom has students with ADHD as well as specific learning disabilities, it is very important you receive training about both ADHD and learning disabilities. You need to understand that these students have neurological, physiologically-based disorders. Awareness training as well as specific skill-building training should be ongoing. You need to have the opportunity to attend workshops, seminars, and conferences that will provide you with the background information you need, and a host of strategies/interventions that can be used in the classroom to help ADHD students (and ALL students) in the classroom.

◆ You must have the space, materials, and resources to set up an environment conducive to learning and to motivating students.

◆ Teaching can be a lonely profession if there isn't the opportunity to meet and team with colleagues, exchange ideas, and re-energize each other. It has been found to be very effective if teachers buddy with each other (find a partner). Some team-teach different subject areas. Other teachers do "guest" lessons and exchange classes to teach and share their areas of strength/interest. Teachers use buddy classes for disciplinary purposes: sending a student for a brief time-out in the buddy teacher's class.

◆ Administrative support is essential. It is very important to find creative ways to provide teachers (and support staff) with the time and opportunity to get together and plan, team, and collaborate with each other.

◆ Administrators can support teachers by providing them with staff-development opportunities that are practical, useful, and meaningful to teachers.

◆ You need to know you are supported by your administrator, and that you can comfortably approach the administrator with concerns, questions, etc.

◆ Administrators can support those wonderful teachers who are willing to take on more than their fair share of "challenging students" by providing some assistance to those teachers (e.g., extra aide time, fewer number of students in the class, more prep time).

◆ You need the responsiveness and assistance from school support team members. You need a knowledgeable and well-trained team that makes every effort to listen to your concerns, and provide appropriate recommendations and interventions. You need support staff to follow through and provide timely feedback.

◆ You need help from support staff in identifying the problems students may be experiencing, strategizing and then developing together a plan of action and intervention.

◆ You need to be allowed and encouraged to "experiment" with various strategies and techniques. Finding what will work for individual students (especially those with ADHD) requires a lot of trial and error and going back to "the drawing board" frequently. You need to be flexible, and so does the administration.

◆ It is very important that you have the support of parents and shared responsibility in the education of their children. Parents need to support by: knowing and understanding school rules/teacher expectations, cooperating with the school in reinforcing appropriate discipline and consequences, communicating with the school regularly, and helping to ensure that the child is coming to school ready to learn.

◆ It is very helpful if there is a lending library of resources that both teachers/staff and parents can access on a number of topics. It is recommended that schools or parent-teacher organizations begin investing in some books, videotapes, and other resources on ADHD, learning disabilities, behavior management, parenting skills, etc.

◆ You need extra assistance in the classroom. When there are children in need of one-to-one assistance in the classroom, it is so helpful if there is another adult to provide that extra support. If possible, instructional aides and teacher assistants are wonderful supports to the teacher and students. Schools that work with a university or teacher's college are able to access student teachers during the school year. This is also quite helpful. Parent volunteers who are willing to donate time to assist in the classroom (or work on projects at home that are requested by you) are excellent sources of very needed teacher support.

◆ It is very helpful if there are schoolwide programs and interventions in place (i.e., organization/study skills program, discipline/behavior plan) that are used with consistency by all staff members.

◆ Schools should have academic supports and interventions available to students in need that are not part of a special education program (i.e., tutorial assistance, extra direct-reading instruction). These supports to students and teachers also serve as pre-referral interventions that can be tried prior to referral for special education.

◆ You should be able to observe other teachers and have mentor assistance if needed or requested.

◆ It is very beneficial to have an idea/material swap and periodic opportunities for exchanging information, lessons, etc.

◆ You need to be cheered on to keep on learning and growing. The best support is being able to associate with positive, upbeat, enthusiastic colleagues who love to teach and are committed to their students.

◆ You need to be treated with courtesy and respect by parents.

◆ You need to be treated as a professional whose opinion and input is solicited and listened to for site-based decision making and district policy.

◆ Being human, we all need to know that our efforts are recognized and appreciated. A positive comment from a colleague, parent, administrator, or student is very much appreciated by teachers. Parents, if your child's teacher is trying hard to help and teach your child, take the time to thank that teacher.

19.   WHAT SUPPORTS DO PARENTS NEED?

Parenting a child with ADHD can be far more challenging and stressful than parenting a child without ADHD. Teachers need to be sensitive to the struggles that may be occurring at home due to the child and family trying to cope with ADHD-related behaviors and issues. Often other parents and family members don't understand the source of the child's behaviors, and tend to blame the parents of the ADHD child—assuming that some of the child's behaviors displayed are due to poor parenting or lack of discipline. Anyone making such unfair judgments needs to be more aware and empathetic. Sometimes there is more than one child in the family with ADHD, and/or a parent who may be struggling to manage his or her own attention deficit disorder, as well.

The following are some of the supports that parents of children with ADHD may need to help them better cope with some of the challenges, and become better equipped to help their child.

◆ Educate yourself about ADHD. Fortunately there is a wealth of resources about attention deficit disorders and information/expert advice specifically for parents on a number of issues. The more you know and understand about the disorder, the better. This knowledge should give you confidence, hope, and many practical, usable skills to make life easier for your child and your family.

◆ Educate yourself by attending conferences or working with a professional specializing in ADHD to train you in effective parenting/behavior management strategies.

◆ Seek counseling if you are having individual/personal problems with stress and coping. It is very common for families of children with ADHD to need counseling at some point. Many families experience marital strife and family crises due to some of the issues surrounding the ADHD child's behaviors. Parents need to support each other and do everything they can to function as a team which means getting professional help when needed.

◆ Family counseling is often necessary to work out problems.

◆ Join support groups for parents of children with ADD/ADHD. Find out information about your local chapter of CH.A.D.D. (Children and Adults with Attention Deficit Disorders; *see Checklist 74 on Recommended Resources and Organizations*). Many communities have other support groups for parents—through schools, agencies, hospitals, as well. CH.A.D.D., a grass-roots organization that developed from parent need and advocacy, is very well-recognized and respected for the quality and amount of up-to-date information and support it provides to parents and professionals interested in ADD/ADHD.

◆ Support groups are very helpful in that parents can network with other parents of children with ADHD and learn from each other. Just hearing that you "aren't alone"—that many others are dealing with some of the same struggles you are—can be reassuring, comforting, and empowering. Other parents are often the best sources for referrals to professionals in the community, as well. Most of the support groups have meetings where they bring in guest speakers to address different topics of interest to parents.

◆ You need to share the load with household responsibilities as well as all of the parenting issues: homework, monitoring, discipline, and so on. Find ways to simplify and reduce some of the additional demands on your time that may take away from your ability to support each other and parent effectively.

◆ Single parents need to find support wherever possible (i.e., friends, relatives, neighbors, after-school tutoring programs).

◆ Providing parents with some respite by volunteering to babysit for a while, or inviting the child to your home for a weekend, is a wonderful gift from a relative or good friend.

◆ With a very challenging child in the home, it may be necessary to hire two babysitters.

◆ It may be necessary to hire help in the home: for housekeeping, to assist with driving carpools, or assisting with homework.

◆ It is very important for families to find ways to have fun together, play games, participate in recreational activities, and appreciate the "good times."

◆ You need to ask for help when needed. It is hard to cope with stress and frustration alone. If you need a break—are on physical or emotional overload—try to find someone who can help you.

◆ You need the support of teachers—their willingness to communicate clearly with you, monitor your child's daily performance, and provide the feedback. You need teacher sensitivity and responsiveness to struggles with homework issues; as well as flexibility regarding modifications and accommodations as needed for your child.

◆ You need the support of other school staff members (e.g., counselor, administrator, special ed personnel, nurse) who provide service or interventions to your ADHD child (i.e., communication and teamwork).

◆ It is highly recommended that any professionals with whom you choose to work (i.e., counselors, physicians, psychologists) have a strong background in ADHD, and are very aware of the surrounding issues.

✔ Checklists for Parents

The following section addresses topics that are of specific concern to parents: behavior management and positive discipline, organization/study skills and homework issues, as well as how to pursue an evaluation for ADD/ADHD, and advocate effectively for one's child. Parenting a child with ADHD can be far more challenging than parenting a child without the disorder. When a child is hyperactive and impulsive, the behaviors can be very difficult to deal with. It is common to have stress and conflict in the home, and for others to be very judgmental—blaming the parent for the child's inappropriate behaviors.

Some of the checklists are designed to help parents better cope with and manage the more challenging behaviors of their children and teens with attention deficit disorders. Behavior management with ADHD children requires structuring the environment for their success, and often increasing the motivation to follow rules and work towards goals. This section includes strategies for prevention of behavioral problems inside and outside of the home, incentives/reinforcers which may be used as part of a behavioral plan, and guidance for dealing with hyperactive/impulsive behaviors. These checklists are just a beginning—parents of children and teens with ADHD are encouraged to turn to other resources as well to expand their knowledge and confidence in effective behavior management/parenting skills.

A very common characteristic of individuals with ADD/ADHD is weakness in organization, study habits, and time management. It is important for both parents and teachers to structure the environment and provide support and assistance. This section provides strategies and guidance for parents regarding how to improve their child's skills in these areas and, consequently, the chances for school success. Included are checklists that address how parents can help organize their child's work space and materials, and strategies for helping to build time awareness and study skills.

Homework issues are often a source of major conflict and frustration in homes of children with ADHD. This section includes checklists with homework tips for parents, and some organizational tools that reduce the home-work hassles ("Homework Supply Kit").

Children who are distractible and inattentive typically have a hard time with listening and following directions. One of the checklists provides tips for parents on effectively giving directions so that the child is more likely to do what he or she is asked to do.

When parents are concerned about their son or daughter, they may wish to pursue an evaluation. Parents are guided in how to go about doing so in one of the checklists. In addition, parents of a child with ADHD or any special needs must be aware of what is happening in their child's life at school and other situations. To ensure that their son or daughter's needs are being met, parents will have to sometimes step in and advocate on their child's behalf. One of the checklists in this section provides strategies for ef-fective parent advocacy.

20. What Children and Teens with ADHD Need at Home

Most children, whether they express it or not, care very much about their parents' approval, trust, and belief in them. Children and adolescents with ADHD can become easily discouraged with the amount of negative feedback and disapproval they receive on a day-to-day basis. Parents can help their children build confidence and self-esteem by fostering a positive environment in the home, and communicating their love and support of their son or daughter. Children and teens need:

✔ The unconditional love and acceptance of their families

✔ The patience, understanding, and tolerance of their parents

✔ To know they are "okay" and not deficient in the eyes of their parents

✔ Forgiveness

✔ Numerous opportunities to develop their areas of strength (e.g., sports, music, dance, arts)

✔ To be able to pursue their interests and participate in extracurricular activities

✔ Special time with parents—not conditional on anything—just time to talk and have fun together, building/strengthening the relationship

✔ To feel safe and comfortable, and able to "let down their guard"

✔ To be treated with dignity and respect

✔ To be able to express their feelings, worries, concerns, and ideas

✔ To feel they have choice(s) and are involved in some decision-making

✔ Parents who are supportive and encouraging

✔ Positive attention and feedback

✔ To be really listened to

✔ A lot of reassurance and building up of self-esteem

✔ Parents to focus on important issues and down-play less critical ones

✔ An emphasis on their own personal best efforts and self-improvement

✔ Ongoing reminders, support, and prompting—without nagging, criticism, or sarcasm

✔ Parents' involvement and close communication with the school

✔ Help with coping skills and feelings of frustration

✔ Parent modeling, guidance, and coaching in appropriate behaviors and skills

✔ Choices, options, and flexibility

✔ Fun and humor

✔ Praise and recognition for what they are doing "right"

✔ To know that it is okay to make mistakes—we all do—and for parents to acknowledge when they do so

✔ Parents to become knowledgeable about ADHD so that they will be well-equipped to advocate effectively on their behalf

✔ To be able to ask for help, and know parents will do what they can to provide it

✔ Buffering from unnecessary stress and frustration

✔ Fair, clear, and reasonable rules and expectations

✔ Structure—not chaos

✔ Supervision and follow-through

✔ Consistency and logical consequences

✔ Predictability of schedules and routines

✔ Help with organization and study skills

✔ Structuring of their work environment, tasks, and materials

✔ Help getting chores, assignments, and projects started

✔ Preparation for changes and time to adapt/adjust

✔ Help with planning ahead, following schedules, and keeping on-target with deadlines and responsibilities

✔ Escape-valve outlets

21. Effective Behavioral Strategies for Parents

◆ Establish a few specific, important rules/expectations that are clearly understood by all members of the household.

◆ Praise and positively reinforce your child for following rules/expectations.

◆ Establish clear-cut consequences (that are logical, reasonable, and fair) in advance with your child for breaking the rules.

◆ Enforce with consistency.

◆ Provide structure, routine, and predictability.

◆ Set limits and let your child know you mean business.

◆ Catch your child behaving appropriately (as frequently as possible). Immediately reinforce that good behavior with a positive consequence. This means something your child likes (e.g., praise, smiles, hugs, privileges, activities, points/tokens earned towards a reward). Use the smallest reinforcers necessary. Don't overdo it. Keep rewards reasonable—no big-ticket items.

◆ Establish rewards and punishments that are easy to do and as simple as possible.

◆ Use a system of rewarding with stickers, stars, points, etc., on a chart (for one or more specific behaviors), working towards earning a prize, privilege, or other reward once they have earned enough to "cash in."

◆ Realize that children with ADHD can't wait very long for reinforcers. Working toward a long-range goal or "pay-off" is not going to be effective. It is better to use more frequent, smaller reinforcers, but ones that are still motivating.

◆ Reinforcers will have to be changed frequently as well. Children with ADHD won't stay interested in the same reinforcers; they respond best to novelty.

◆ Consequences should be enforced as immediately following the infraction of rules as possible—usually one warning, not several.

◆ Keep in mind to always reward or give positive attention to the behaviors you want to increase or continue to occur.

◆ Negative consequences or punishments are also effective in changing behavior. (Use, however, far more positives than negatives.)

◆ Punishments should not be harsh. The purpose is to **teach** your child through its use and enforcement.

◆ Some effective punishments include: **ignoring** (particularly attention-getting behaviors), **removal of privileges, response costs** (receiving a "fine" or penalty such as removal of some points, stars, tokens earned), **time-out** (isolation for a brief amount of time), and **verbal reprimands** (not yelling and screaming).

◆ If using a "time-out," use a location that is boring for your child, safe, but away from the reinforcement of other people and activity. It should be clear to your child what behaviors will result in time-out. Typically, a reasonable amount of time is one minute per year of age (6-year-old = 6 minutes). Set a timer.

◆ Punishments must have a clear beginning and ending that you are able to control.

◆ Anticipate and plan in advance (with your spouse) how to handle challenging behaviors. Avoid responding and punishing when you are very angry. You don't want to dole out a punishment you will regret later because it is too harsh, inappropriate, or impossible to enforce.

◆ Avoid getting pulled into a power struggle or a shouting match with your child. Disengage. Don't be afraid to say, "I'm too angry to talk about this right now. We will discuss this later." Take time to step back, calm down, and think before you act.

◆ When punishing, be careful to focus on the *behavior* that is inappropriate. Don't attack the child as "being bad" or criticize his or her character.

◆ Prioritize and focus on what's important. You can't make an issue out of everything.

◆ Use "do" statements rather than "don't" statements. ("Walk in the house" rather than "Don't run in the house.")

◆ When delivering consequences, do so in a calm but firm voice. State the consequence without lecturing. Be direct and to the point.

◆ Try lowering your voice rather than raising it.

◆ Talk about, acknowledge, and label feelings—your child's and your own.

◆ No matter how exhausted or frustrated you are, maintain your authority as a parent and follow through on what you need to do.

◆ It is far more difficult to manage the behaviors of children with ADHD than most other children. Be willing to seek professional help to find more effective strategies and guidance. Get referrals from other parents of children with similar needs. Find a mental health professional who is very familiar with ADHD and experienced in dealing with hyperactive/impulsive behaviors.

NOTE:

There are many outstanding books on behavior management and positive discipline, specifically geared for parents of children with ADHD. It is recommended to learn as much as possible about the specific techniques and strategies effective for dealing with challenging behaviors, and the best ways to implement rewards and punishments.

22. PREVENTING BEHAVIOR PROBLEMS IN THE HOME

◆ Establish and provide the necessary structure: rules/expectations and consequences as described in *Checklists 21-23 and 29*.

◆ Set limits; be clear and consistent.

◆ Your responses to your child's behaviors/misbehaviors should be predictable, not random.

◆ Organize and arrange the home environment in a way that will optimize the chances for success and avoid conflict.

◆ Anticipate problem situations and avoid them.

◆ Set up routines and adhere to them as closely as possible. For example: morning routines for getting ready for school, mealtime routines, homework routines, bedtime routines.

◆ Try to keep calm and avoid discipline that is reactive, not thought out in advance.

◆ Remove items or objects you don't want your impulsive/hyperactive child to touch or play with. "Child-proof" the house.

◆ Anticipate stressors and frustrating expectations and circumvent them.

◆ Avoid fatigue—your own and your child's.

◆ Focus on your child when he or she is behaving appropriately. Make it your goal to catch your child doing things right with high frequency and *praise*. Identify and specifically point out the positive behavior(s) and positively reinforce at those times. *(See Checklist 25 on Positive Incentives and Reinforcers for Home—social, activity, material ones.)* Parental approval is very important to most children. Knowing that you are aware of their efforts to exhibit self control and that they can earn your approval and other awards is a strong incentive.

◆ Try to give your ADHD child as much of his or her own space as possible.

◆ Plan ahead which behaviors you will work towards increasing and how you will reward (positively reinforce those behaviors).

◆ Plan ahead how you will deal with inappropriate, challenging behaviors—what you (both parents) agree to be the consequences/

punishments for those specific behaviors. Make sure all of these expectations and the consequences are spelled out to your child and clearly understood.

◆ Be observant. Notice when your child is becoming agitated, overly stimulated, angry, etc., and intervene. Try redirecting your child's attention and focus on something else.

◆ Only give your child chores and responsibilities that he or she is developmentally able to handle. For your child that means what he or she is capable of, not what other kids of his or her age or other siblings may be able to do.

◆ Provide the supports to enable your child to follow-through with chores and responsibilities. Remember that forgetfulness, procrastination, and disorganization are part of the ADD picture. Your ADHD child will need reminders, help getting started, etc.

◆ Provide physical outlets. Your child needs to be able to release energy and participate in physical activities (running, swimming, gymnastics, dancing, riding bike, playing ball).

◆ Maintain flexibility and a sense of humor!

◆ Avoid sarcasm, ridicule, criticism, nagging, yelling, and screaming or physical punishment.

◆ Monitor and supervise.

◆ Prepare your child for changes in the home, such as redecorating, change in parent work schedules, visitors/house guests. Talk about the change and avoid surprises.

◆ Purchase toys, books, games, etc., that are developmentally appropriate for your child—not too frustrating.

◆ Avoid competitive activities and/or prepare for games and activities that involve competition. Walk your child through the strategies of what to do if he or she loses a game. Reinforce good sportsmanship—and that when playing games, he or she can't always win. Praise and reward behavior when playing games that require your child to display self control.

◆ Provide a limited number of choices. Don't allow your child to dump out all of his or her toys, or choose from all the music/video tapes, or examine all the books before choosing one for you to read with him or her. Allow your child to choose from only a few at one time.

◆ Be aware of siblings who are teasing and provoking your ADHD child, and intervene.

◆ *See the checklists on Giving Directions—Tips for Parents (28) and Homework Tips for Parents (27) for more strategies that will prevent behavioral problems and conflict at home.*

23. Preventing Behavior Problems Outside of the Home

Many parents of children with ADHD dread having to take their son or daughter shopping with them, or to other places outside of the home where behavior issues often emerge. The behavioral controls expected in some of these environments can be more than a child with ADHD is able to handle. Children who are overactive and impulsive will engage in behavior that is often quite embarrassing to the parent, as well. The following are some recommendations for preventing, or at least reducing potential behavior problems which can occur:

◆ Teach, model, and practice appropriate behaviors and manners that you expect your child to display outside of the home (e.g., follow directions, clean up after self, walk/don't run in the house/building, say "please" and "thank you").

◆ Anticipate and prepare for potential problems.

◆ Give your child time to get ready and talk about what to expect. Give advance notice. Remember how any change of routine can be stressful and unnerving. Children with ADHD need preparation; avoid catching them off guard.

◆ Before going into public places (stores, doctor's offices, restaurants, church, movie theaters) or visiting other people's homes, talk to your child about behavioral expectations. State the rules simply. Review. Have your child repeat them back to you.

◆ Establish reward(s) that your child will be able to receive if he or she behaves appropriately and follows the rules.

◆ Don't put your child in situations that are too taxing on his or her self control and attention span.

◆ Avoid shopping without building in the opportunity for your child to get something small.

◆ Let your child know the consequences if he or she behaves inappropriately. Mean what you say!

◆ Give written directions if appropriate.

◆ Don't take your child to places that you know will be too stimulating or difficult to manage the behavior and supervise.

◆ Remove your child from the situation when he or she is behaving inappropriately or showing signs of losing control.

◆ Supervise. Supervise. Supervise.

◆ Talk with your child about the natural consequences of inappropriate behavior (e.g., friends or their parents won't want to invite him or her to their house again, other children will get angry and not want to play).

◆ Be prepared with a "bag of tricks." Knowing the nature of ADHD—how children bore easily and need to be kept busy—don't leave the house without toys, books, audiotapes, games, etc., that can occupy your child and keep him or her entertained. Keep the "bag of tricks" replenished and changing to maintain novelty and interest.

◆ Give your child feedback when you are with him or her outside of the home. "I'm proud of how you are . . . . It looks like you'll probably earn the . . . we talked about."

◆ Avoid fatigue. Don't take your child out when he or she is tired and needs a nap.

24. Dealing with Hyperactive/Impulsive Behavior at Home

◆ Impose the necessary **structure** (rules, expectations, limits/boundaries, positive and negative consequences, organization, etc.) that is absolutely crucial to the management, well-being, and success of your child.

◆ *See Checklist 21 on Effective Behavioral Strategies for Parents, Checklist 25 on Positive Incentives and Reinforcers for the Home, and Checklist 29 on Environmental Modifications that Make a Difference at Home.*

◆ Know your child's behavioral tendencies and temperament. Understand the source of these behaviors which are difficult to manage and deal with. Learn everything you can about ADHD and the manifestations of the disorder. This knowledge and awareness is so important for those living with ADHD. It helps us be more tolerant and empathetic, and to maintain our sense of humor when we really understand that the challenging behaviors are not deliberate—that the lack of impulse control and difficulty regulating behavior and activity level is physiological—not willful.

◆ Seek professional help and a proper diagnosis. *(For more recommendations, see Checklist 4 on Characteristics of Predominantly Hyperactive/Impulsive Type of ADHD, and Checklist 11 on Making the Diagnosis: What Is a Comprehensive Evaluation for ADHD? Checklist 30 on Pursuing an Evaluation for Your Child.)*

◆ Implement all interventions and strategies possible to PREVENT behavioral issues that are likely to occur due to your child's impulsivity and/or hyperactivity. *(For more recommendations, see Checklist 22 on Preventing Behavioral Problems in the Home and Checklist 23 on Preventing Behavioral Problems Outside of the Home.)*

◆ Look for warning signs of your child's agitation, becoming over-stimulated, becoming frustrated, having difficulty sitting, controlling self, etc., and intervene early (i.e., redirect, remove from situation, change the focus, try calming techniques, remind about rewards/consequences).

◆ Teach your child strategies for relaxation and anger control. *(See Checklist 68 on Relaxation, Guided Imagery, and Visualization Techniques.)*

◆ Once your child has been taught a few strategies, practice them often, model their use, prompt, and cue to use those strategies.

◆ Catch your child when he or she is exhibiting behaviors that are appropriate and reward immediately. For example, **use positive reinforcement** when your child: shows good self-control, sits appropriately, takes turns in games, exhibits good sportsmanship, performs a task without rushing through it carelessly, doesn't interrupt, etc. Specifically point out what you noticed your child doing right, thank him or her, and reward.

◆ Take immediate action and enforce negative consequences (i.e., time-out, loss of privileges, other response costs) that your child knows are to occur for inappropriate behaviors.

◆ Provide time and a place to calm down, get under control, avoid escalation of conflict. (For you as well as your child.)

◆ Prioritize your focus on behaviors. Ignore minor misbehaviors or those that are just annoying and irritating. Clearly deal with the important behaviors (i.e., those that are a matter of safety, those that infringe upon the rights of others, and so forth).

◆ Provide as many opportunities as possible for your child to socialize and play with other children in situations that don't tax his or her ability to maintain self control. For example, invite a friend over to the house or allow your child to visit a friend at his or her house for a few hours, not for a full day. Communicate with the parents of your child's friend. Let them know that they may call you if any problems arise.

◆ Encourage friendships and association with children who are good role models.

◆ Teach your child positive strategies for resolving conflicts, coping and dealing with frustrations, stopping and thinking before acting.

◆ Anticipate the probability of breaking things and having accidents. Arrange the environment accordingly to minimize this occurring. For example, buy plastic, not glass. Move expensive, valuable items out of reach. If an accident occurs, downplay it. Explain that accidents happen, and avoid reacting strongly.

◆ Model patience, talking/not screaming, problem solving, and calmness whenever possible.

◆ Supervise closely.

◆ Encourage your child (and model within the family) how to express feelings, share emotions, and talk about issues and problems.

It is hard to do so in the midst of a situation when emotions run high. However, at a later time—a more teachable moment—it is easier and more productive.

◆ Set up situations in which your child has a better chance of success. For example, don't make him or her sit at the table a long time after eating. Teach a proper way to ask to be excused. Play games that engage participation without having to wait excessively for a turn.

◆ Play board games and other games together—talking about and teaching how to lose a game like a good sport—and the importance of doing so when with peers.

◆ Provide your child with plenty of exercise and opportunities to release his or her energy. Children with ADHD are often more successful in sports such as soccer (where everyone is running around as a pack) as opposed to being an outfielder on a baseball team (having to stay and wait for a ball to come to you). Swimming, track and field, martial arts, dance, and gymnastics are often excellent physical activities for children with ADHD because they teach self discipline and control, concentration and focus, and are less competitive than many other sports.

◆ Find every opportunity for your child to build areas of strength and interest. Try to provide activities that are enjoyable and motivating to your son or daughter. Not only will this build self-esteem and confidence, but it will also reduce behavioral issues (as one is less likely to engage in misbehavior when doing activities that are fun).

◆ Employ proper treatments for ADHD that can greatly improve your hyperactive/impulsive child's chances for success. Monitor the treatment plan and make adjustments as necessary. *(See Checklist 13 on A Comprehensive Treatment Program for ADHD.)*

◆ Adjust your expectations to be reasonable. Know that your child's behaviors are often that of a much younger child. Change your mindset and don't expect your child to be able to "act his or her age." A child is only able to function as he or she is developmentally able to do so. **Note:** It is very common for children with ADHD to get along better with and prefer playing with younger children.

◆ Living with a hyperactive/impulsive child (especially one whose behaviors are more on the severe end of the scale) is extremely difficult. Learn effective coping strategies. Find support systems to help you! *(See Checklist 74 on Recommended Resources and Organizations.)*

25. POSITIVE INCENTIVES AND REINFORCERS FOR HOME

Social Reinforcers

✔ Positive attention

✔ Hugs

✔ Kisses

✔ Placing arm around child

✔ Smiles

✔ Thumbs-up sign

✔ High five

✔ Piggyback ride

✔ Cheering

✔ Specific praise such as:

"I like it when you . . . "

"That sure was grown up of you when . . . "

"That was great the way you . . . "

"It makes me so happy when you . . . "

"I'm so proud of how you . . . "

"Thank you for . . . "

"I can really tell you worked hard on . . . "

"Let's show mom . . . "

"Let's make a copy of this for grandma . . . "

"Let's hang this up somewhere special . . . "

"Great job on how you . . . "

"I can't wait to tell dad how you . . . "

"I knew you could do it!"

Activity Reinforcers

✔ Playing a special game

✔ An outing (park, restaurant, beach)

✔ Inviting a friend to visit

✔ Extended bedtime

✔ Extra TV time, phone privilege, time on computer, play time

✔ Special time alone with parent (out for breakfast, shopping, ice cream, ball game, building something)

✔ Freedom from a chore(s)

✔ Drawing or painting

✔ Using playground equipment

✔ Selecting meal for dinner

✔ Baking cupcakes, cookies

✔ Riding bike—alone or with parent(s)

✔ Swimming, skating, bowling, golfing

✔ Renting a movie

✔ Craft project

✔ Playing board game(s)

✔ Camping

✔ Spending time with special person (grandparent)

✔ Playing Nintendo™

✔ Computer games

✔ Staying overnight at a friend's or relative's house

✔ Inviting someone to sleep over

✔ Inviting friend for lunch/dinner

✔ Extended curfew

✔ Participating in school activity that costs money (e.g., ski trip)

Material Reinforcers

✔ Toys

✔ Art supplies

✔ Snacks

✔ Trinkets

✔ Jewelry

✔ Books/magazines

✔ Games
✔ CDs/tapes/videos
✔ Clothing
✔ Accessories
✔ Puzzles
✔ Pets
✔ Sports equipment
✔ Wanted items for room
✔ Money

26. WHAT PARENTS CAN DO TO HELP THEIR CHILDREN GET ORGANIZED

Disorganization and lack of time awareness are common character-istics of ADHD. Your child or teen is likely weak in these skills and will need your help, support, and "coaching" in order to be success-ful in school. Try not to be critical; instead, keep in mind that this is part of the disorder.

Helping to Organize Your Child's Work Space and Materials

Note: See recommendations to teachers regarding use of 3-ring binder and required school supplies/materials.

◆ Provide your child with a backpack and notebook/binder ac-cording to teacher's specifications.

◆ Provide all necessary supplies for school and homework. *(See Homework Supply Kit recommendations at the end of this checklist.)*

◆ Label your child's materials and possessions with his or her name.

◆ Together with your child choose a place in the home that has adequate lighting, is comfortable for working, and is as free from distractions as possible.

◆ Together with your child, carefully examine his or her work space. Make sure there is available a large working surface (desk-top) free from clutter. If your child has a computer, don't place it on the desk, which cuts down considerably on his or her working surface area. Instead, place the computer on a separate desk or table.

◆ Have your child clear out desk drawers and shelves of work, projects, and papers that were from different school years. Together, decide on what you would like to keep and store out of the way (in colored boxes, or zipper portfolios) in order to make room for cur-rent papers and projects.

◆ Provide your child with a corkboard and pins to hang up im-portant papers.

◆ Dry-erase boards and markers are helpful to hang in the kitchen and your child's room for important notes and messages.

◆ Provide a file with color-coded folders in which your child can keep papers stored categorically.

◆ Keep trays and bins for storing supplies/materials that will remove some of the clutter from the desktop.

◆ Keep a 3-hole punch and electric pencil sharpener easily accessible.

◆ Besides a master calendar (in kitchen), provide your child with a desk calendar that serves as an overview of important dates, activities, and events.

◆ Assist your child with cleaning and organizing by getting him or her started.

◆ Make the time to help your child clean and organize his or her backpack, notebook, desk, and room.

◆ Provide the necessary supplies to help your child be organized at school. (You will likely have to replace and replenish supplies often.) Have your child take inventory of what needs replacement or ask the teacher.

◆ Provide the necessary storage space (shelves, closet space, bins, trays, drawers) for organizing your child's room efficiently.

◆ Besides supplies/materials in the room (e.g., on the desk), maintain a Homework Supply Kit.

◆ Encourage and help your child get in the habit of putting all books, notebooks, signed notes, and other necessary materials inside the backpack before bedtime. Place in the same spot every night.

Helping with Time Management and Awareness

◆ Teach your child how to tell time and read a non-digital clock.

◆ Teach your child how to read calendars and schedules.

◆ Assist your child with prioritization of activities and workload.

◆ Give your child advance notice whenever possible.

◆ Help your child break down longer assignments into smaller, manageable increments.

◆ **IMPORTANT:** Your assistance with time management and structuring of long-term school projects (i.e., book reports, science projects, research projects) will be critical for the success of your child. See the suggestions to teachers as to how they should structure and provide supports to students.

◆ Pay close attention to due dates. Post the project requirements. Together with your child, record on a master calendar the due date of the final project and plan when to do the steps along the way (i.e., going to the library, getting resources and materials). Ask the teacher for feedback. Don't assume your child is working on projects at school, even if he or she is given some time in class to do it. Avoid procrastination and last-minute scrambling to complete projects.

◆ Expect your child to record assignments (see the teacher for help) and monitor that this is being done. Ask to see their assignment calendars/sheets every day.

◆ Teach your child to use "things to do" lists (writing down and then crossing out accomplished tasks).

◆ Help to plan a "things to do" list when your child comes home from school—scheduling for the evening, and estimating together with your child how long each assignment/activity should take.

◆ Help with preparing and following schedules.

◆ Set a schedule for homework. Some children like to come home and immediately get part or all of their homework done and out of the way. Others need a break before tackling any homework. Together with your child plan a schedule or time for homework that can be adhered to as consistently as possible.

◆ Post a master calendar or wall chart for important events and activities. Remember to refer to it often.

◆ Help transfer important extracurricular activities/scheduling onto your child's personal calendar/planner.

◆ Get your child a watch to wear and a clock that is accurate in his or her room. Providing your child with a watch that has an alarm set is very helpful, especially if your child takes medication and needs to go to the nurse's office during school.

◆ Consider "no phone call" times in the evening.

Other Ways Parents Can Help

◆ Establish a daily routine with expectations clearly defined and discussed in the family (i.e., getting ready for school, chores, homework, bedtime routine).

◆ Adhere as closely as possible to a schedule during the school week.

◆ When giving chores or responsibilities around the house, be sure they are reasonable, limited in number, and developmentally appropriate for your ADHD child.

◆ Write down and post all chores/responsibilities in a highly visible place.

◆ Support your child from being distracted by the TV by turning it off.

◆ Use self-stick notes to place on mirrors, doors, and other visible places for reminders.

◆ If possible, be available when your child is doing homework to help as needed; but don't get in the habit of having your child rely on you. However tempting it may be, DON'T DO THE WORK for your child.

◆ Ask to see how your child is recording assignments. Praise all efforts at being organized.

◆ Expect your child to have all assignments recorded. If your child is one who tends to have difficulty keeping up with assignments, turning work in on time, following through with projects and daily homework, see the teacher! Let the teacher know that this is an area of weakness for your child, and that you want to be in a position to help. Request the teacher's help in making sure all assignments are recorded daily. Then be sure to follow through by reviewing the recorded assignments with your child.

◆ Reinforce with your child the need to not leave school until they check their assignment sheet/calendar. Make sure they have any necessary books and materials needed to do the homework.

◆ Have your child take the phone numbers of a few responsible students that he or she can call if there is a question about school work. Ask the teacher to assign a responsible buddy for this purpose.

Some accommodating teachers are willing to share their own home phone number.

◆ Be sure to ask for progress notes that keep you appraised as to how your child is doing. If you haven't received any communication or feedback for a while, call the teacher or write a note.

◆ Help your child divide the workload and assignments into manageable chunks. Ask to see what he or she has accomplished after a certain amount of time, or to show you when a particular assignment is done.

◆ Consider using a timer if your child has difficulty staying on task. Sometimes a "beat the clock system" is effective in motivating children to complete a task before the timer goes off. Ask to see the completed task, and reward if it was done with relative accuracy and neatness. Even more effective is having the child self-monitor, requiring that he or she take a few minutes more to check over the work and self-correct as needed.

◆ Communicate your expectations that homework is a priority. In today's busy society, many families are over-extended with the number of extracurricular activities that they are involved in. If there is very little time in an evening to devote to schoolwork, perhaps you need to re-examine your commitments and activities— "something has to give."

◆ Only a reasonable amount of time should be spent on homework. If homework assignments seem to be taking an inordinate amount of time and your child is struggling, make an appointment with the teacher. Special modifications may need to be arranged (i.e., shorter assignments, oral rather than written projects, child dictates and you transcribe for him or her). Make sure the teacher understands your efforts and the extraordinary difficulty your ADHD child is having surrounding homework. If the teacher is unwilling to accept any reasonable adjustments or make modifications, see the administrator.

◆ Encourage your child and emphasize **effort** as the most important criteria.

◆ Praise your child for being on-task, getting to work, and taking responsibility. Give extra praise for accomplishment and progress. Rewards and incentives are effective and appropriate.

◆ *See these checklists for more tips and strategies: Homework Tips for Parents (27), Environmental Modifications that Make a Difference at Home (29), and What Teachers Can Do to Help Build Organization and Study Skills (38).*

The Homework Supply Kit

Parents can help their child considerably in cutting down on wasted time spent searching the house for necessary homework supplies and materials. Not only is it a frustrating waste of precious minutes, but it also causes a major break in productivity, pulling children unnecessarily off-task.

This Homework Supply Kit can be stored in anything portable, preferrably a lightweight container with a lid. Some children work at their desks, others on kitchen or dining room tables, others prefer to spread out on their beds or the floor. With this system, it doesn't matter the location of where your children choose to study. The necessary supplies can accompany them anywhere.

Recommended Supplies (Depending on Age of Your Child)

- ✔ Plenty of paper
- ✔ Sharpened pencils with erasers
- ✔ Pencil sharpener
- ✔ Ruler
- ✔ Crayons
- ✔ Paper hole reinforcers
- ✔ Glue stick
- ✔ Colored pencils
- ✔ Colored pens and markers (thick and thin points)
- ✔ Stapler with box of staples
- ✔ Paper clips
- ✔ Single-hole punch
- ✔ Three-hole punch
- ✔ Dictionary
- ✔ Thesaurus
- ✔ Electronic spell check
- ✔ Self-stick notepads
- ✔ Highlighter pens
- ✔ Index cards
- ✔ Calculator

27. HOMEWORK TIPS FOR PARENTS

◆ Establish a routine and schedule for homework (a specific time and place) and adhere to the schedule as closely as possible. Some children prefer to start homework shortly after they come home from school, while others need time to play, relax first and then start homework later. Don't allow your child to wait until the evening, though, to get started.

◆ Examine assignment sheet/calendar with your child after school. Help with planning a things-to-do list of tasks for the evening. Some prefer to do the easiest, quickest tasks/assignments first; others like to tackle the hardest ones first.

◆ Limit distractions in the home during homework hours (such as reducing unnecessary noise, activity and phone calls; and turning off the TV).

◆ Encourage your child to cross off tasks as they are accomplished.

◆ Allow your child a break between homework assignments. In fact, your child can reward him- or herself with a snack and play/ exercise break after completing each assignment or two.

◆ If your teen has his or her own phone, restrict use during homework hours, and consider using an answering machine during these times.

◆ Make sure your child has a quiet work space, with minimal distractions and adequate lighting and ventilation.

◆ Be sure your child has the necessary supplies handy. *(See Checklist 26 on What Parents Can Do to Help Their Children Get Organized, including The Homework Supply Kit recommendations.)*

◆ Assist your child in dividing assignments into smaller parts or segments that are more manageable and less overwhelming.

◆ Assist your child in *getting started* on assignments (i.e., reading the directions together, doing the first items together, observing as your child does the next problem/item on his or her own). Then get up and leave.

◆ Monitor and give feedback without doing all the work together. You want your child to attempt as much as possible independently.

◆ First get your child started. Then have your child continue with a short amount to accomplish independently (a row or two, the next few items or sentences to be written, etc.). Check over that amount of work to make sure your child is doing it accurately. Continuing in this format (checking and giving feedback on small amounts) is preferable to sitting next to your son or daughter as he or she is working.

◆ Look over the homework, checking for completion, careless errors, and legibility.

◆ Praise and compliment your child when he or she puts forth good effort. In a supportive, non-critical manner it is appropriate and helpful to assist in pointing out and making some corrections of errors on the homework.

◆ It is not your responsibility to correct all of your child's errors on homework or make him or her complete and turn in a perfect paper.

◆ If the homework is too confusing or difficult for your child to be able to do (or for you to understand from the directions what is expected), let the teacher know.

◆ Remind your child to do homework and offer incentives: "When you finish your homework, you can watch TV, or play a game."

◆ A contract for a larger incentive/reinforcer may be worked out as part of a plan to motivate your child to persist and follow-through with homework. ("If you have no missing or late homework assignments this next week, you will earn . . .").

◆ If homework is a frequent cause of battles, tears, and frustration in your home, seek help! Request modifications and adjustments in homework assignments.

◆ Let the teacher know your child's frustration and tolerance level in the evening. The teacher needs to be aware of the amount of time it takes your child to complete tasks, and what efforts you are making to help at home.

◆ If your child's teacher is not willing to make reasonable accommodations, go to the administrator.

◆ Be available to answer questions, support, and help your child stay on task.

◆ Some children prefer and do better working on homework in a location with you in the vicinity (e.g., dining room table) rather than away in their room.

◆ Being around to help and assist as needed is good. However, try not to get in the habit of having your child rely on you overseeing every minute.

◆ Try using a kitchen timer to challenge your child to stay on task, rewarding work completed with relative accuracy during that time frame.

◆ Use the kitchen timer and tell your child that you will come back to check his or her progress on homework when the timer rings.

◆ Experiment with music softly playing in the background because it helps some children to concentrate. Try various types of instrumental music and environmental sounds. *(See Checklist 29 on Environmental Modifications that Make a Difference at Home).*

◆ One of the best possible investments you can make is the purchase of a computer and printer. Being able to do written assignments on the computer will make life much easier for your child, and greatly improve the appearance of projects/assignments.

◆ Help your child study for tests. Study together. Quiz your child in a variety of formats.

◆ If your child struggles with reading, help by reading the material together or reading it to him or her.

◆ Help your child with reading and comprehending content area textbooks by photocopying the chapter of the book your child is studying. It is much easier to write notes directly on the pages, underline or color-highlight key vocabulary, main ideas, and so forth.

◆ Allow your child to dictate to you while you do the writing and recording of responses for him or her. These accommodations to help bypass writing difficulties are reasonable for children with ADHD. Speak to the teacher.

◆ Work a certain amount of time and then stop working on homework. Don't force your child to spend an excessive and inappropriate amount of time on homework. If you feel your child worked enough for one night, write a note to the teacher and attach it to the homework.

◆ Again, communicate with the teacher and try to come to a reasonable agreement about daily homework expectations.

◆ Make sure your child has all papers, books, notebooks, etc., in the backpack before going to bed, placed so that he or she can't miss seeing it or tripping over it when leaving the house in the morning.

◆ **Note:** It is very common for students with ADHD to fail to turn in their finished work. This is very frustrating to know your child struggled to do the work, and then never gets credit for having done it. Papers seem to mysteriously vanish off the face of the earth! Supervise that completed work leaves the home and is in the notebook/backpack. You may want to arrange with the teacher a system for collecting the work immediately upon arrival at school.

◆ If your child is on medication during the school day, but *cannot* get through the homework, consult with your doctor. Many children with ADHD are more successful with a small dosage of medication in the late afternoon.

◆ Many parents find it very difficult to help their own child with school work. Find someone who can. Consider hiring a tutor! Often a junior or senior high school student is ideal, depending on the need and age of your child.

◆ Make sure your child has the phone number of a study buddy—at least one responsible classmate to call for clarification of homework assignments.

◆ Some schools are modernizing their communication systems with homework hotlines, recording daily assignments on teachers' voice mail, and establishing school websites with teachers all being on-line and able to enter all homework assignments.

◆ If your child frequently forgets to bring home textbooks, ask if you can borrow another set for home. If not, consider purchasing one.

◆ Parents, the biggest struggle is keeping on top of those dreaded *long-range homework assignments* (reports, projects). This is something you will need to be vigilant about. Ask for a copy of the project requirements. Post at home and go over it together with your child. Write the due date on a master calendar. Then plan how to break down the project into manageable parts, scheduling steps along the way. Get started AT ONCE with going to the library, gathering resources, beginning the reading, and so forth.

◆ Praise and reward work completion.

◆ Again, as tempting as it may be, DON'T do the work for your child.

◆ *See all of the checklists in the academic strategy section for home and school, as well as the organization and environmental modifications checklists in this parent section for additional strategies to help with homework.*

28. GIVING DIRECTIONS—TIPS FOR PARENTS

◆ Get your child's attention directly before giving directions. This means face to face and direct eye contact (not just calling out what you expect your child to do).

◆ You may need to walk over to touch or physically cue your child prior to giving directions.

◆ Don't attempt to give directions or instructions if you are competing with the distraction of TV, music, video games, etc. First turn those off to gain their attention and focus.

◆ Show your child what you want him or her to do. Model and walk through the steps. Check that your child understands.

◆ Depending on the developmental skill of your child, one direction at a time is often all your son or daughter is capable of remembering and following through on. Don't give a series of directions.

◆ Provide multisensory instructions. Use a visual chart of tasks or chores your child is to do.

◆ A helpful technique for young children is to draw or cut out pictures on a chart hanging in the room that shows the sequence of morning activities or evening activities: (1) clothing—to get dressed, (2) cereal bowl—to show eating breakfast, (3) hairbrush and toothbrush—grooming. As your child completes the task, he or she moves a clothespin down the chart next to that corresponding picture.

◆ For older children write down directions in addition to giving the directions orally.

◆ Always check for understanding of directions. Have your child repeat or rephrase what you asked him or her to do.

◆ Use color to get your child's attention with anything you put in writing (key words, pictures, etc.).

◆ Try putting down on paper the task you want done with words or pictures, and giving that visual direction to your child.

◆ Keep directions clear, brief, and to the point.

◆ Give directions as statements, not questions. Say, "Lights off in 15 minutes." Don't say, "Are you ready to turn off the lights?"

◆ Be sure to give frequent PRAISE and POSITIVE FEEDBACK when your child follows directions and/or is making a good attempt to do so.

◆ Provide the follow-up when you give directions (i.e., inspect, check your child's work, and praise a job well done).

◆ REWARD your child for following directions as appropriate. For example, "You did a great job straightening up your room as I asked. You get to . . . (choose a game, have a snack)."

◆ Try not to lose your temper when your child fails to follow directions. Remember that it is characteristic of ADHD to have difficulty:

 – disengaging from activities, especially fun ones that they have not finished

 – responding and following through without structuring, adult prompting, and cueing

 – with recall/memory

◆ Examine what you asked your son or daughter to do and see if you provided enough structure and assistance to enable him or her to follow through with the directions given. It's easy to forget that even though they are at an age where they *should* remember and be able to do a task independently, developmentally they are not able to do so, and need some of the supports that a younger child would normally require.

◆ Break down tasks into smaller steps that you want to get done. Give one step at a time.

◆ Avoid vague directions that your child can interpret differently than you (e.g., "Clean up your room"). Be specific in defining what you expect done (clothes hung in closet or folded/placed in drawers, bed made, toys in storage bins).

◆ Provide needed support by working alongside your child on a task together. Try turning unpleasant chores/tasks into more pleasant or motivating experiences by making a game of it when possible; for example, *Beat the Clock* challenges such as, "Let's see if you can finish picking up your toys and get in your pajamas while the commercials are on, or . . . before the alarm goes off . . . or by the end of the song . . . "

◆ Once you have provided the necessary support and guidance, it is important that your child work independently to the best of his or her ability. You don't want to establish co-dependent behaviors that can be disabling to both you and your child.

29. Environmental Modifications that Make a Difference at Home

◆ Provide as much structure and predictability in the home as possible. Establish some rules, routines, and schedules to help life run smoother.

◆ Plan with your child a routine/schedule (e.g., for getting ready for school in the morning, homework, mealtime, bedtime).

◆ Your child needs to know what is viewed as acceptable and unacceptable behavior at home, and the consequences (positive and negative) for both.

◆ Help your child to organize his or her room for ease in locating, using, and cleaning up his or her belongings, and for creating a sense of order.

◆ Provide your child with his or her own space for doing homework and studying (that will be removed from noisy siblings, and other constant distractions and interference).

◆ Design your child's work space with easy access to necessary supplies and materials.

◆ Provide well-labeled storage bins, containers, shelving, drawers, and trays.

◆ Provide sufficient, uncluttered desktop space and storage space.

◆ Provide a work space that is well-lit and ventilated.

◆ Use *color* strategically to organize.

◆ Post calendars and use master schedules. Write each family member's name and activities in different colors.

◆ Minimize distractions that will interfere with your child's ability to focus and do his or her homework.

◆ If your child has his or her own TV, restrict its use during homework hours or remove from the room.

◆ Try turning the family TV off in the house during homework hours.

◆ If your child has his or her own phone in the room, you may need to restrict its use during homework hours. Consider an answering machine for teens.

◆ Keep in mind that children with ADHD need their own *space*, and as much space as possible.

◆ *See the checklists on What Parents Can Do to Help Their Children Get Organized (26) and Homework Tips for Parents (27) for more ideas on how to establish a home environment conducive to studying.*

◆ Experiment with playing a variety of music in the home. Different kinds of music can increase productivity, and stimulate our ability to think and be creative. Other kinds of music are calming, relaxing, and healing. Consider purchasing instrumental cassettes/CDs including environmental sounds (e.g., ocean sounds, rain forest), classical, jazz, etc. There is some research demonstrating the effectiveness of music with ADHD children that has 60 beats per minute (such as instrumental compositions by Gary Lamb). *See Checklist 68 on Relaxation, Guided Imagery, and Visualization Techniques.*

◆ Realize that we all have our own learning styles and preferences. Some of us don't like to work at a desk/chair, and are more comfortable and productive sitting on the carpet or propped up against a back rest—writing with paper attached to a clipboard or on a laptop desk.

◆ Design informal areas for study and relaxation in the house. Consider big cushions, beanbag chairs, low tables (with chairs like stadium seats).

◆ We all need a time/place for *quiet*. Children with ADHD particularly need to be able to have a "quiet area" to be able to go and regroup and calm down. Try to establish some room/space in the home with quiet colors, perhaps placing an aquarium (to quietly watch the fish), and equipped with relaxing music (and earphones). Any member of the family should be able to "escape" to that quiet room when needed.

◆ Some children are too distracted in their room to do homework there, or don't work productively isolated. Allow your child to do his or her homework in another area of the house (e.g., dining room, den) where parent(s) are in the same vicinity.

◆ If your child shares a room with a sibling, consider allowing your ADHD child to do his or her homework in your room (perhaps on a card table).

◆ If your child tends to be accident-prone or destructive, buy with this in mind, and place furniture and items strategically.

◆ Consider covering a desk/table top with butcher paper for doodling/drawing.

◆ If possible, design an area of the house—such as the basement—with furniture (or lack of), where rambunctious behavior is tolerated.

◆ Many children with ADHD are skilled at and *love* to construct, build things/take them apart, do arts and crafts, and other hands-on activities. These activities should be encouraged, although they can be messy. Supply the necessary materials, tools, and storage containers.

◆ Many working parents with late schedules restrict their children to the house after school (as it is unsafe to let them play outside unsupervised). Children with ADHD particularly need to be able to release their energy with vigorous activity (i.e., playing outside, riding bikes, participating in organized sports). Explore ways for your child to have this opportunity, such as after-school programs at a recreation center.

30. PURSUING AN EVALUATION FOR YOUR CHILD

At what point would a parent consider pursuing an evaluation for ADHD? There is no need to seek an evaluation for possible ADHD if the child's symptoms/behaviors are not causing a problem in functioning. If your son or daughter is displaying some of the characteristics of ADHD and you question whether or not it may be ADHD, unless those characteristics are affecting how well your child is performing academically, socially or behaviorally in daily life, having the "label" of ADHD serves no purpose. The behaviors associated with ADHD should be problematic to go through the evaluation process.

◆ It is very common for parents to become aware and concerned about their child's problematic behaviors when the child starts school, and faces the demands of an academic environment; or in third or fourth grades when the academic work gets much harder, and it is expected that the child be able to work independently, initiate and complete tasks, and so on. Sometimes the student manages to function adequately in an elementary school setting, but falls apart at the middle school level. When looking at the student's elementary school history, the behaviors/symptoms were evident, but under control. Now, clearly something needs to be done to help the child.

◆ At whatever stage you may become concerned about your child's functioning, and suspect that it may be the result of ADHD, there are several steps you may take in pursuing an evaluation:

– Speak to the classroom teacher(s). Ask for their input and observations regarding your child's performance/production, achievement, and behavior. Ask the teacher to implement a few reasonable interventions to help with any of the above concerns; and find out how you can assist/support from your end.

– Let the teacher know you want to have your child evaluated and why. Then go speak with the school counselor, principal, school nurse, or school psychologist with your request. At many schools the first step is scheduling a Student Study Team meeting. *(See Checklist 70 on The Student Study Team [SST] Process.)* At that time information and concerns are reviewed as a team (classroom teacher, support staff, administrator, and parents). This is recommended protocol—particularly if your child has never been referred before, and an intervention plan to address some of the student's needs has not been done at the school site.

- A school-based evaluation may be initiated at the time of the Student Study Team (SST) meeting. Parents will be asked to sign a release of information and permission for the school to begin the process. **Note:** A parent can put in writing a request for testing which begins the formal process for evaluation, as well. However, it is *highly* recommended to channel your concerns and request for testing through a team process (SST) if one exists at your school site. Be aware that the school evaluation team determines how in-depth of an assessment to provide. In some cases they will conduct a full psycho-educational evaluation; in other cases a less comprehensive assessment will be done. *(See Checklist 71 on What Is an IEP?)*

- Many parents prefer to have their child evaluated outside of the school. *(See Checklist 11 on Making the Diagnosis—What Is a Comprehensive Evaluation for ADHD?)* Find professionals in the community who have expertise and experience assessing/treating children (and/or adolescents) with ADHD. Before choosing who will evaluate your child, do your homework. Ask for referrals from those who are knowledgeable. Speak with the school nurse, psychologist, or school counselor for names of specialists in the field. Question parents of other children/teens who have ADHD. Contact local support groups for parents of children with attention deficit disorders (i.e., CH.A.D.D. chapters) or children's hospitals, local mental health agencies, etc.

- The school will still be called upon to supply the necessary data (i.e., records, reports, observation forms, rating scales, work samples) to the doctor, psychiatrist, social worker, psychologist—or whoever the medical/mental health professionals may be conducting the evaluation. *(See Checklist 12 on What Parents Should Expect from the School in the Diagnostic Process.)*

31. ADVOCATING FOR YOUR CHILD:
POSITIVE STRATEGIES FOR PARENTS

◆ If your child has ADHD, you will need to educate yourself about attention deficit disorders. It will be your responsibility to step in and intervene on behalf of your child whenever the situation arises that he or she is in need of extra support and understanding.

◆ Make every effort to learn about ADD/ADHD and any other coexisting disorders or difficulties your child may have (e.g., learning disabilities). Fortunately, over the past few years a great deal of information has become available about attention deficit disorders. Before that time there were very few resources available to parents. Now you can find books, magazines, videotapes, and other published materials on ADD/ADHD in most bookstores and through vendors who specialize in this area, websites, and libraries. *(See Checklist 74 on Recommended Resources and Organizations.)* In many communities there are workshops, training sessions, conferences, resource centers, and services available to parents, educators, and others interested in learning about ADHD.

◆ Learn about your child's rights under the law to a free, appropriate education; and to accommodations and/or direct special services if the ADHD is affecting your child's ability to learn or perform successfully at school. *(See Checklist 71 on What is an IEP? and Checklist 72 on What Is 504? for more information.)*

◆ To be an effective advocate, you will need to establish a partnership with the school. You will have to communicate with school staff regarding your ADHD child to a far greater degree than necessary for most other children. Your level of involvement with the school greatly increases when you have a child with any special needs.

◆ Many parents feel uncomfortable at school meetings, particularly team meetings that involve several members of the school staff. Try to enter meetings/conferences with an open mind and cooperative attitude. Be willing to share your opinions, feelings, observations, suggestions, and any information about your child/family that may help in planning and intervention.

◆ Don't be afraid to ask many questions, and to request that any language (educational jargon) be explained. Ask for clarification on anything you don't understand. At meetings such as Student Study

Team meetings and IEP meetings, you should receive a copy of any reports or paperwork that staff members are referring to. If not, request a copy.

◆ Take some notes during meetings anyway. It is helpful if you enter meetings prepared with a few notes to yourself, regarding items you wish to share, discuss, or ask about. You are welcome to bring someone with you to the meeting/conference if you prefer. It is most helpful if both parents are able to attend school meetings together. If parents are divorced but share custody, it is very beneficial to have both parents attend. Schools are used to working with sensitive family situations, and will do what they can to effectively communicate and work with parents and guardians.

◆ Avoid becoming defensive, aggressive, accusatory, or hostile with school personnel. Try to remain polite and diplomatic.

◆ One of the most effective ways to help your child is to provide resources and information about ADHD to teachers, coaches, and other adults directly working with and interacting with your son or daughter on a regular basis. Much of the teacher training and public awareness about ADHD in this country and others is a direct result of parents' strong efforts (through organizations such as CH.A.D.D.) to educate others about the needs of their children.

◆ It is highly recommended to join organizations such as CH.A.D.D. to learn how to help your ADHD child, and keep updated about what is new in the field. Local chapters provide the opportunity to learn from and network with others in your situation: parents of children/teens, other adults with ADHD, professionals interested in and working with individuals who have ADHD. Generally there are meetings with guest speakers from the community addressing a number of relevant topics and issues. Their publications have excellent articles on a variety of topics of interest, and information on numerous resources, state and national conferences on ADHD, and so forth. Besides CH.A.D.D. chapters, there are other parent support groups, organizations, and resources available in many communities. *(See Checklist 74 on Recommended Resources and Organizations.)*

◆ Parents will find that often the best way to establish a positive relationship with the school is to be a helpful, involved parent who gives of his or her time and service to the school. There are countless ways that schools can use the direct or indirect services of parents. All schools are seeking parent involvement in the classroom or various school committees/programs and projects. Volunteer your time. Become more involved in the school community and get to know staff members.

◆ Let teachers or other staff members who are making a strong effort on behalf of your child know that you are appreciative. It is generally the little things that make a difference.

◆ Communicate frequently with the classroom teachers. Find out as much as you can about how your child is functioning at school and ways you can support at home.

◆ You have a right to have your child's educational needs assessed by the school district. If you want your child evaluated, speak with the classroom teacher, special education teacher, other members of the Student Study Team, the principal, or director of special education. Ask how to go about getting your child evaluated. Every district has procedures in writing that parents can receive a copy of. Parents suspecting their child may have a disability may request a formal evaluation from their school. Put your parental request for assessment in writing, date it, and submit it to the school. This will begin the IEP process and timeline. This evaluation will determine whether or not your child qualifies for special education or related services, based upon an identified area of disability. It is generally recommended to first proceed through the Student Study Team process before requesting formal testing, if this process is used at your school site. It is not a requirement, however, to do so. *(See Checklist 12 on What Parents Should Expect from the School in the Diagnostic Process and Checklist 70 on The Student Study Team Process.)*

◆ Read the paperwork regarding procedures, the assessment plan, and your rights under the law. If you have any questions, ask.

◆ Once your child is tested, there will be a meeting called an IEP meeting at which time the results of the evaluation will be shared with you and other members of the team. It will be determined at that time whether or not your child has been identified as having a handicapping condition. *(See Checklist 71 on What Is an IEP?)* If your child qualifies for special education or related services, an individualized education program (IEP) will be written with specific goals and objectives to meet his or her needs. Again, be sure to ask questions regarding any of the test data, interpretations, or recommendations you don't understand.

◆ If your child qualifies for services or special education programs, ask for information about those services/programs. If the recommendation of the team is a different placement for your child (e.g., a special education class), ask to visit and make observations of those programs or special education classes. You do not have to accept any services, programs, or placements. As your child's advocate, you will want to make sure the program or placement is appropriate. Know that you also have the right to discontinue any services/programs at any time. If you disagree with any part of the IEP, you don't have to sign it; you may also write your areas of disagreement on the IEP. If you wish to include other information on the IEP or request additional goals/objectives be written to address the needs of your child, ask for the inclusion of those goals on the IEP. *(See checklists 71 and 72 for more information about your rights under IDEA and 504.)*

◆ Keep a file on your child that includes all copies of testing, reports, IEPs, report cards, and other important data. It is amazing how thick these files become! In addition to official papers and records, it is a good idea to keep a log of general communication with the school and other professionals working with your child. Having an easy way to remind yourself of dates of conversations, meetings, doctor appointments, recommendations, interventions put into effect in and out of school, etc., may come in handy.

◆ Seek professionals in the community whom you feel comfortable with and confident in. Get referrals from others who may be in the best position to recommend specialists dealing with ADHD-related issues. Be assertive in checking out their level of expertise and experience specifically with ADHD. If you are uncomfortable with their treatment approach, express your reservations and concerns. If they don't appear to be committed to a team approach, you will probably be better off finding someone else. Your child's doctors and therapists should be in close communication with you and the school.

◆ To be an effective advocate for your child, you will need to monitor the plans and your son's or daughter's progress. Request update meetings or conferences. If something isn't working, it can always be changed. Attempt to solve problems using a cooperative team approach. Any plan—informal or formal (i.e., 504, IEP)—can be reviewed at any point during the school year. You do not have to wait until an annual review meeting or a quarterly/semester parent-teacher conference. You can request a review of the plan or any services, programs, or special placements whenever you wish. The best is to remain in close communication on an ongoing basis to monitor growth and progress and implement changes/modifications as needed.

✔ Checklists for Teachers

The following section addresses topics of specific concern to teachers. Engaging the attention of students is not an easy task, particularly those with ADHD. Strategies for getting, focusing, and maintaining students' attention, as well as techniques for keeping students on-task during seat work times, are among the checklists in this section. Students who are distractible and inattentive don't listen or follow directions well, and they need a lot of extra teacher cueing, prompting, and support. One of the checklists shares tips for giving directions in the classroom, and another provides specific strategies for helping our distractible, inattentive students.

Students with ADHD often present behaviors that are problematic in the classroom and other school settings. Teachers need to effectively use behavior-management techniques that focus first on problem prevention. Some of the checklists provide specific strategies for preventing behavioral problems in the classroom, and avoiding/preventing behavior problems during "those challenging times" of the school day (i.e., transitions, changes of activity, playground, lunchroom). Behavior management with ADHD children requires structuring the environment for their success, and often increasing the motivation to follow rules and work towards goals. This section includes a checklist of positive incentives and reinforcers to select from at school for increasing the motivation, specific strategies and recommendations for dealing with hyperactive/impulsive students, and a list on environmental modifications that make a difference in the classroom.

Many of our students with attention deficit disorders are weak in organization, time awareness/management, and general study skills. Lacking the internal structure, it is important that we impose some external structures to help in these areas both at home and school. Teachers need to provide the necessary supports and assistance for students to achieve success. Some of the checklists in this section address organizing students' work space and materials, helping students with time management and awareness, and other ways teachers can help.

In the homes of children with ADHD homework is often a tremendous struggle—far more so than in the homes of other students. It is often a monumental task for our ADHD students to complete their homework—taking hours longer than the average student to accomplish. One of the checklists in this section offers tips for teachers when assigning homework to students with ADHD.

Students with special needs, including those with attention deficit disorders, should be allowed access to the same curriculum as their peers whenever possible. It is very important for classroom teachers to know how to make modifications and adaptations in their lesson presentations, materials, and testing. By doing so, they will enable all of the students in their classrooms to receive the information, and demonstrate their knowledge/mastery of skills. Checklists in this section address these specific topics.

Classroom teachers are often in the best position to notice when a student is having attention, academic, behavior, or social/emotional problems. This section contains checklists on what a teacher should do if he or she suspects a student has ADHD, how to go about referring a student whom the teacher is concerned about, and typical teacher referral form questions and information to gather.

32. WHAT DO STUDENTS WITH ADHD NEED?

✔ A structured, positive classroom that is welcoming, inclusive, and well-managed

✔ A teacher who is a good role model—one who is firm, fair, and clearly in charge

✔ To feel "safe" and comfortable in the classroom environment (knowing that they will be treated with dignity and respect, and not deliberately criticized, embarrassed or humiliated in front of their peers)

✔ To feel confident that their teacher cares about their needs and can be trusted

✔ Opportunities to voice their feelings, worries, concerns, and ideas

✔ To feel they have choice and are involved in some decision-making

✔ Instruction and materials that motivate, engage their interest, and keep them involved—therefore, minimizing both boredom and frustration—the source of many behavior problems in the classroom

✔ Positive attention from teachers and peers

✔ Ongoing support, encouragement, and "coaching" in skills they are weak in

✔ An emphasis on their own personal best efforts and self-improvement, rather than on competition against one another

✔ Clarity of expectations

✔ Structuring of their work environment, tasks, and materials

✔ Assistance through transitions

✔ Assistance in helping to focus and maintain attention

✔ Cueing, prompting, and reminders

✔ Active learning and high response opportunities

✔ Help with organization, time-management, and study skills

✔ Multisensory instruction

✔ Learning-style accommodations

✔ Written output modifications

✔ Escape-valve outlets

✔ Predictability of schedules and routines

✔ Extra time to process information and output/perform tasks

✔ Creative, interesting, and challenging curriculum

✔ Engaging and effective instruction

✔ Help with coping and feelings of frustration

✔ Adaptations and modifications of the curriculum and environment

✔ A great deal of modeling and teacher-guided instruction

✔ Meaningful learning experiences that help them to make connections and see the relevancy

✔ Choices, options, and flexibility

✔ Teaching strategies that build upon their strengths and help bypass their weaknesses

✔ Teachers who maintain high expectations, yet provide the support enabling them to achieve those expectations

✔ Teachers who have a sense of humor, and make learning experiences both novel and fun

✔ Teachers in their lives who are positive and flexible . . . who are encouragers and motivators, and are able to see past the behaviors to the "whole child"

33. Effective Behavioral Strategies for Teachers

Structural

♦ Establish a clear routine.

♦ Maintain a well-structured classroom.

♦ Establish a few clearly defined rules and expectations.

♦ Post the rules and review frequently.

♦ Ask individual students to state the appropriate rule when there is an infraction.

♦ Teach, model, and practice all the behaviors you want students to exhibit.

♦ Establish reasonable, realistic consequences that are clearly understood by students, and enforce them with consistency.

♦ Implement a classroom behavior-management plan/system that is clearly defined (verbally and in writing) so that it is easily understood by students, parents, classroom aides, and other parties.

♦ Role-play appropriate behaviors and social skills.

♦ Define concretely what behaviors sound like and look like (i.e., what are "inside voices"; what does "on-task" during seat work look like and sound like).

♦ Give positive attention, such as praise, a small privilege or token, etc., to students who are engaged in appropriate behaviors.

♦ Praise specific behaviors. ADHD students are always being told what they are doing wrong. Let the student know exactly what he or she is doing right. Give specific, descriptive feedback. For example, "I like the way Michael is standing in line quietly with his hands and feet to himself. Thank you, Michael."

♦ Use preventive tactics—anticipating problems, looking for warning signs, and avoiding through careful planning.

♦ Remind students of your expectations with established visual/auditory prompts and signals.

♦ Remind students of expectations before each activity.

◆ Arrange individually some private signals and cues between you and the student with ADHD to remind him or her of appropriate behavior.

◆ Greatly increase the degree of positive reinforcement, as well as the amount and frequency of positive reinforcers (rewards and privileges) the student can receive with appropriate behaviors.

◆ Increase the immediacy and frequency of positive feedback and positive reinforcement.

◆ Communicate with parents frequently.

◆ Prepare for and provide structure and supervision during transition times, changes of routine, and unstructured situations.

◆ Reward smooth transitions. *(See Checklist 37 on Positive Incentives and Reinforcers for School for more ideas.)*

◆ Use praise significantly more than reprimands; and reward with far greater frequency than you punish.

◆ Greatly increase positive comments and attention to ADHD children who receive a far greater percentage of negative comments and reprimands than average on a daily basis.

◆ Remind yourself frequently to "catch them being good"!

◆ Use proximity control—teacher positioning himself or herself near the student (seating closer to teacher, standing near student's desk).

◆ Redirect whenever possible to a different activity or situation (when student is becoming agitated, disruptive, frustrated, or losing control). Allow the child some time-away to "regroup" by running an errand to the office, straightening the library shelf, etc.

◆ Redirect in a calm, firm voice.

◆ Use a hierarchy of negative consequences or mild punishments that are clearly established in the classroom and reinforced (i.e., head down, loss of some recess time, time owed after school, five-minute time-out, ten-minute time-out, etc.).

◆ Whenever possible, use natural consequences. For example, mishandling classroom equipment results in not being able to use the equipment the rest of the day or next day.

◆ When having students "owe time," determine and teach the class in advance what offenses will result in owing time. Have procedures for what they need to do if they owe you time (e.g., sit quietly, no talking). Set a timer and keep it brief. A typical rule of thumb is one minute of time for each incident.

◆ Use behavioral charts and contracts, and short reinforcing periods with teacher evaluation of the effectiveness of the plan. **Note:** Re-evaluate at least every two weeks how well the behavior plan you are using is working; readjust as needed.

◆ Change rewards if they are no longer effective or motivating.

◆ Have a changing array and variety of positive reinforcers. *(See Checklist 37 on Positive Incentives and Reinforcers for School.)*

◆ Use a "token economy system" (i.e., specific rewards earned for points/tokens) to motivate the student in achieving goals.

◆ Response costs can be built into the token economy system (i.e., loss of tokens, points, privileges when unacceptable behavior occurs). **Note:** When using response costs, be sure student is earning far more points than he or she is losing, or the incentive to meet the behavioral goal will disappear.

◆ Selectively ignore minor inappropriate behavior that is not intentional. Not every behavior warrants teacher intervention. Teachers will have to be tolerant and flexible with ADHD students—allowing extra movement, fiddling with objects, and behaviors of which they have significant physiological difficulty controlling!

◆ Teach the class to ignore some of the minor inappropriate behaviors and praise/reinforce positive behaviors.

◆ "Time-out" as a punishment/consequence should be used judiciously, and for specific behaviors that are clearly defined and understood by the class. Plan what the child is to be doing during "time-out"; the length of time in that location needs to be appropriate for the age or developmental level of the student. The purpose is to briefly isolate the child or remove him or her from the positive reinforcement of class participation; when he or she returns from time-out, the child is fully included again with the class activities.

◆ Develop contracts, as needed, with individual students and his or her parents, working on one or two specific target behavioral goals. **Note:** When using contracts, define the positive behavior that will replace the inappropriate behavior. Make sure the goal is achievable. Determine the time/frequency that the contract will be reviewed; and remember to reinforce contingent upon the behavior.

Environmental

◆ Use preferential seating with ADHD students. Seat by well-focused, good role models. Avoid seating near students with whom they may get in conflict. Position ADHD student so that you can have direct eye contact and will be able to cue/prompt throughout the day.

◆ Change student's seating (close to center of instruction, close to teacher, away from distractors) when necessary.

◆ Remove distracting items/objects from students (i.e., toys or objects with which they are playing). **Note:** In some cases fidgety children who seem to need having something in their hands actually are better able to focus and perform when given something they can squeeze or hold. Some children with ADHD need to keep their hands busy to stay alert. In this case it might be helpful trying a special arrangement for this child to be given a small piece of clay, squeeze ball, or an object attached to a key ring (perhaps clipped out of sight) for the student to hold as needed.

◆ Try using music for transitions and for calming/relaxing students.

◆ Arrange the environment for easy access to all parts of the room, and visibility of all students.

◆ Circulate and move around the room frequently. Use proximity control to cue and physically prompt students (i.e., hand placed gently on shoulder, gain eye contact, tap desk).

◆ Seat disruptive students closer to you.

◆ Examine environmental variables for students' individual needs. *(See Checklist 46 on Environmental Modifications that Make a Difference in the Classroom for more ideas.)*

Affective Variables and Personalized Efforts

◆ Offer personal support, encouragement, and coaching to help students who struggle behaviorally.

◆ Provide teacher assistance to individual students on a personal, one-to-one level.

◆ Acknowledge and validate what students are thinking and feeling.

◆ Try to be as empathetic and understanding as possible.

◆ Talk with former teacher(s) regarding strategies and interventions they may have found effective, and check the cumulative records for information that may be significant in trying to help certain students.

◆ Make eye contact and use pre-arranged teacher signals and cueing. This can be a specific trigger word or nonverbal signal/gesture that the teacher sets up privately with individual students. These are used as a way of warning or redirecting the student without having to nag or call negative attention to that student.

◆ When delivering consequences, do so unemotionally, in a matter-of-fact voice, and as soon as possible after the misbehavior occurs.

◆ When giving verbal reprimands, don't lecture; keep it brief.

◆ Address only the child's behavior, not the child him- or herself.

◆ Provide a cooling-off period for students who are becoming agitated or angry. This is not "time-out" as a consequence.

◆ Discuss situations individually with students in a calm, quiet voice.

◆ Try to remove student from an audience of peers when discussing misbehaviors with him or her.

◆ Maintain positive expectations for students' success.

◆ Use humor to de-escalate problem situations and to provide student support.

◆ Avoid lecturing, nagging, criticism, and sarcasm.

◆ Try lowering your voice, rather than raising it to gain and keep student's attention.

◆ Don't take the child's inappropriate behavior personally.

Instructional

◆ Have clear choices and options of activities for students who complete work early to avoid problems that arise out of boredom.

◆ Be careful not to assign seat work or independent tasks that a student is not capable of doing—a prime invitation to acting out from frustration!

◆ Make sure lessons and activities are engaging and motivating, and students understand the relevancy.

◆ Utilize effective questioning techniques.

◆ Provide for many legitimate opportunities to get up and move around.

◆ Provide frequent breaks between activities.

Other

◆ Have class meetings and practice/model problem-solving strategies.

◆ Teach conflict-resolution skills (how to peacefully resolve differences through mediation and compromise.) Students need to explicitly be taught how to talk about a problem, listen to the other party and reach a mutually acceptable agreement.

◆ Teach cooperative skills (e.g., taking turns, sharing, participating in the group activity, working towards a common goal).

◆ Use calming and relaxation techniques *(See Checklist 68 on Relaxation, Guided Imagery, and Visualization Techniques).*

◆ Teach self-monitoring skills (children periodically stop and self-evaluate: "Am I using my inside voice?" "Am I on-task?"; or whatever the specific behavior is that is being monitored and encouraged). Some teachers use an audiotape that is completely quiet except for a beep that sounds at various intervals. When the beep goes off, student(s) reward themselves with a point on their self-monitoring card if they were engaged in the appropriate behavior at the time of the beep.

◆ Use "cognitive mediation." Question the child: "What did I ask you to do?" "What should you be doing right now?" "Where are your feet supposed to be?"

◆ Utilize your school support staff. Consult with the school counselor for help establishing behavioral plans and documentation. See the school nurse and/or refer the student to the Student Study Team if you suspect he or she has ADHD. *(For more recommendations, see Checklist 47 on If You Suspect Your Student Has ADHD.)*

34. Preventing Behavioral Problems in the Classroom

◆ Create a classroom where students want to be—that is, structured, welcoming and inclusive, yet is flexible enough to accommodate individual needs of students.

◆ Model respectful language, tone of voice, body language.

◆ Open lines of communication with parents. Encourage parent feedback and partnership.

◆ Establish 4–5 positively stated rules that are taught, practiced, modeled, posted in words/pictures, and referred to frequently.

◆ Clarify all expectations through modeling, guided practice, and clear communication of those expectations to students and parents.

◆ Provide structure and routine.

◆ Review behavioral expectations prior to activities.

◆ Provide for frequent breaks and opportunities to get up and move around.

◆ Provide fair consequences and enforce with consistency.

◆ Scan the room frequently. Stay alert as to what students are engaged in at all times, and provide positive feedback to students. ("I like the way . . .")

◆ Use proximity control (standing next to or seating students in need of closer management closer to teacher—within cueing distance).

◆ Redirect students. (Mention their name, get eye contact, use physical proximity and cueing.)

◆ Utilize effective questioning techniques that are inclusive and engage all students.

◆ Prepare students for transitions, changes of routine, and unstructured activities. Children with ADHD often need extra guidance and assistance through transitions.

◆ Examine environmental factors in the classroom (e.g., arrange for visibility of all students).

◆ Seat distractible students away from high traffic areas, doors, noisy heaters/air conditioners, pencil sharpeners, drinking fountains, learning centers, etc.

◆ Carefully arrange seating of disruptive students (surrounded by and facing good role models, close to the center of instruction, closer to the teacher—within teacher cueing and prompting distance).

◆ Carefully assign peer partners.

◆ Use nonverbal signals to cue "I need help!"

◆ Use humor to de-escalate potential problems.

◆ Avoid lag time when students have nothing to do.

◆ Provide instructional activities that are motivational and engaging.

◆ Have clear choices and options of activities for students who complete their work early. This avoids problems that arise out of boredom.

◆ Use private, pre-arranged cueing and signals for students (gesture or trigger word) to remind students of appropriate behavior in an unobtrusive way.

◆ Ask students to repeat rules and expectations.

◆ Position yourself at the door and greet students as they enter the room.

◆ As they enter the room, immediately direct students to routine warm-up activities (journal entries, interpreting brief quotation on board, writing sentences using vocabulary words, 2–3 math problems) to avoid students having to wait undirected for instruction to begin.

◆ Give positive, specific, descriptive feedback to students. For example: "I see that Alicia is in her chair facing forward with her book open to the right page. Good job, Alicia."

◆ Many older students would be humiliated if teachers praised openly in front of peers. However, they still need the positive feedback (through notes, quiet statements before/after class, etc.). Try using a self-stick pad to jot down comments to students and place these on their desk.

◆ Anticipate problems and avoid them through careful planning.

◆ Delay instruction until it is quiet and students' attention is focused.

◆ Increase ratio of positive to negative comments and feedback to students to at least three-to-one.

◆ Increase the immediacy of rewards and consequences.

◆ Make eye contact and use prearranged signals with individual students for cueing. This can be a specific trigger word or nonverbal signals/gestures that you set up privately with individual students and use as a way of warning or redirecting the student.

◆ Have clear choices and options of activities for students who complete work early to avoid problems that arise out of boredom.

◆ Make sure independent seat work is developmentally appropriate and within the student's capability of doing successfully without assistance. **Note:** Many teachers give assignments for seat work that children are incapable of doing independently because they lack the prerequisite skills to do so. Prevent students' acting out due to frustration by either assigning a peer buddy to work together with on these tasks, giving easier seat work, or alternative tasks until you can directly assist that student.

◆ Watch for signs of students beginning to "lose it" and redirect or divert by assigning tasks such as straightening the library shelves, passing out papers, or running an errand to the office.

◆ Watch for what triggers the student's misbehavior (such as the time of day, the activity/expectations) and begin a plan of early intervention (i.e., change the antecedents).

◆ Provide a cooling-off period for students who are becoming agitated or angry. Sometimes just the act of walking to another area of the room with the opportunity to look through books or magazines, or to go out for a drink of water, etc., is enough to break the tension and have the student regain composure.

◆ No matter how much you are provoked to responding out of anger, try to remain calm. Plan in advance how to deal with certain situations. Disengage from any kind of power struggle.

◆ Use behavioral contracts, behavior charts, and behavior-modification techniques. These strategies are often necessary for children with ADHD. Keep in mind, however, that any plan is short-term and often doesn't maintain effectiveness for more than a few weeks. Use for two weeks and evaluate: change plan, revise the incentive, etc., together with the child.

◆ Maintain close communication with parents. Let them know what strategies you are using to help with behavioral issues in the classroom. A coordinated home/school plan and reinforcement are the most effective.

◆ Pace your instruction to avoid both boredom and frustration.

◆ Provide the support and any necessary modification on academic tasks to enable each student to achieve success.

35. Preventing Behavior Problems During Those "Challenging Times" of the School Day

Changes in activity and transitions are typically the most challenging times for children with ADHD. These students often can function well within the structure of the classroom, but have major problems during recess, in the lunchroom, between passing periods, riding the bus, and so on.

◆ Prepare for changes in routine (such as assemblies, substitute teachers, field trips) through discussion and modeling expectations. Avoid catching students off-guard.

◆ Praise and reward appropriate behavior and problem-solving skills.

◆ Communicate clearly when activities will begin and when they will end.

◆ Give specific instructions, not general instructions about how students are to switch to the next activity.

◆ Use **signals** for transitions (e.g., playing a bar of music on the piano, strumming a guitar, flashing lights, ringing a bell). The signal indicates that an activity is coming to an end and children need to finish whatever they are doing. Some teachers signal and tell students they will have a brief amount of time (3–5 minutes) to finish what they are working on before the next activity, or to clean up. They then set a timer for that amount of time.

◆ Provide direct teacher or aide assistance and support during these changes of activity.

◆ Assign a buddy or peer helper to assist during these transitional periods and out-of-classroom times.

◆ Always maintain a visual schedule of activities and routine for students to see. Young children should have a schedule of pictures displaying the sequence of daily activities.

◆ Build in stretch breaks and brief exercise between activities, particularly ones that require a lot of sitting or high level of concentration.

◆ Be prepared for the next activity with necessary materials, directions, etc., so students don't have to wait, and you can avoid instructional lag time.

◆ Teach and practice procedures for how to: enter/leave the room, stand in line, get a drink, line up, change activity centers, carry a chair, move from desks to group activities, and so forth.

◆ Teach, model, and practice appropriate behaviors and expectations for out-of-classroom activities (i.e., in assemblies, cafeteria, hallway).

◆ It is very important to have schoolwide rules of behavioral expectations so that there is consistency among staff members.

◆ Schoolwide incentives and positive reinforcers (e.g., "caught being good" tickets redeemable for school prizes) are helpful in teaching and motivating appropriate behaviors outside of the classroom.

◆ For ADHD students riding the bus and having difficulties, a behavioral chart/incentive may need to be arranged with the cooperative efforts of the school, bus driver, and parent. Special contracts/incentives may also need to be arranged for playground or cafeteria behavior.

◆ Use relaxation and imagery activities and exercises for calming after recess, lunch, and P.E. Playing music, singing, and/or reading to students at these times is also often effective. *(See Checklist 68 on Relaxation, Guided Imagery, and Visualization Techniques.)*

◆ Reward smooth transitions. Many teachers use individual points or table points to reward students or rows/table clusters of students who are ready for the next activity. The reward is often something simple like being the first row/table to line up for recess, etc.

◆ Increase supervision outside of the classroom, and provide more choices of activities that children can engage in (i.e., hoola hoops, jump rope, board games, library/computer, supervised games). **Note:** It is important that all staff are aware of the struggles children with ADHD have in nonstructured environments. Awareness training in ADHD (what it is and is not) should be provided for personnel involved with supervision outside of the classroom.

◆ Increase supervision during passing periods, lunch, recess, and school arrival/dismissal.

◆ It is helpful to have organized clubs and choices for students before and after school, and during the break before/after lunch.

◆ It is helpful for teachers to meet their students after lunch, PE, recess, and other activities outside of the classroom, and walk them quietly into the classroom.

◆ Often children with ADHD need someone guiding them, prompting and giving direct assistance during transitions.

◆ One of the biggest transitions children face is the move from one grade level to the next (particularly the change from elementary to middle school, and middle school to high school). It is very helpful to prepare students (especially those with ADHD) by visiting the new school, meeting with counselors and/or teachers, practicing their locker combination, receiving the schedule of classes in advance, and practicing the walk from class to class.

◆ Staff members should identify and positively target those students in need of extra support, assistance, and careful monitoring outside of the classroom.

36. DEALING WITH HYPERACTIVE/IMPULSIVE BEHAVIORS AT SCHOOL

♦ Impose the necessary structure (i.e., rules, expectations, limits/boundaries, positive and negative consequences, organization) that is critical to the management and success of *all* students—especially those with ADHD.

♦ *See checklists on Effective Behavioral Strategies for Teachers (33), Positive Incentives and Reinforcers for School (37), and Environmental Modifications that Make a Difference in the Classroom (46) for additional tips and strategies.*

♦ To deal effectively with the behaviors of children who are hyperactive and impulsive, it will take FLEXIBILITY, A SENSE OF HUMOR AND PERSPECTIVE, and a good deal of TOLERANCE on your part.

♦ Learn everything you can about the nature of ADHD. Knowing what ADD/ADHD is and is not (*see Checklists 2 and 3*) helps us to be more understanding and tolerant. Attend professional conferences and workshops, read books and articles, view videos, talk to other educators. Arm yourself with knowledge/training, and learn how to employ specific strategies and techniques that are effective with ADHD students.

♦ Seek help from your school's support staff. Talk to the school counselor, school psychologist, school nurse, special education teacher(s). Bring your concerns to their attention early in the school year. They should help you (formally or informally) with strategies, guidance, and support. (*See checklists on What Supports Do Teachers Need? (18), If You Suspect Your Student Has ADHD (47), Typical Teacher Referral Forms (48), and The Student Study Team (SST) Process (70).*)

♦ Implement all interventions and strategies possible to PREVENT behavioral issues that are likely to occur due to the students' impulsivity and/or hyperactivity. (*See Checklist 34 on Preventing Behavioral Problems in the Classroom and Checklist 35 on Preventing Behavioral Problems During Those "Challenging Times" of the School Day.*)

♦ Teach strategies for relaxation and anger control. Practice those strategies often, and model their use.

◆ Establish a close partnership with the parents of students with ADHD. Win their trust that you are going to do your best to help their children to be successful. Encourage frequent communication and mutual support. Talk about and plan strategies that can be used at home and school.

◆ If a student is receiving outside counseling, work with mental health professionals on behavioral strategies. Ask parents for permission (signed consent) to communicate. It is very helpful if you are aware of strategies your ADHD students are being taught to employ (such as coping strategies, relaxation strategies, anger control). That way you can reinforce and assist in cueing the student to utilize those specific techniques.

◆ Watch for warning signs of the ADHD student becoming overly stimulated, upset, frustrated, agitated, restless, or beginning to lose control—and intervene at once. Divert and redirect, change the activity/expectations, lend direct support and cueing/signaling, employ calming techniques and remind about rewards/consequences.

◆ Catch students exhibiting behaviors that are appropriate and REWARD immediately. Call attention to appropriate behavior and **positively reinforce** when a student with ADHD: shows good self-control, sits appropriately, performs tasks without rushing through carelessly, doesn't interrupt/blurt out, remembers to raise hand before speaking, keeps hands/feet to self.

◆ Take immediate action and enforce negative consequences that students clearly know are to be expected when class rules are broken and inappropriate behaviors occur (i.e., time-out, response costs, loss of privileges).

◆ Provide time and a place for students to be able to regain control, calm down, refocus, and avoid escalation of emotions and conflict.

◆ Prioritize your focus on behaviors. Be tolerant and willing to ignore some minor behaviors that are basically annoying and irritating. Clearly deal with those more disruptive, destructive behaviors that are a matter of safety and infringement upon the rights of others.

◆ Set up behavioral charts or contracts specifically focused on one or two behaviors you want the student to improve (e.g., staying in seat). Determine the baseline behavior; what is typical, normal behavior for the child at this time. (How long can he or she stay seated generally?) Set your goals to increase the length of time gradually and reasonably, so the student has a chance of success and will be motivated to try his or her best.

◆ Be sensitive to social issues and difficulties that are occurring in and out of the classroom. Facilitate friendships when possible. Set up situations that increase chances of success by pairing ADHD students with other children who tend to be kinder, more patient and tolerant. Seek assistance from the school counselor or guidance aide who can help with problem solving, keeping an eye on social situations/interactions on the playground, lunchroom, etc.

◆ Teach and model positive strategies for conflict resolution, dealing with frustration, and stopping/thinking/planning before acting.

◆ Establish a relationship with the student, letting that child know that you will be doing everything you can to help him or her succeed. Set up some signals and cues together that will serve as warnings and private communication between you and the ADHD student so as not to embarrass in front of peers.

◆ Arrange the room environment and design/schedule lessons and activities with the awareness that students (particularly those with ADHD) need active involvement, quiet and calming times, many opportunities for movement and hands-on participation, preparation for and help through transitions. *(See Checklist 35 on Preventing Problems During "Those Challenging Times" of the School Day, Checklists 40-42 on Getting Students' Attention, Focusing It, Maintaining It, and Checklist 46 on Environmental Modifications that Make a Difference in the Classroom.)*

◆ Continuously scan and monitor student behavior in the classroom. Provide direction, redirection, and close supervision.

◆ For impulsive work habits, provide support such as editing assistance, extra time for checking over work, and use of rewards/incentives for neatness, completion of tasks, and accuracy.

◆ Require impulsive students to repeat directions (to a peer, an aide, or teacher) before being allowed to start a task.

◆ Provide a visual reminder of behavioral expectations (i.e., list of rules or picture of student engaged in appropriate behavior). Try taping the list or picture to the child's desk. Point to it as a means of cueing.

◆ Use preferential seating and proximity control (close to you, so as to be able to easily cue/signal and make eye contact, and away from peers who tend to get in conflict with the ADHD student).

◆ Teach specifically the criteria of your expectations. Instead of "Talk quietly" say, "Use your indoor voices." Determine what that looks like and sounds like. Model and practice "indoor voices" frequently. What does "sitting appropriately" mean to you? Define it—what it looks like and point out good models of that behavior.

◆ Provide ADHD students many opportunities to legitimately get up and move. Assign tasks that will enable them to leave their seats.

◆ Build in many breaks and opportunities to stretch, get a drink, go to the restroom, have a snack, exercise, hear music.

◆ Students who are impulsive are often most successful with a combination of *reward* (i.e., for remembering to raise hand and wait) along with a *response cost* (i.e., being fined—losing a token or a few points for blurting out without being called on).

◆ Allow logical consequences to occur if a student is continuously falling out of the chair causing a disruption (for example, chair is removed and student must do work standing for certain amount of time.)

◆ Clear the desk or work area of all materials except those needed for the activity.

◆ Some children are better able to remain seated and control behavior if they are permitted to doodle/draw/color or be allowed to touch/hold objects in their hands while listening in class.

◆ Establish boundaries on the rug or floor area with masking tape that you want the very hyperactive young child to stay within if he or she tends to intrude on others' space (i.e., pushing their desks into those of peers, crowding them out).

◆ If certain areas of the room are off limits, be sure that is clear and enforce those limits.

◆ Provide more space to this child if possible (and consider even assigning two seats).

◆ If a student is on medication for ADHD, ask the school nurse and/or parents about time of day administered and when it should be at its peak effectiveness, as well as when it will start to wear off. Scheduling prime instruction at optimum times and more support/less demands during times when medication is less effective may be helpful. *(See Checklist 17 on If a Child/Teen Is Taking Medication.)*

◆ Alert administrators or school counselor/nurse if student arrives at school angry, out of control, or exhibiting behaviors that clearly predict he or she will need intervention early. If the child takes medication at home before leaving for school, parents should be called to see if it was administered that morning. Perhaps the student can have a chance to talk to the counselor or other designated support person, or someone can follow the child into class and stay there a while until settled down.

◆ Adjust your expectations to be reasonable. Change your mindset—ADHD children don't have the physiological controls to enable them to sit so long, focus so long as others their age/grade. They can't control their fidgetiness noises/talking. So make adjustments accordingly without being punitive.

◆ It is not easy to live with a hyperactive/impulsive child at home or school. When there is only one or two children with challenging behaviors in the classroom, it is manageable. However, many teachers have a number of students with special needs, who require a great deal of teacher support, monitoring, and intervention. In order to be effective and not "burn out" from the effort, teachers need support. *(See Checklist 18 on What Supports Do Teachers Need? for more information.)*

37. Positive Incentives and Reinforcers for School

Social Reinforcers

✔ Positive teacher attention and verbal praise

✔ Praise given in writing (e.g., notes written on student's papers, on self-stick note placed on student desk or mailed to student)

✔ Positive phone call directly to student

✔ Positive notes and calls to parents

✔ Teacher smiles, gentle pat on back, thumbs up, high five, shaking hand

✔ Class applause or cheering of student

✔ Choosing book to read to class, game to play, etc.

✔ Class privilege like ball monitor, team captain, etc.

✔ Special assemblies, awards, and recognition for good or improved behavior

✔ Choice of seating for the day or week

Activity Reinforcers

✔ Tutoring a younger child

✔ Playing a game with friend(s)

✔ First in line for dismissal (to lunch, recess, etc.)

✔ Early dismissal of 1–2 minutes for lunch/recess/passing to next class

✔ Special activity, field trip, party, assembly, movie at end of month

✔ Special game (in class or recess/PE time)

✔ Lunch-time activities that are special

✔ Earning time in class or period to catch up on work while listening to students' choice of music

✔ Extended lunch time

✔ Extra P.E., music, art, computer time

✔ Breakfast or lunch with teacher, VP, principal, other staff member

✔ Ice cream party or pizza party for class or group of students arriving at certain goal

✔ Privileges (office assistant, taking care of class pet, taking attendance, ball monitor, passing out papers, sharpening pencils, operating AV equipment)

✔ Awarded a "no homework pass" for the evening or good for one assignment

✔ Release time to go to gym (to shoot baskets), go to library, use computer, etc.

✔ Free time (individual or class earned) for games, talking with neighbors, listening to music, drawing, doing activity of choice

✔ Listening to music or stories on tape in the classroom

✔ Playing with clay

✔ Working at art center

✔ Taking off one bad grade from daily assignments recorded

✔ Taking one problem off a test

✔ Extra-credit opportunity to raise grades

✔ Studying with a friend

✔ Choice of seating

✔ Leading a game

✔ Free time in class or time to do homework in class

✔ Awards and certificates for improved behavior

✔ Drawings/raffles for donated prizes by local merchants

Material Reinforcers

✔ School supplies (special pencils, erasers, folders)

✔ Stickers

✔ Food—preferably healthy snacks such as pretzels, popcorn, crackers, fruit, cold juice, breakfast cereal, low-fat cookies, frozen ice sticks

✔ Treasure-chest items (small toys, trinkets, etc.)

✔ Magazines/books

✔ Class money or points redeemable at auctions/lotteries or class stores

✔ Free tickets awarded to school dances, concerts, plays, sporting events

✔ Class-/or school-store credit

✔ "Caught being good" coupons to be used for school or classroom raffles

NOTE:

Many teachers pass out tickets or tokens of some form or another for appropriate behavior, homework turned in on time, etc. These are later redeemed for auctions, classroom purchases of material, and/or activity reinforcers at the end of the week/biweekly.

Many teachers use a point system and have a 15- to 25-minute activity time at the end of the day (every other day/once a week). The choice of activities students may choose from during the activity time is dependent on the number of points earned. Some of the more enticing activities/choices have a higher point value attached.

Many teachers use *behavioral charts or contracts*—identifying one or two behaviors they want the child to try to achieve (staying in seat, staying on-task, etc.). Then the teacher places either a sticker, star, smiley face, check mark, teacher initials, points, etc., on the chart for successfully displaying the behavior(s) during identified time intervals throughout the day. These systems can be very effective for ADHD children. However, it is important that teachers make the time intervals manageable for observing and within the child's ability to achieve success. Depending on the child, the positive reinforcer may need to be given twice a day, at the end of the day, every other day, etc., in order for the ADHD child to maintain the interest and effort to work towards achieving his or her specified behavioral goals.

Remember:

ADHD children lose interest in the reinforcer with high frequency, so it should be changed to maintain novelty and interest. Also, they cannot wait for long-term reinforcers—shorter time frames with more immediate reinforcement work better.

38. What Teachers Can Do to Help Build Organizational and Study Skills

It is very common for students with ADHD to have significant difficulty with organization skills and time management. There is a lot that both parents and teachers can do to help organize our children, which will allow them a far greater chance for success throughout their lifetime. For children who have weakness with internal organizational skills, teachers need to provide this assistance and structure.

Helping to Organize Students' Work Space and Materials

◆ Require the use of a 3-ring binder or notebook (starting in third or fourth grade the latest).

◆ Require the use of subject dividers and a pencil pouch for the notebook (to include a few sharpened pencils with erasers, highlighter, and other essentials).

◆ Require students to carry a backpack or bookbag and to bring the notebook/binder to and from school daily.

◆ Require the use of a monthly assignment calendar or daily/weekly assignment sheet, utilize consistently with regular teacher modeling and monitoring.

◆ Encourage your school site to establish a schoolwide expectation and organization/study skills program for consistency.

◆ Provide handouts to students that are always 3-hole punched in advance.

◆ Teach how to organize papers, desks, and materials.

◆ Provide time and assistance as needed for cleaning out/sorting students' messy desks, backpacks, notebooks, and lockers.

◆ Have periodic desk and notebook checks.

◆ Positively reinforce (prizes, certificates, privileges such as "no homework tonight passes") for passing inspection of notebook/workspace checks as an incentive.

◆ Provide assistance (another student or adult) to help them sort through desks, backpacks, and notebooks. It helps to dump everything into a shopping bag and bring to another area while working on this. Unnecessary papers can be recycled, paper reinforcers placed on ripped out papers, miscellaneous papers can be re-filed appropriately, pencils sharpened, old pens thrown out, etc.

◆ Provide students with the necessary supplies and time to get organized.

◆ Clearly identify certain places in the room (trays, shelves, color-coded folders or boxes) where students know consistently where to turn in assignments or store unfinished work.

◆ Encourage child to organize materials first thing in the morning when entering the class, or before going home in the afternoon.

◆ Send home an extra set of books for the parents to keep at home.

◆ Utilize brightly colored file folders for different subjects.

◆ At the end of the day check that the student has necessary books/materials in the backpack to take home.

◆ Color-code books, folders, and materials.

◆ Give student a clipboard for papers on the desk.

◆ Provide bins, pencil cases, boxes, and/or organizing trays for supplies and materials if possible.

◆ Require labeling of materials/supplies with students' names.

◆ Give personal reminders (verbally or notes) about materials needed for class assignments.

◆ Allow for natural consequences of not having materials. DO NOT positively reinforce students who are unprepared with materials/supplies by giving them a new pencil, notebook paper, etc. Instead, give LESS DESIRABLE materials for those who need to borrow and are unprepared. Many teachers keep a box of golf pencils and/or old pencils for this purpose, and keep a stack of used papers (so students without paper can use the backside of the page).

Helping with Time Management and Awareness

◆ Teach students how to tell time and read a non-digital clock.

◆ Teach students how to read calendars and schedules.

◆ Establish a daily routine and schedule for the classroom.

♦ Post all schedules and refer to them with the class.

♦ With younger students, use a pictorial schedule depicting the daily routine.

♦ Call close attention to due dates. Post those due dates and frequently refer to them as reminders.

♦ Assist with prioritization of activities and workload.

♦ Break down longer assignments into smaller, manageable increments, providing a lot of structure, monitoring, and follow-through.

♦ Make sure you know at what stage your ADHD students are on long-term projects (i.e., book reports, research projects, science fair projects). Personally check that they have materials needed. Ask to see what they have accomplished so far. Call parents to make sure they are aware of these projects, and have a copy of all the guidelines/deadlines at home.

♦ Provide advanced notice about upcoming projects and reports. Consider allowing ADHD student(s) to get a "head start" (especially with research and planning).

♦ Help students to plan for short-term assignments.

♦ Utilize "things to do" lists, modeling for the class and providing for students, and teaching how to write down and cross off accomplished tasks.

♦ Attach a "things to do" list on the student's desk, and monitor the practice of crossing off accomplished items.

♦ Provide checklists and schedules.

♦ Keep a master monthly calendar posted in the classroom that contains all the activities and assignments given.

♦ When using an assignment calendar, teach students to write the assignments on the day they are DUE. Walk them through recording on the correct date.

♦ Monitor the assignment calendars (particularly monthly calendars of ADHD students). They tend to write things on the wrong date.

♦ Model the writing of assignments on the calendar using a transparency of the calendar.

◆ Communicate and maintain the clear expectation that all assignments are to be recorded on students' assignment calendars, and monitor that this is occurring.

◆ Provide additional assistance either directly or from peer partners/study buddies.

◆ Routinely ask table partners or groups seated together to check each other that everything is accurately recorded on calendars.

◆ Assign study buddies to help each other. These partners can be responsible for checking each other to make sure assignments are recorded on calendars; and when absent to have the buddy collect all handouts, notices, and assignments. Buddies exchange phone numbers to call each other when the other is absent and communicate about what was missed that day in class.

◆ Use timers for seat work.

◆ Set timers for transitions. (First state: "You have 5 minutes to finish what you are working on and putting away your materials." Then set the timer.)

◆ Teach students how to self monitor on-task behavior, so that they are using class time effectively for getting work done.

◆ Use frequent praise and positive reinforcement. Reward for meeting deadlines, finishing in-school assignments, etc.

◆ Encourage students taking medication at school to have a beeper watch set for the time they need to go to the nurse's office.

Other Ways Teachers Can Help

◆ Make sure ALL assignments, page numbers, due dates, etc., are presented to students both verbally and visually.

◆ Record all assignments in a consistent place in the room (e.g., corner of the board).

◆ Keep assignments posted on the board for students to copy.

◆ Take a few moments at the end of the subject period or school day to lead students in the recording of assignments on their calendars.

◆ Prepare important notices and handouts on colored paper, preferably color-coded for certain categories. For example: weekly/monthly newsletters in blue, spelling lists in pink, etc.

◆ Reward students who are organized and prepared.

◆ Try using a contract for work completed in class with positive reinforcement.

◆ Provide models of well-organized papers, projects, science boards, etc.

◆ Provide in-school help and adult assistance for putting together projects. Many of our students with ADHD and/or learning disabilities have a hard time with laying out the pieces of projects, and impulsively gluing papers to boards without first planning for the amount of space they have. By providing help with the little 'extras' (nice lettering on the computer, mounting on contrasting colored paper, cutting papers straight with a paper cutter rather than scissors), student projects look so much better. This gives students a greater sense of pride in their work.

◆ Provide enough time during transitions to put material away and get organized for the next activity.

◆ Be sure to collect homework daily.

◆ Use visual/graphic organizers with high frequency (i.e., sequence charts, story maps, sentence maps, webs, clusters, flow charts, Venn diagrams).

◆ Provide framed outlines for filling in missing words and phrases during instruction.

◆ Use brightly colored paper for project assignments, providing details and due dates. Give two copies (one for the notebook, and one to be posted at home).

◆ Help students organize their ideas (pre-writing, planning) by using self-stick notes, dry-erase boards and pens, tape recorders, and questioning/prompting.

◆ Encourage students to use and, if necessary, provide them with self-stick notepads for marking pages in books, jotting down key words and notes.

◆ Teach note-taking skills (using index cards, standard outline form, and webbing/cluster techniques).

39. Homework Tips for Teachers

◆ Keep in mind how much longer it typically takes for a student with ADHD (and/or learning disabilities) to do the work. What takes an average child 15–20 minutes to complete often takes 3–4 times that long for this child!

◆ Be responsive to parents reporting great frustration surrounding homework. Be willing to make adjustments so that students with ADHD and/or LD spend a reasonable, not excessive, amount of time doing their homework.

◆ Realize that for students with ADHD who receive medication during the school day (to help them focus and stay on-task), they are typically *not receiving* the medication after school or in the evening hours. It is an *unreasonable* expectation that parents be able to get their child to produce at home what you weren't able to get them to produce all day at school.

◆ Many teachers have a practice of sending home unfinished class work. Avoid doing so with ADHD students. Instead, provide the necessary modifications and supports so that in-school work is in-school work, and homework is homework.

◆ Remember that homework should be a time for REVIEWING and PRACTICING what students have been taught in class. Don't give assignments involving new information that parents are expected to teach their children.

◆ Homework SHOULD NOT be "busy work." Make the homework relevant and purposeful so that time spent isn't on obscure assignments that aren't helping to reinforce skills or concepts you have taught.

◆ Don't add on homework as a punishment or consequence for misbehavior at school.

◆ Make sure you have explained the homework and clarified any questions.

◆ Supervise ADHD students before they walk out the door at the end of the day. Make sure they have materials, books, and assignments recorded and in their backpacks.

◆ Assign a study buddy (or two) to your students with ADHD. They should have one or two classmates who are responsible and willing to answer questions, who they can phone in the evening about homework if necessary.

◆ One of the most important things you can do to help ALL students (and their parents) keep on top of homework, tests, and long-term projects is to *require* use of an assignment calendar or sheet. Then *guide, walk-through,* and *monitor* the recording of assignments. If this is a daily expectation and routine, it will help everyone.

◆ With some students, require that parents initial the assignment calendar daily. With this system, it is a good way for you to communicate with parents, as well. You may write a few comments or notes to the parent on the assignment sheet and vice versa.

◆ Modify, modify, modify the homework for students with special needs. Ask yourself: "What is the goal?" "What do I want the students to learn from the assignment?" "Can they get the concepts without having to do all the writing?" "Can they practice the skills in an easier, more motivating format?" "Can they practice the skills doing fewer?"

◆ Think in terms of *shortening, cutting the work load, reducing the amount of written output required.*

◆ Communicate regularly with the parents of students who are falling behind in homework. Work out a system of letting the students and parents know that they are not getting the homework turned in (i.e., monitoring homework chart/form).

◆ When you assign a long-term major project or report, consider calling the parents of some students. Just because you have talked about it a lot in class, and provided written information, doesn't mean the parents know a thing about it. You may call to ask parents to check the notebook for the written information about the project, or volunteer to send another copy to post at home. A few well-meaning phone calls—offering your support and assistance—can make a big difference.

◆ Communicate with other teachers in your team. Students who have several teachers are often assigned a number of tests, large projects, and reading assignments all at the same time from their different classes. Be sensitive to this. Stagger due dates, and coordinate whenever possible with other teachers to avoid the heavy stress of everything being due at once.

◆ Be sure to collect homework and give some feedback. It is very frustrating to students and parents to spend a lot of time on assignments that the teacher never bothers to even collect.

◆ If you have extra copies of texts to loan parents, do so for those students who are always leaving the books they need at home or school.

◆ Work out a contract or incentive plan (with rewards) for turning in homework. Discuss with student and parent(s).

◆ Finally, realize how *critical* it is for students with ADHD and/ or learning disabilities to participate in extracurricular activities. They need every opportunity to develop areas of strength (athletics, arts/crafts, music) that will be their source of self-esteem and motivation. These after-school activities are just as—if not more—important to the child's development as academics. Also keep in mind that many students with learning/attention difficulties have tutors, work with other professionals in the community (e.g., counseling), and participate in additional academic training programs outside of school.

40. Getting Students' Attention

◆ Ask an interesting, speculative question, show a picture, tell a little story, or read a related poem to generate discussion and interest in the upcoming lesson.

◆ Try "playfulness," silliness, a bit of theatrics (props and storytelling) to get attention and peek interest.

◆ Use storytelling. Students of all ages love to hear stories, especially personal stories. It is very effective in getting attention.

◆ Add a bit of mystery. Bring in an object relevant to the upcoming lesson in a box, bag, or pillowcase. This is a wonderful way to generate predictions and can lead to excellent discussions or writing activities.

◆ Signal students auditorily: ring a bell, use a beeper or timer, play a bar of music on the piano or guitar, etc.

◆ Vary your tone of voice: loud, soft, whispering. Try making a louder command "Listen! Freeze! Ready!" followed by a few seconds of silence before proceeding in a normal voice to give directions.

◆ Use visual signals: flash the lights or raise your hand which signals the students to raise their hands and close their mouths until everyone is silent.

◆ Frame the visual material you want students to be focused on with your hands or with a colored box around it.

◆ If using an overhead, place an object (e.g., little toy car or plastic figure) to be projected on the screen to get attention.

◆ Clearly signal: "Everybody . . . Ready . . . "

◆ *Color* is very effective in getting attention. Make use of colored dry-erase pens on white boards, colored overhead pens for transparencies and overhead projectors, and colored paper to highlight key words, phrases, steps to computation problems, spelling patterns, etc.

◆ Model excitement and enthusiasm about the upcoming lesson.

◆ Use eye contact. Students should be facing you when you are speaking, especially while instructions are being given. If students are seated in clusters, have those students not directly facing you turn their chairs and bodies around to face you when signaled to do so.

41. Focusing Students' Attention

◆ Employ multisensory strategies when directions are given and a lesson is presented.

◆ Maintain your visibility.

◆ Project your voice and make sure you can be heard clearly by all students.

◆ Be aware of competing sounds in your room environment (such as noisy heaters or air conditioning unit.)

◆ Call students up front and close to you for direct instruction (e.g., seated on the carpet by the board).

◆ Position all students so that they can see the board and/or overhead screen. Always allow students to readjust their seating and signal you if their visibility is blocked.

◆ Explain the purpose and relevance to hook students in to your lesson.

◆ Incorporate demonstrations and hands-on presentations into your teaching whenever possible.

◆ Use a flashlight or laser pointer. Turn off the lights and get students to focus by illuminating objects or individuals with the light.

◆ Use study guides/sheets that are partial outlines. While you are presenting a lesson or giving a lecture, students fill in the missing words based on what you are saying and/or writing on the board or overhead.

◆ Use visuals. Write key words or pictures on the board or overhead projector while presenting. Use pictures, diagrams, gestures, manipulatives, and high-interest material.

◆ Illustrate, illustrate, illustrate: It doesn't matter if you don't draw well to illustrate throughout your presentation. Give yourself and students permission and encouragement to *draw* even if you lack the skill or talent. Drawings don't have to be sophisticated or accurate. In fact, often the sillier, the better. Have fun with it. These silly illustrations get and maintain attention and help students understand and remember the material (sequence of events, key points, abstract information, etc.).

◆ Point with a dowel, a stick/pointer, or laser pointer to written material you want students to focus on. If you can find a pointer/dowel with a little hand/finger on it, even better.

◆ **Note:** Overhead projectors are the best tools for focusing students' attention in the classroom. You are able to write down information in color without having to turn your back on the students, thus improving classroom management and reducing behavioral problems. On the overhead, you can model easily and frame important information. Transparencies can be made in advance, saving you time. Then it can be partially covered up, blocking out any distracting, visual stimuli.

◆ Block out material by covering or removing from the visual field that which you visually don't want students to focus on. Remove the distracting clutter from the board or screen.

◆ Have students write down brief notes or illustrate key points during instruction.

42. MAINTAINING STUDENTS' ATTENTION AND INVOLVEMENT

◆ Move around in the classroom to maintain your visibility.

◆ Teach thematically whenever possible, allowing for integration of ideas/concepts and connections to be made.

◆ Present at a lively, brisk pace.

◆ Be prepared and avoid lag time in instruction.

◆ Use pictures, diagrams, gestures, manipulatives, and high-interest materials.

◆ Use higher-level questioning techniques. Ask questions that are open-ended, require reasoning, and stimulate critical thinking and discussion.

◆ Decrease the amount of time you are doing the talking. Make all efforts to greatly increase student responses (saying and doing something with the information being taught).

◆ Use direct instruction techniques and other methods of questioning that allow for high response opportunities (i.e., unison responses, partner/buddy responses).

◆ Structure the lesson so that it can be done in pairs or small groups for maximum student involvement and attention.

◆ Alter the way students are called on to avoid calling on students one at a time. Instead, have students respond by "telling their partner," writing down or drawing their response, or other alternative way.

◆ Make frequent use of group or unison responses when there is one correct and short answer. While presenting, stop frequently and have students repeat back a word or two.

◆ Use the proper structure of cooperative learning groups (i.e., assignment of roles, accountability). It is *not* just group work. ADHD students do not typically function well in groups without clearly defined structure and expectations.

◆ Allowing students to use individual chalkboards or dry-erase boards throughout the lesson is motivating to students and helps maintain attention. If used properly it is also effective in checking for students' understanding and determining who needs extra help and practice.

◆ Use motivating computer programs for specific skill building and practice (programs that provide for frequent feedback and self-correction).

43. KEEPING STUDENTS ON-TASK DURING SEAT WORK

◆ Check for clarity. Make sure directions are clear and understood before sending students back to their seats to work independently.

◆ Make sure necessary supplies are available.

◆ Give a manageable amount of work *that the student is capable of doing independently.*

◆ Give other "failproof" work that student can do in the meantime if he or she is stumped on an assignment and needs to wait for teacher attention or assistance.

◆ Study buddies or partners may be assigned for any clarification purposes during seat work, especially when you are instructing another group of students while part of the class is doing seat work.

◆ Have students use signals to the teacher/aide for "I need help!" Some teachers use a sign or a colored signal that students may place on their desk that alerts any adult scanning the room that the student needs assistance.

◆ Scan classroom frequently. All students need positive reinforcement. Give positive comments with high frequency, praising students specifically whom you observe to be on-task. This serves as a reminder to students who tend to have difficulty.

◆ Consider using a timer for some students who work well with a "beat the clock" system for work completion.

◆ Use contracts, charts, and behavior-modification systems for on-task behavior.

◆ Reward for the certain number of completed items that are done with accuracy.

◆ Provide desk examples for reference.

◆ Use response costs and natural consequences for off-task behavior. Students might "owe you time" at the end of the day, before school, or for part of recess time. If they are on a point system, they may be fined points if a reasonable amount of work isn't accomplished.

◆ Make use of study carrels or quiet office areas for seat work.

◆ Teach students to self-monitor their own on-task behavior. Some teachers use an auditory signal (e.g., audio tape with intermittent beeps) and students reward themselves with points if they are on-task when the beeps go off.

44. Tips for Giving Directions in the Classroom

◆ Wait until it is quiet and you have everyone's attention before giving instructions. Don't talk over students' voices.

◆ You may need to walk over to touch or physically cue certain students for their focus prior to giving directions.

◆ Face students when you talk.

◆ A signal used in class that indicates students are to stop what they are doing and look at/listen to teacher is useful prior to giving instructions.

◆ Provide multisensory instructions. Provide visuals and graphics along with simple verbal explanations. Write on the board a few key words, picture cues, phrases, page numbers.

◆ Speak in simple, short sentences avoiding a lot of unnecessary language.

◆ Write assignments and directions needed on the board—in a consistent spot—and leave there for reference.

◆ Always check for understanding of directions. Have individual students repeat or rephrase your directions to the whole class. Ask for volunteers to repeat directions given.

◆ It is helpful to use a partner/buddy for clarification of directions—"Tell your partner what we are going to be doing on page 247."

◆ Provide for a discreet means of clarifying directions without calling attention to and embarrassing individual students who need extra help (e.g., use of private signals).

◆ Use color or underlining to highlight key words in written directions.

◆ Model what to do. Show the class. Leave visual models in the classroom as reference.

◆ Read written directions to the class and have students color-highlight or circle/underline key words in the directions.

◆ Don't overwhelm with too many instructions at one time.

◆ Keep directions clear, brief, and to the point.

◆ Give frequent praise and positive feedback when students are following directions and/or making a good attempt to do so.

◆ Follow-up after giving directions. Check the students' work.

◆ Break down tasks into smaller steps.

◆ Avoid vague directions (such as "Get ready for the next activity."). Define exactly what you expect: "Take out your Writer's Corner book and a sharpened pencil. Clear your desk of everything else."

◆ Keep in mind that you may often need to provide more assistance and structure to enable students with ADHD to follow directions. Remember, it is characteristic of ADHD to have difficulty:

- disengaging from activities (particularly fun ones) that they have not completed

- responding and following through without structuring, adult prompting, and cueing

- with recall/memory

◆ Make sure to give complete directions, including what you expect them to do (a) if they have any questions and (b) when they are finished with the task/assignment.

45. Helping Your Inattentive, Distractible Students

◆ Provide preferential seating—up front, within cueing distance of the teacher, and away from doors, windows and high-traffic areas of the room.

◆ Seat distractible students surrounded by well-focused students, and with good role model(s) facing them.

◆ Increase physical prompting of student (e.g., hand on shoulder or back).

◆ Make direct eye contact with this student.

◆ Use behavior-modification techniques with positive reinforcement/incentives for motivating and reinforcing attentive, on-task behavior (e.g., table points, individual charts for teacher initials, stickers, points, contracts).

◆ Utilize an individual contract for on-task behavior with positive incentives and perhaps response costs.

◆ Use private signals and cues that have been arranged with this student to help focus attention. Example: When a teacher points to and taps his or her chin it means "watch my face and pay attention."

◆ Make use of nonverbal signals (e.g., flashing lights, ringing bell) to cue students prior to transitions, or to stop all activity and focus on teacher.

◆ Increase visual prompting/cueing of student (direct eye contact, private hand signals).

◆ Increase auditory cues and signals to student (private signal words to serve as reminders).

◆ Increase teacher proximity to student (standing near or seated close by).

◆ Praise the student when focused (e.g., "I like the way Dequan is following along and is on the right page." "See how nicely Laticia is sitting up and looking at the board.").

◆ Vary your tone of voice when presenting to students. Avoid monotone!

◆ Present at a snappy, lively pace.

◆ Keep brevity in mind (i.e., brief instruction, brief explanation).

◆ Utilize a high degree of multisensory teaching strategies (color, movement, graphics).

◆ Provide for more variety throughout instruction, and movement between activities.

◆ Provide study carrels or partitions. (**Note:** These privacy boards or "office areas" should not be used if they are viewed by the students in the class as punitive measures, or as accommodations for students with special needs only.)

◆ Provide earphones for students to reduce auditory distractions as appropriate—preferably not the kind that have cords as part of a listening post. Have four or five sets of earphones available and encourage experimentation among *all* students.

◆ Have student clear desk of distractors (allowing only essential items to the task on the desk).

NOTE:

Some children—especially those with ADHD—have the need to touch objects for stimulation to keep alert and focused. Experiment after making private arrangements with the student. It may be necessary to remove all of these toys/objects or it may be helpful to allow their use if controlled. For example: Allow some children with a need to have something in hand to try holding a small piece of clay, playdough, squishy ball—as long as it stays within their hand and is not a distractor to others. Perhaps allow this child to attach something to a belt loop (e.g., a key chain with small object attached) to accommodate this need to touch/fidget.

◆ Use a timer to complete certain tasks and then reward for completion or on-task behavior during that time segment.

◆ Actually cut assignments or work pages in half, giving only one half at a time.

◆ "Block" pages of work assigned as seat work so that it doesn't overwhelm or cause a student to give up or completely avoid the task. Blocking pages means to cover up part of the page or fold the page in segments so that lesser amounts are visible at one time. Very helpful is if someone can monitor/give feedback after the shorter blocks of work are completed. Breaking the assignment into these smaller chunks helps keep students more motivated and on-task, as well as reduce frustration.

◆ Reward students for a certain number of completed items that are done with accuracy.

◆ Teach students to self-monitor on-task behavior/work completion; and to set individual short-term goals to self-monitor.

◆ Color-highlight directions and important words in the assignment.

◆ Provide guided practice before having students work independently on task.

◆ Provide a study guide or some graphic tool for students to use accompanying verbal presentation. **Note:** It is helpful for maintaining attention to be jotting down a few words or filling in missing words in a guided format.

◆ Allow students to ask buddies for clarification on seat work.

◆ Significantly increase opportunities for active student involvement in the lesson, and utilize questioning techniques that engage all students.

◆ *See checklists on Getting Students' Attention (40), Focus Students' Attention (41), Maintaining Students' Attention and Involvement (42), and Tips for Giving Directions in the Classroom (44) and Environmental Modifications that Make a Difference in the Classroom (46), for more strategies.*

46. Environmental Modifications that Make a Difference in the Classroom

◆ Design the room to accommodate the different learning styles of your students.

◆ Physically arrange the classroom with options of seating. Alter the seating with: staggered arrangements of desks and rows, semi-circle or horseshoe arrangement of desks, a mix of desk clusters and individual desks/rows.

◆ Increase the distance between desks/tables when possible.

◆ Avoid "open classrooms" or loft-type situations.

◆ Have informal areas of the classroom (e.g., carpet area, soft cushions, beanbag chairs).

◆ Use carpet squares for seating at times if the room is not carpeted or if sitting outside.

◆ Establish rules and procedures for movement within the classroom (when it is okay to get up and get a drink, sharpen pencils, etc.).

◆ Define areas of the room concretely.

◆ Make use of storage bins for "center" activities and materials.

◆ Store materials in clearly labeled bins, shelves, tubs, trays, and/or folders.

◆ Provide easy access to materials and independent learning activities.

◆ Post all schedules, calendars, and assignments.

◆ Have pictures and/or a list of rules and daily routine.

◆ Use furniture, shelves, and partitions to divide space.

◆ Have comfortable lighting and room temperature.

◆ Keep a portion of the room free from distractors. Provide desk organizers to help children easily locate materials.

◆ Seat ADHD students closer to the center of instruction, surrounded and facing positive role models/well-focused students, within teacher cueing and prompting distance.

◆ Seat ADHD students away from high traffic areas and distractors (e.g., noisy heaters/air conditioners, the door, windows, pencil sharpeners).

◆ Have models and visual displays for student reference.

◆ Use tools such as timers of various kinds, bells, etc., for signaling changes of activity.

◆ Use a minute timer to designate how much time is alloted for transitions. Meeting the expectation can result in class/table privilege(s); failure to meet expectation may result in time owed.

◆ Allow ADHD student(s) an alternative desk or chair in the room (two-seat method).

◆ Reduce visual distractions (e.g., a lot of unnecessary writing on the board).

◆ Reduce or minimize auditory distractions when possible.

◆ Use a listening post for books on tape, stories, and music as appropriate.

◆ Be sure desks/tables are positioned so all students can see the board and overhead screen (at least be able to move their chairs easily to do so).

◆ Permit the student who can't sit for very long to stand near the desk while working at certain times (if productive).

◆ Build in stretch breaks or exercise breaks after sitting any length of time.

◆ Experiment with background music at different times of the day and for various activities/purposes (i.e., to calm and relax, to motivate, to stimulate thinking). Try a variety of instrumental cassettes/CDs including environmental sounds (e.g., rain forest), Baroque music, classical, jazz, show tunes. There is some research demonstrating the effectiveness of music with ADHD children that has 60 beats per minute (e.g., instrumental compositions by Gary Lamb. *(See Checklist 68 on Relaxation, Guided Imagery, and Visualization Techniques.)*

◆ Permit students to use earphones to block out noise during seat work, test taking, or other times of the day. Some teachers purchase sets of earphones to be used for this purpose. It is encouraged that *all* students experiment with and be allowed to use these tools (not just students with special needs).

◆ Have designated quiet times of the day.

◆ The room environment should be well organized, visually appealing, arranged for maximum use of space, and showing student work/ownership.

◆ Be aware of glare in the classroom and its effects on visibility.

◆ Be sure desks are raised/lowered so that each student can sit at a desk/chair of the appropriate height. Make sure furniture is stable, not wobbly.

◆ Reduce the clutter and unnecessary visual overload in the classroom.

◆ Provide "office areas" or "study carrels" for seating options during times of the day as needed. These should be encouraged and experimented with by *all* students in the class so seating in these areas is never viewed as punitive or for students with special needs only.

◆ Purchase or construct privacy boards to place on tables while taking tests, or other times of the day to block visual distractions and limit the visual field.

◆ Provide some students extra work space and/or storage space.

◆ Turn off the lights at various times of the day for calming (particularly after PE and recess).

◆ Provide a lot of opportunities for hands-on learning, exploration, using manipulatives, artistic expression, and using a variety of supplies/materials.

◆ Design instruction for frequent opportunities to interact with peers.

◆ Structure activities so that built-in opportunities for movement are provided.

◆ Kidney-shaped tables are ideal for small-group instruction.

◆ Allow students to move to a quiet corner or designated area of the room if needed.

◆ Create an environment of safety, inclusiveness, success, emotional well-being, acceptance, tolerance, calmness, high interest, fun, and humor.

◆ Pair students or establish cooperative groups carefully to avoid conflicts and increase chances of success.

◆ Be open, flexible, and willing to make changes in seating when needed.

◆ Be sensitive to the physical needs of students that may interfere with learning: need for a drink of water, a snack, use of restroom, movement/stretching.

47. If You Suspect Your Student Has ADHD

When you observe a student displaying inattentive, hyperactive, and impulsive behaviors in the classroom, you should automatically attempt to deal with those behaviors by using strategies that are generally effective in doing so. This would include providing more structure, positive reinforcement, and teacher assistance. Obviously, this is simply good teaching practice—to provide behavioral and academic interventions for any student displaying the need.

◆ You should begin keeping records of interventions you are attempting, as well as any phone contacts/conferences with parents.

◆ You should have a general knowledge base about ADHD (what it is and isn't), and recommended strategies and interventions for students with attention deficit disorders. This information will be necessary in guiding how you instruct the student, organize the environment, and use behavioral interventions that may be helpful. Many school sites have resources (books, manuals, videos, audiocassettes, magazine/journal articles) that teachers can access to learn more about ADHD, and also share with parents.

◆ It is helpful if you communicate with the previous year's teacher(s) to see if the areas of concern were also of issue the prior year; and if so, what strategies and interventions were used successfully or unsuccessfully by that teacher.

◆ If the student continues to be having difficulty, you should communicate with staff members from the support team sharing your concerns about the student. Tell the school counselor, school nurse, psychologist, or special education teacher your concern and ask for assistance. This support staff member may arrange to observe the child in the classroom, look at work samples, and suggest other strategies/interventions that can be tried.

◆ Many schools use a Student Study Team (SST) process for this next step. You sign up on a master calendar for a Student Study Team meeting to discuss the child with the whole team. Often, by just alerting one of the support team members it will be suggested to proceed by scheduling a SST meeting on the child. *(See Checklist 70 on The Student Study Team Process.)*

◆ In most districts the SST process requires that the teacher have documented all interventions he or she has tried, and has already shared concerns with parents prior to bringing the child to the team. Parents are typically invited to SST meetings, as they are a valued member of the team whose input is necessary for helping the student.

◆ You will be asked to fill out a referral form and to bring to the SST meeting any documentation/data collected on the student that may be helpful in sharing with the team how the child is functioning academically, behaviorally, socially, and emotionally. *(See Checklist 48 on Typical Teacher Referral Forms.)*

◆ At the SST meeting, support staff, the classroom teacher(s), parents, and administrator often review the student's school history and discuss interventions implemented both in the past and currently. After discussing the student's strengths and weaknesses, a plan of action is written at the SST meeting. Typically, support team members will plan to observe the student in different school environments, implement some more interventions (sometimes school-based such as counseling, social skills group, nonspecial ed academic support, behavioral contracts/plans, etc.). This is often the time/place that parents will be told that the child exhibits behaviors that indicate he or she may have ADHD. Information (i.e., articles or other resources) will be given to parents if they are interested in learning more about ADHD. They are told what the diagnostic process involves and given the options of how to proceed with an evaluation for ADHD—if interested.

◆ It is explained to parents that diagnosing ADHD is not simple; it requires the collection of a lot of data that needs to be interpreted. For educational purposes we can evaluate at a school site. For a clinical/medical diagnosis of ADHD to be made, the parents would need to have the school supply evidence/data to the physician/mental health professional conducting the assessment.

◆ Parents are asked to sign a release of information, permitting the school to communicate with the physician or any professionals working with the child outside of school. If parents wish to pursue any evaluation (school-based or clinically based), they may be asked to sign permission forms to enable the school to start gathering information (e.g., teacher rating scales, questionnaires, observation forms, screening devices, informal/formal diagnostic testing).

◆ If it is decided to proceed with a formal school evaluation, the procedures and paperwork for an IEP will be initiated. *(See Checklist 71 on The IEP Process for more information.)*

Cautions to Teachers

- ✔ Do *not* tell parents that you think their child has ADHD.

- ✔ Do *not* send the parent to see their doctor because you suggest the child has ADHD.

- ✔ Do *not* attempt to diagnose ADHD.

- ✔ Do *not* recommend that the child be placed on medication.

- ✔ Learn as much as you can about ADHD. Utilize a team approach and make any referrals/suggestions that the child has ADHD through the team.

- ✔ Teachers need to objectively describe what they see regarding the child's behavior and performance in the classroom. Dr. Sam Goldstein, one of the leading national experts in the field, strongly suggests: "Teachers should describe not diagnose."

48. Typical Teacher Referral Forms

When teachers have concerns about students in their classrooms, typically there is a system in place for referrals to be made to the school support team to discuss the student's needs and develop a plan of action. *(See Checklist 70 on The Student Study Team Process.)* Teachers or other staff members (as well as parents) may also make a direct referral for a student to be evaluated for possible special education services. However, it is generally recommended to first go through the SST process (if available at the school site) before making a special eduction referral. The following are typical items that you may be asked to respond to on a referral form/checklist.

Health/Physical Factors

_____ Health problems

_____ Frequent physical complaints

_____ Appears pale, listless, apathetic

_____ Extremely active and restless/fidgety

_____ Possible vision deficit

_____ Possible hearing deficit

_____ Poor fine motor coordination (small muscle movements such as using pencil, scissors)

_____ Poor gross motor coordination (running, jumping, skipping)

_____ Growth or development lag

_____ Physical injuries (appears accident-prone)

Speech/Language Factors

_____ Limited speaking vocabulary

_____ Difficulty relating own ideas

_____ Incomplete sentences

_____ Poor grammar

_____ Responses are inappropriate

_____ Difficulty following directions

_____ Articulation: mispronunciation of speech sounds

_____ Stuttering: speech blocks, breaks, poor rhythm

_____ Voice: Quality is _____ hoarse _____ harsh _____ too soft

Education Factors

_____ Reading difficulties in word recognition

_____ Reading comprehension difficulties

_____ Spelling difficulties

_____ Math computation difficulties

_____ Math applications/conceptualization difficulties

_____ Written language difficulties

_____ Poor retention of subject matter

_____ Poor handwriting

_____ Makes reversals (b/d, p/q) and inverts letters/numbers within a word

_____ Messy, disorganized work

_____ Difficulty staying on task

_____ Inattentive

_____ Difficulty comprehending directions

_____ Difficulty comprehending subject matter

_____ Difficulty changing activities

_____ Easily discouraged; often frustrated

_____ Work completion: rushed

_____ Work completion: slow

_____ Does not complete assignments

Personal/Social Factors

_____ Generally withdrawn, timid, fearful

_____ Poor self control

_____ Temper outbursts

_____ Inappropriate language

_____ Poor peer relations

_____ Fights/physically aggressive

_____ Disturbs others

_____ Seems unhappy

_____ Seems moody

_____ Cries easily

_____ Feelings of inadequacy: _____ low self-concept

_____ Fantasizes: _____ exaggerates _____ lies

_____ Challenges authority: _____ defiant

_____ Impulsive

_____ Shows little empathy/concern for others

Student Strengths

◆ In addition to checking your areas of concern, you would be asked to identify the student's strengths:

_____ Creativity

_____ Sense of humor

_____ Physical strength and coordination

_____ Cooperative

_____ Enthusiastic

_____ Good motivation

_____ Highly verbal

_____ Confident: socially/academically

_____ Compassionate

◆ Identify other areas of strength/interests of the student:

_____

_____

◆ You will also be asked to document the parent contact dates—at which time concerns have been shared; and the various interventions that have been implemented (including length of time and effectiveness of those interventions).

49. A LIST OF DON'TS FOR TEACHERS

♦ **DON'T** assume the student is lazy in the classroom. Students with attention deficit disorders (or with learning disabilities) are typically *not* lazy. There are other reasons for their nonperformance in the classroom.

♦ **DON'T** be fooled by inconsistency, or assume the student is deliberately not performing because you have observed that at times he or she is able to perform that kind of task/assignment. Students with ADD/ADHD have *inconsistency* as a hallmark characteristic of their disorder. Sometimes they can do the work, sometimes they cannot.

♦ **DON'T** give up on any student. These children need your persistence and belief in their ability to succeed no matter how difficult and frustrating it may be.

♦ **DON'T** give up using behavior-modification techniques. Students with ADHD often do not respond well to behavior modification and positive reinforcements for any extended period of time. You will need to revamp, revise, and modify your behavior-management system frequently. It is still worth the effort!

♦ **DON'T** be afraid to ask questions. Classroom teachers are not expected to be experts on teaching children with special needs. Ask for information, advice, and support from staff members who may be able to help you.

♦ **DON'T** forget to involve your support staff. Communicate with school support personnel. Bring students to the Student Study Team for assistance. Your team should support you in making observations, helping with behavioral management and classroom strategies, attending meetings with parents, providing information, suggesting any school-based interventions that may be available and appropriate, and making necessary referrals. Networking with the other professionals at your school site eases the load.

♦ **DON'T** neglect to involve parents. Start early in the school year to invite parents to visit the school, observe their child in the classroom, and meet with you to plan strategies for working together on behalf of their child. Be sensitive to parents' frustration and fears. Let them know that your primary goal is helping their child to succeed, and that you welcome a partnership/team effort in order to accomplish this.

◆ **DON'T** surround yourself with negative peers who are critical of students, aren't open or receptive to new techniques and strategies, and are not updating their skills.

◆ **DON'T** listen to previous teachers who only want to pass on the negative traits and characteristics of their students to you. Assume the best of the child. Allow each student to start the year with a fresh, clean slate.

◆ **DON'T** forget the quiet student in the background who can easily go through the school year unnoticed and anonymous. Often these are the students in greatest need of support and intervention.

◆ **DON'T** work alone. Find buddies, share with colleagues, collaborate!

◆ **DON'T** put yourself in the position of suggesting to parents that their child has ADHD and needs to be evaluated. **DO** state your objective observations regarding the child's behavior and performance in the classroom. Tell parents you will share your observations/concerns with the School Support Team. Allow the team to share information about ADHD with parents and to make recommendations for evaluation.

◆ **DON'T** be afraid to modify, make exceptions, and alter assignments for students as needed. Your goal is the student's success and building/maintaining self-esteem. That requires flexibility and special arrangements with certain students. It is *okay* and *fair* to make accommodations for individual students with special needs.

50. Assessment/Testing: Modifications and Adaptations

The following is an extensive list of possible adaptations to be considered when trying to provide a fair assessment of students' learning. Included are some recommendations you should keep in mind when preparing exams for *all* students. Some of the other interventions should be considered as special accommodations for students with moderate to severe reading, writing, or attention difficulties, who are unable to demonstrate their comprehension or mastery of the content material under normal testing conditions and criteria.

♦ Prior to testing, *review, review, review.*

♦ Provide students with all handouts/test copies that are easy to read (typed, clear language, at least double spaced, clean copies, ample margins).

♦ Avoid handwritten tests.

♦ Eliminate unnecessary words and confusing language on the test.

♦ State directions in clear terms and simple sentences.

♦ Underline or color-highlight directions or key words in the directions.

♦ Provide many opportunities for short-answer assessment (e.g., multiple choice, matching).

♦ On vocabulary tests give the definition and have student supply the word, rather than providing the word and student needing to write out the definition.

♦ For fill-in-the-blank tests, provide a word bank from which students may select the correct word for the blanks.

♦ Allow extended time for completing the test.

♦ Take the exam in the classroom, and then in a small group or with special education teacher. Average the two grades.

♦ Provide students with examples of different types of test questions they will be responsible for on the exam.

◆ Provide more work space on the test (particularly for math tests).

◆ Allow students to use graph paper or other paper to solve math problems and attach to test, rather than require that computation be done on the limited work space directly on the test.

◆ Enlarge the print.

◆ Divide a test in parts, administering each part on different days rather than rushing students to complete lengthy tests in one class period.

◆ Allow students to retake the test orally after given in written form to add points to their score if they are able to demonstrate greater knowledge/mastery than shown on written test (especially for essay questions).

◆ Administer frequent short quizzes throughout the teaching unit, reviewing the next day, and thus providing feedback to students on their understanding of the material. These short quizzes do not need to be graded for a score, but to help students in their learning and confidence prior to the exam.

◆ Substitute oral for written tests as appropriate.

◆ For a change of routine, assign take-home tests on occasion.

◆ Allow taped tests if needed, and permit student to tape-record answers to essay questions rather than write them.

◆ Read test items orally to student(s).

◆ Don't penalize for spelling, grammar, etc., on tests that are measuring mastery of content in other areas.

◆ Give credit for what is done correctly.

◆ Read aloud the directions for the different parts of the test before students begin the exam.

◆ Read the directions again to those students who need additional clarification.

◆ Before providing the final grade on a test, point out test items that you spot are incorrect, and allow student to try self-correcting careless errors before scoring.

◆ Give reduced spelling lists for students who struggle with spelling (for example, 15 words rather than 20 or 25). When dictating the words on the test, dictate those 15 words in any order first; then continue with the other words for the rest of the class. Those students on modified lists have the option of trying the additional words for bonus points.

◆ Score tests for number correct/total number assigned per student (which can be shortened assignments or tests for individual students).

◆ Eliminate need for students with writing difficulties to copy test questions from the board or book before answering.

◆ Teach students the strategies and skills for taking a variety of tests (true/false, multiple choice, fill-in-the-blank, essay, fill-in-the-bubble, etc.).

◆ Give students the opportunity to write their own test questions in a variety of formats.

◆ Practice all types of testing formats—sharing and discussing "test-taking strategies."

◆ Use more short-answer testing formats (fill-in-the-blank, matching, multiple choice). When giving essay questions, be willing to make accommodations for students with written output disabilities.

◆ Collaborate with special educators to rewrite the tests for students with special needs (e.g., shorter sentences, simplified vocabulary, easier-to-read format).

◆ Test what has been taught.

◆ Avoid questions that are worded in a way to deliberately trick the student.

◆ Write multiple-choice questions with choices listed vertically rather than horizontally (as it is easier to read).

◆ Utilize portfolio assessment (progress evaluated on individual performance and improvement as opposed to comparing with other students).

◆ Reduce weight of a single test grade. Have several shorter and more frequent quizzes rather than a lengthy unit test.

◆ Color the processing signs on math tests for students who don't focus well on details and make careless errors due to inattention (e.g., highlight: yellow = addition, green = subtraction, blue = multiplication).

◆ Utilize privacy boards at desks during test-taking time, and/or find other means of reducing distractions when students are tested.

◆ Allow calculator and multiplication charts/tables on math tests that are assessing problem-solving skills, not computation.

◆ Encourage students to double and triple check their tests for careless errors (i.e., skipping items, getting mixed up on numbering, writing numerals and letters/words legibly, filling in next to the correct corresponding number).

◆ Administer the test if necessary in a separate location either individually or in a small group.

◆ Administer the test in shorter intervals in a few different sessions.

◆ Revise the test format as needed for certain students (e.g., reducing number of items on a page, enlarging print, increasing the spacing between items).

◆ Allow student to directly write in test booklet if needed.

◆ *See Checklist 60 on Strategies for Bypassing Writing Difficulties for more information.*

51. Lesson Presentation: Strategies and Modifications

◆ Relate information to students' prior experiences and background information.

◆ Have students share what they already know about a topic before instructing on that topic.

◆ Limit the number of new concepts introduced at one time.

◆ Pause during oral presentations/lectures, and allow students a few minutes to work with partners in order to briefly discuss the content and share their understanding.

◆ Summarize key points, and let students know what is important for them to remember.

◆ Pause throughout instruction to question their understanding of concepts.

◆ Frequently monitor and assess (formally and informally) students' understanding and mastery, re-teaching and providing intervention when necessary.

◆ Allow extra time for students to process the information presented.

◆ Increase "wait time" to *at least* five seconds when asking a student to respond to a question.

◆ Use questioning strategies that encourage student success without humiliation; such as probing techniques, providing clues, asking student if he or she would like more time to think about the question, and so forth.

◆ Expand on students' partial answers (i.e., "Tell me more.")

◆ Ask open-ended questions that allow for a variety of acceptable answers and encourage sharing of different perspectives.

◆ Speak slower and avoid giving directions when not directly facing the class.

◆ Be aware of your use of complex sentence structure and sophisticated vocabulary, and which students may have difficulty comprehending.

◆ Paraphrase using similar language.

◆ Adjust lessons in response to student performance.

◆ Increase student response opportunities significantly (e.g., unison responses, partner responses, small group responses).

◆ Teach with fewer words/greater use of visuals.

◆ Monitor and vary your rate, volume, tone of voice.

◆ Move throughout the room and provide individual assistance (clarification, cueing/prompting, redirection, feedback) as needed.

◆ Use a variety of graphic organizers and techniques such as webbing, graphing, clustering, mapping, and outlining.

◆ Use a lot of role playing, demonstrations, and experiential learning.

◆ Alternate activities to allow for variety and change of pace.

◆ Teach from concrete to abstract.

◆ Introduce lessons with strategies to gain students' attention and interest and "set the stage" for learning.

◆ Clearly state lesson purpose and relevance, and what students will be learning.

◆ Set learning and behavioral expectations for the lessons as well as materials needed.

◆ Review prior concepts/material presented with high frequency.

◆ Allow students to preview new material.

◆ Show students the connection between concepts/lessons taught.

◆ Teach thematically across the curriculum whenever possible since students better grasp the connection and learn most effectively when information is integrated and interrelated.

◆ Supplement verbal presentation with visuals, graphics, and demonstrations.

◆ Significantly increase use of hands-on, active learning.

◆ Model enthusiasm and interest in lesson/topic.

◆ Increase the amount of teacher modeling and guided practice.

◆ Increase use of gestures, hand signals, and other forms of nonverbal communication.

◆ Increase the amount of immediate feedback to students.

◆ Repeat important information.

◆ Move around, yet remain visible throughout lesson presentation.

◆ Present lessons in short, brief segments and time blocks—giving students opportunities to respond in some format with high frequency throughout the lesson.

◆ Provide as many opportunities as possible for small-group instruction with the teacher.

◆ Design lessons so that students experience a high rate of success.

◆ Vary the structure of presentation and student response opportunities: direct teacher instruction (whole class or small group), cooperative (fours, triads, partners), independent, verbal/nonverbal responses, etc.

◆ Provide audiotapes of lessons, lectures, literature read in class, and content book chapters as needed.

◆ Use an overhead projector with transparencies of key points during lesson presentation, or write/illustrate main information/topics on the board.

◆ Project an outline of the lesson on the overhead or write topic outline on the board for students to follow.

◆ Give students framed outlines to follow your lectures, and have them fill in the key points during the lecture. This framed outline can be projected on an overhead with you or individual students filling in directly on the transparency throughout the lesson.

◆ Teach students about "multiple intelligences" and "learning styles"—how we all learn differently, and have strengths and weaknesses in different areas. Provide numerous opportunities for student choices and options (projects, activities, tools/materials) to accommodate individual learning styles and interests.

◆ Increase use of cooperative learning activities and formats. Utilize triads and partner structures with high frequency.

◆ Student projects and assignments should have options that may include: music, drama, art, construction, designing, writing, speaking, use of technology, research, and any means of creative expression.

◆ Use multisensory techniques throughout the lesson.

◆ Use a lot of color, movement, and graphics.

◆ Be certain that each student in the classroom is able to access the information. For example, if asking students to silently read in class and be prepared to discuss or respond, is every student capable of reading that text independently? If not, perhaps consider partner reading. Consider having parts be read or re-read orally or summarized orally. Perhaps some students can have the option of listening to the book on tape (at a listening post).

◆ Utilize peer tutoring in the classroom, allowing students to work together and help each other.

◆ Vary instructional techniques. Remember to incorporate VARIETY and NOVELTY into lesson presentations.

◆ Utilize a variety of audio-visual materials and resources.

◆ Present many models and examples.

◆ Teach strategically and model effective thinking, questioning, and planning/organizing processes.

◆ Know the skill level of your students, and assign tasks at an appropriate level.

◆ Design instruction and activities that can span developmental skill and ability range of students—providing choices and levels of complexity in assignments to meet needs of ALL students in an inclusive classroom.

◆ Highlight in COLOR important concepts, vocabulary, and key points.

◆ Provide some texts as needed that are color highlighted for main ideas and vocabulary.

◆ Modify the objectives and mastery levels when needed.

◆ Utilize people supports (aides, cross-age tutors, peer tutors, parent volunteers, special education teacher or aide) for more intensive direct assistance.

◆ Use technological tools, computer software, and other means of individualized or programmed instruction as appropriate.

◆ Use a game format for drill and practice activities.

52. Adaptations/Modifications of Materials

◆ Use the tape recorder as an excellent adaptive device for a number of purposes such as:

✔ recording directions/specific instructions to tasks for students to listen to as many times as necessary

✔ recording text chapters or literature for students to listen to (as they follow along in the text if possible)

✔ recording test questions for students to respond to verbally or in writing

◆ Permit the student to use his or her own tape recorder in class for:

✔ recording lectures

✔ recording class reviews prior to exams

✔ recording assignments

✔ giving self-reminders

✔ alternative methods of presentation such as oral presentations with use of sound effects

Math Material Supports and Adaptations

◆ Reduce the number of problems on a page.

◆ Use frames, boxes, or windows to separate and space problems on a page.

◆ Use graph paper to structure placement of numerals and help with alignment and organization of problems on a page.

◆ Use an assortment of colorful, concrete, manipulative materials (i.e., pattern blocks, tiles, cubes, counters, number lines, more than/less than spinners, dice, beans/cups) to teach and reinforce number concepts of whole numbers/fractions, geometry, quantity, patterning, and so forth.

◆ Use calculators for problem solving and for checking work after paper/pencil computation skill practice.

◆ Allow the use of and provide students with multiplication tables/charts, a chart of formulas, and list of measurements/conversions.

◆ Use compensatory techniques and materials for computation such as Touch Math™ (Innovative Learning Concepts, Colorado Springs) which enables students to compute rapidly and accurately through the technique of touching or visualizing the strategically-placed "touch points" for numerals 1–9. *(See Checklist 61 on Math Difficulties and Interventions.)*

Make Use of the Computer

◆ Educational software, particularly interactive CDs and programs are excellent for teaching and reinforcing academic skills. The element of self-correction, self-pacing, and competition against oneself or the computer (not another peer) is much less threatening for children with learning difficulties and low self-esteem. The immediate feedback and reward, color and sound, exciting graphics, and novelty in the programming is very motivational—perfect for holding the interest of children with ADHD.

◆ Use computer programs for drilling and practicing all basic skills (i.e., spelling, word recognition, math facts, grammar and vocabulary).

◆ Let students create materials on the computer—written projects, graphics, charts/graphs, lettering.

◆ Provide access to information/resources available through computers (CD encyclopedias, Internet, etc.).

Enhance Students' Attention and Focus

◆ Block the page or fold in such a way that only part of the print is shown at one time.

◆ Frame the material.

◆ Highlight, underline, circle, draw arrows, draw a box around in vivid COLORS.

◆ Provide clear, clean copies of handouts that are well organized and easy to read.

◆ Use illustrations and graphics.

◆ Enlarge the print/font size and spacing on the page.

◆ Provide markers (strips of cardboard or index cards) to students when reading.

Structuring the Materials

◆ Provide an outline of the lesson.

◆ Reduce the amount of reading required.

◆ Simplify the vocabulary.

◆ Reduce the readability level.

◆ Tape-record the reading material.

◆ Rearrange the page format to simplify.

◆ Provide for short amounts of material to be learned, reviewed, and checked for understanding/mastery.

◆ Provide study guides and graphic organizers.

◆ Color-highlight a few texts (important ideas, vocabulary and other material to be studied) for students to borrow.

◆ Remove pages from a workbook or make a copy rather than giving the student the whole text or workbook to work from.

◆ Provide students with partially filled-in materials, maps, graphs, etc., that are already semi-prepared.

Compensating for Writing Difficulties

◆ Permit writing directly on a page or test booklet rather than having to copy answers onto another page or answer sheet.

◆ Try a variety of pencil grips.

◆ Use a mechanical pencil.

◆ Use a clipboard.

◆ Use a computer/word processor.

◆ Experiment with different sized graph paper and lined paper. Some children with writing difficulties can write neater and easier within smaller/narrower lines; others do better with wider lines. Paper that has vertical spacers is helpful for many students. Computer paper is excellent for writing—especially rough draft copies. (Write on the green lines/edit above on the white lines or vice versa.)

◆ Provide photocopied pages rather than requiring copying from the book/board onto paper.

◆ If it is easier and faster for an upper-grade student to write in manuscript (print) rather than cursive, allow him or her to do so.

◆ *See Checklist 60 Strategies for Bypassing Writing Difficulties and other writing checklists in the academic strategy section.*

Increase the Rate and Immediacy of Feedback

◆ Use well-designed programmed materials for independent work.

◆ Give students access to answer keys to self-correct.

◆ Collect work and correct/return as quickly as possible.

◆ Use computer software programs.

◆ Use flash cards with answers on the back for immediate check/correct.

Other

◆ Provide as many visual models and concrete/graphic examples as possible.

◆ Use creative learning center activities for students to work on independently, with partners, or small groups. These centers can include materials that are already set up in an area of the room (stations), or they can be taken out for easy set-up and use by the students. Directions should be simple and clear. Activities should all have been explained and modeled first so students know what to do.

◆ Organize your materials by placing in tubs/bins, self-locking plastic bags, or colored boxes and clearly labeling them for students (in words or pictures).

◆ Teach thematically, and within that theme have an array of learning materials, books, and activities that span the developmental levels of your students. For example, if studying about *inventors*, have biographies/books on inventors available for students at an easy reader level through more challenging reading levels. Regardless of the readability level, students can learn the same concepts and information.

◆ Create as many hands-on activities, games, puzzles, etc., as possible that teach and reinforce skills.

◆ Design a classroom with materials and activities that build upon the strengths/learning styles of *all* students. Use music, art, discovery/free exploration, construction, audio-visuals, etc., with high frequency.

◆ Use word walls of vocabulary.

◆ Use tactile materials (i.e., writing/tracing on various surfaces and textures, salt/sand trays, pudding, frosting, carpet).

◆ Use GAMES, GAMES, GAMES.

◆ Use high-interest supplemental materials.

For more recommendations see Checklists 40, 41, and 42 on Getting, Focusing, and Maintaining Students' Attention, Checklist 54 on Reading Strategies and Interventions for Home and School, and Checklist 57 on Multisensory Spelling Activities and Choices.

✔ Academic Strategies for Home and School

This section provides information about academic difficulties that are common for children/adolescents with attention deficit disorders. Writing tends to be the area that causes those with ADD/ADHD the most difficulty. This section addresses why writing is such a struggle, and contains checklists with strategies for how to help with pre-writing, organization, handwriting, legibility, spelling, editing, and general written production.

When written output is slow and tedious, it is important to allow the struggling writer to bypass some of his or her difficulties. Children with this disability are often unable to demonstrate their mastery of skills and knowledge because they can't effectively express it on paper. This section includes a checklist of bypass strategies that will alleviate some of the frustration, and enable the child or teenager with ADHD to show what he or she knows.

Other checklists in this section explain common reading and math problems of those with ADD/ADHD. Included are strategies and techniques for improving skills in those areas. All of the information in this section is intended for parents and teachers, as the strategies and recommendations are applicable both at home and school.

53. Common Reading Difficulties of Children/Teens with ADHD

◆ Silent reading is often difficult for individuals with ADHD. They often need to subvocalize or read quietly to themselves in order to hear their voice and maintain attention to what they are reading. If you observe students doing this, permit them to do so. Many students need the auditory input and can't get meaning by reading the passages silently.

◆ Maintaining attention during whole-class instruction is an area of difficulty for many students with ADHD. They often have a hard time paying attention to stories and text being read out loud in class. When one person is orally reading, and the rest of the class is supposed to be following along in their book and listening to the reader, it is common for students with ADHD to have a hard time doing so. They are frequently on the wrong page in the book, and struggle to follow the reader (particularly if the oral reader lacks fluency and expression). It is often more beneficial to listen to the text being read with fluency and expression in a large-group setting, and then reread with partners and small groups after the initial reading. It is also helpful to read passages first alone, with partners or small groups, and then to reread sections in whole group. If possible, seat ADHD students among well-focused students during this part of instruction.

◆ Many poor readers (often those with ADHD) struggle because they are not using what is called "metacognitive strategies" while they are reading. This means they aren't actively thinking about the reading material. They are not processing what they are reading to get meaning. Reading is an interactive, strategic process that must be taught.

◆ Losing their train of thought and not being able to concentrate on what they are reading is a common problem. A large percentage of individuals with ADHD report this difficulty. They may have excellent decoding skills and fluency. However, due to their distractibility and difficulty sustaining the mental effort, they struggle tremendously with focusing on what they are reading—particularly if they find it dry, uninteresting, or difficult material. They report having to read and reread numerous times. Metacognitive strategies and techniques such as paraphrasing, retelling, summarizing, brief note taking, and self-questioning while reading are helpful strategies to teach your students. Any techniques that require active involvement and thinking about/responding to what is being read help maintain focus and attention. *(See Checklist 54 on Reading Strategies and Interventions for Home and School.)*

◆ Many struggling readers don't have a strong word bank of vocabulary they recognize in print. They are not fluent readers because they don't recognize words at the automatic level—even the most common, high-frequency words. Therefore, they attempt to sound out every word, are slow and choppy in their reading, and lose the meaning of what they are trying to read.

◆ A number of students have difficulty with the language/ vocabulary of books being read. This is naturally one of the disadvantages of having everyone read from the same book or piece of literature. Some students will find the story or book far too difficult for independent reading or decoding. For part of the reading program, this is okay. Children should have the opportunity to hear and discuss literature that is interesting and motivating, even if they can't read the text independently.

◆ Through teacher-guided reading and alternative strategies, struggling readers can have the same exposure to stories and literature as the rest of the class—although the vocabulary may be difficult and challenging. These students will benefit from listening to the stories/passages, the oral discussions, and re-reading the material in different formats. They will definitely gain from all of the creative, motivational whole language techniques and activities related to the literature; and being able to participate along with their classmates.

◆ However, students need to have a classroom rich in reading material that is at their independent level as well—books that they are capable of reading with a fair amount of success on their own or with minimal help. Elementary classrooms should have books for students to choose from with vocabulary that spans the developmental range and reading level of the students in the classroom.

◆ Many children with ADHD also have specific reading disabilities. There is a high correlation between ADHD and learning disabilities. Some children have specific processing problems (i.e., weaknesses in perceptual skills, short-term memory skills) that affect their acquisition of reading skills. They will require special training and intervention. It is very common for those who struggle with reading to be weak in word recognition/decoding skills. If so, they very likely need more *word attack/phonics* training than they may be receiving in their reading programs. They need to develop strategies for independently decoding new, unfamiliar words. These children generally need a systematic approach to learning the sounds/symbols in the English language. They also need to be taught how to see and recognize the structure and common patterns in words, and be taught through a well-designed program that uses a variety of multisensory strategies and mnemonics (memory clues and associations).

◆ Poor readers who struggle to decode unfamiliar words are generally weak in one or more of the cueing systems—knowing how to use semantic clues ("Does that make sense?"), syntactic clues ("Does that sound right grammatically?"), and grapho-phonic clues ("What does that word look like?" "How do I sound out that word?"). *(For more recommendations see Checklist 54 on Reading Strategies and Interventions for Home and School.)*

◆ Difficulty with visually focusing on the print and losing their place when reading (tracking) is a common problem for students with ADHD. Encourage students to use strips of cardboard for markers or to use their finger to track, if needed. Some students may benefit from using a "window box" (or card with a cut-out opening large enough to view a limited number of words at a time).

◆ Many children need more one-to-one assistance and small group work in order to learn how to read, practice and review skills/strategies, and receive corrective feedback. Each school site needs to use all of its resources to provide additional assistance to students who need more help (reading specialists, basic skills teachers, aides, parent volunteers, cross-age tutors, peer-tutors, teacher-directed skill groups, tutoring before or after school, computer-lab assistance, tape-recording selections for students to listen to and follow along with). Some communities have wonderful volunteer programs (e.g., Everyone a Reader—Rolling Reader Volunteer Tutoring Program) which train parent/community volunteers in effective reading strategies and methods, then assigning them at-risk readers in the schools to work with. Such programs have a very high rate of success because of the high level of commitment and the one-to-one support and attention the students receive.

54. Reading Strategies and Interventions for Home and School

◆ **What do good readers do?** Good readers know how to read for a purpose. They draw on personal experience and access prior knowledge. They use whatever background knowledge they have about the subject to make meaning out of what they are reading. They utilize effective metacognitive strategies to think about what they are reading. They are able to visualize when they are reading, and make mental connections. They are constantly predicting and changing their predictions as they read. Effective readers use all cueing systems to figure out unfamiliar words or language, focus on the main content, and interact with the reading material. They check for their own comprehension and use self-correcting strategies.

Improving Fluency and Oral Reading Strategies

The following are some recommended techniques for increasing fluency and practicing oral reading.

◆ *Choral reading:* Everyone in the class or group reads together at the same time. This is an excellent strategy when using a short piece to focus on. You may make a transparency of a poem or passage from the text and read it together in unison. After first modeling the oral reading (e.g., of a humorous poem), students read along with you in different variations (every other verse, line, boys/girls, left side of room/right side, etc.).

◆ *Cloze technique:* You read or reread the material, but leave out key words. The students fill in the missing words aloud.

◆ *Mirror (echo) reading:* You read while students follow along visually (in book or on overhead). You read a sentence or part of a passage, and the student(s) repeat it. After reading a few paragraphs or pages, stop and have students orally reread certain passages.

◆ *Repeated readings:* Given a short, interesting passage, the student reads and re-reads the passage until he or she achieves a certain level of fluency. This technique is helpful for students to have errors recorded, and graph their progress (fewer number of errors) as they become more fluent in reading the passage. It is motivating to students to tape record their improved reading fluency.

◆ *Students reread in a variety of situations:* The process of rereading passages that have already been heard before increases fluency and comprehension and is particularly helpful for students with reading difficulties. Rereading can be done with partners, individually, in small groups, into a tape recorder, in chorus, to an adult (teacher, aide, parent volunteer). Have students locate information in response to your prompts and questioning and orally reread those passages.

◆ *Buddy or partner reading:* Students read orally with partners, taking turns alternating (paragraphs, pages, together in unison). It is often effective for students to share one book that is placed between them. One reader can point to the words while the other is following along. Partners help each other with words and suggesting strategies for figuring out unfamiliar words. They can question, discuss readings, and summarize. You can assign questions that each pair of students will need to be able to answer at the end of the reading assignment to encourage focus.

◆ It is helpful to first listen to a story/passage, before having to read as a group in class. Special educators often assist struggling readers by previewing the material with them, allowing the student(s) the opportunity to first hear it read (by a fluent reader), and practice/discuss before the reading in the classroom.

◆ *Improving silent reading:* Another very important strategy for building reading skills is to incorporate into the day a short period of time (i.e., 15–20 minutes) of uninterrupted time for everyone to be engaged in reading self-choice material at their independent reading level. In schools this has a variety of names including Sustained Silent Reading (SSR), or DEAR (Drop Everything and Read). For those students who cannot read silently, they may be allowed to listen to a book on tape while following along at a listening post.

Building Reading Vocabulary and Word Recognition Skills

Children who struggle to identify words need to be taught different strategies and cueing systems to recognize words in print.

◆ *Graphic clues:* the shape of the word, visual similarities to other words, pictures, maps, or other visual clues near the words in print that will help clarify the meaning of the unknown word

♦ *Semantic clues:* determining if the word makes sense in the context of what is being read, and being able to self-correct (substitute a different word if it doesn't make sense)

♦ *Syntactic clues:* determining if the word sounds right grammatically, and being able to self-correct (substitute a different word that does grammatically fit in the context of what is being read)

♦ *Grapho-phonic clues:* using recognition of the printed letters (graphemes) and their corresponding sounds (phonemes) to figure out what a word is. Phonetic awareness of the sound associations for consonants, vowels, digraphs, etc., is critical in word recognition. So is being able to take isolated sounds, and blend those sounds into words.

♦ Children with reading disabilities are generally deficient in one or more of their cueing processes. They typically struggle with grapho-phonics and need a highly multisensory approach (using all of their senses) that incorporates mnemonic (memory) clues to help them learn and remember the sound/symbol associations.

♦ There are some excellent programs and multisensory strategies that teach in this format, and have a high success rate with children who have learning disabilities affecting their ability to read and spell. Project Read is one such program. The Stevenson Program is another. *(See Checklist 74 on Recommended Resources and Organizations.)*

♦ *Observing the patterns of words:* Awareness of how words can be grouped by rhyming sound families or visual patterns (rock/stock/flock, right/might/flight/bright) is necessary to being a proficient reader and speller.

♦ *Structural clues:* Many students are helped by directly teaching structural analysis (recognition of prefixes, suffixes, base words, and their meanings). Focusing on the visual configuration of the word is a useful strategy for many readers: "Does this word look like any other word you know?" Knowing how to break a word down into its component parts and syllables is important in word recognition.

♦ *Sight-word recognition:* In order to be a fluent reader it is necessary to be able to identify high-frequency words at an automatic level. Most people can recognize and recall words that are commonly found in print. They generally learn to do so through a whole word approach. High-frequency words and those words that cannot be sounded out phonetically are taught this way. Many struggling readers—especially those with visual sequential memory problems—do not have a very large bank of words they know at the automatic level. It is recommended you provide frequent drill, practice, and repetition in motivating game formats, through multisensory strategies, and *color* to help lock these words into the memory bank for instant recognition. *(See Checklist 64 on Strategies for Aiding Memory Skills.)*

◆ There are numerous strategies to build students' word banks—and improve their recognition and understanding of reading vocabulary. Label words in the environment. Have children maintain their own card file of vocabulary words they are learning or have mastered. Use charts, posters, and as many visual displays as possible to enable children to recognize the printed word and its meaning.

Teaching Reading Comprehension

To read for meaning and to gain comprehension, there are a number of strategies that are helpful and effective prior to reading, during reading, and after completing the reading assignment.

◆ *Pre-reading strategies* are necessary to aid comprehension and stay focused on text. Prior to reading, you should relate the stories or reading material to the students' experience and background knowledge through: class discussions, brainstorming, and charting prior knowledge. ("What do we already know about . . . ?") You should set the stage, and establish the purpose for what students are about to read. Then give time to students to preview the visuals in the text. Lead the class through making/listing predictions prior to reading. To generate interest and increase students' background knowledge and frame of reference before reading, every effort should be made to incorporate visuals/audio-visuals (maps, music, filmstrips) related to the topic of reading material.

- It helps to preview key information (the illustrations, captions, headings, chapter questions) in the text before reading through the chapter/text. Previewing can also involve students listening to passages read aloud first before independently studying and rereading.

- Discuss selected vocabulary that may be challenging for students.

◆ There are many strategies that need to be taught, modeled, and encouraged for use *during the reading*. These strategies involve the reader actively; they require thinking about and interacting with the reading material. This is crucial for comprehension and for remaining focused on text.

- Teach students how to paraphrase a paragraph, putting into their own words the main idea and significant details. Some students find that paraphrasing each paragraph and stating into a tape recorder is a very helpful technique.

- Teach textbook structure (significance of bold, italic print, headings, subheadings).

- Teach how to find introductory paragraphs and summary paragraphs.

- Teach students how to rephrase main ideas and headings into their own words.

- Teach how to find the subject, main ideas, and sift out the key facts and important details from the irrelevant and redundant words/text. An outstanding program for teaching this skill is the comprehension component of Project Read.

- Provide students with a pad of self-stick notes. As they are reading they can jot down notes, vocabulary words to clarify, write questions by items they don't understand, and place directly on the text. The self-stick paper can be placed directly next to key points and main ideas for fast/easy reference.

- Teach story-mapping: identifying the setting (time/place), characters, conflicts/problems, action/events, climax, resolution of conflicts.

- There are many other teaching techniques that are very helpful for improving reading comprehension (i.e., story mapping, reciprocal teaching). *Reciprocal teaching is a comprehension-oriented process that involves children in prediction, question generalization, clarification or defining of unfamiliar terms/phrases, and summarizing. Students are taught each of these strategies through direct modeling and guided practice, and then they take over the 'teacher role' in their cooperative groups.

- Encourage students to activate their imaginations while reading and to visualize. Having students illustrate the scenes they visualize is a very helpful technique.

- Most critical during reading is to be questioning and self-questioning throughout the process. "Where does the story take place?" "What is the problem?" "What will the character do next?" "How does the character feel about . . . ?" "What's the main idea?" "Does this make sense?"

- Teacher-directed guided reading may involve setting a purpose, sharing prior knowledge, making predictions, having students read silently a certain amount of time to find the answer to a question the teacher posed, then discussing, using the text to validate responses.

- Use peer tutors, partner reading, and cooperative strategies in reading texts.

- See if a reading marker or strip helps to focus students who lose their place in reading, and have difficulty visually focusing on text.

- Teach clustering and semantic mapping (graphic Charts/Webs) to pull out the main idea and supporting details from the text.

- Enlarge a page of the book and make a transparency of it. Have students come up to the overhead and locate certain information by underlining it.

- Photocopy chapter pages and have child highlight important information.

- Provide study guides to aid in looking for important information in the text.

- Underline or circle important points in text.

- Color-code a master textbook for lower readers. Important vocabulary can be highlighted in one color. For example: vocabulary in one color, definitions in another color, important facts and topic sentences in a third color.

- Tape-record textbooks for individual use or group listening at a listening post. Use a good quality tape and a recorder with counter numbers. For ease in following text that is being read at a listening post, have clear signals on the tape for when to turn the page, or include periodically on the audio recording the chapter and page number of the book. Pages can be marked with the cassette player's counter number at the beginning of each chapter.

- Teach the SQ3R technique. This strategy, for increasing comprehension and retention of textbook material, involves the following steps:

1) *Survey*—briefly viewing the reading assignment, survey-ing the titles, looking at the chapter headings, skimming through the assignment and reading the chapter summary and/or end-of-chapter questions

2) *Question*—turning the headings and subheadings of the text into questions; examples: *Producing Antibodies* can become "How do our bodies produce antibodies?" *Organic motor fuels* can become "What are the different organic motor fuels?"

3) *Reading*—asking questions to self while in reading process (i.e., "What is the author trying to tell me?"); jot down any questions or unknown vocabulary

4) *Recite*—stating in some form in own words what was read. **Note:** Restating or summarizing into a tape recorder is often very effective.

5) *Review*—seeing how much you remember; check for impor-tant information that you may have forgotten.

– *Graphic Organizers to Aid Reading Comprehension:* There are nu-merous graphic displays to accompany reading of literature and textbook material. The following are a few that are useful in increasing comprehension of text:

1) *Framed outlines*—Students are given copies of a teacher-prepared outline that contains missing information. As the student reads or through subsequent discussion, students fill in the missing information. Ideally, this can be mod-eled on the overhead to teach the skill.

2) *Advance organizers*—Prepare study guides to help focus stu-dents on important points, present information in a logical sequence, and help direct attention to essential information.

3) *Venn Diagrams*—Overlapping circles that help students in visualizing the similarities and differences between two characters, places, topics, objects in the book.

4) *Comparison charts*—Similar to a Venn Diagram, it is used for comparing and contrasting (i.e., of 2 or 3 characters).

5) *Cluster maps*—These are used to categorize or identify re-lated information.

6) *Storyboards*—Divide sections on a board or piece of paper and have students draw or write story events in sequence in each box/frame.

7) *Story frames*—This graphic includes essential elements of a story (setting, characters, time, place, problem or conflict, sequence of important events, resolution of conflict).

8) *Timelines*—These are used to help visualize the chronological sequence of events in the text.

9) *Plot charts*—Somebody . . . Wanted . . . But . . . And So

10) *Response logs*—Students record their thoughts, feelings, and questions about what they are reading.

◆ *After reading* it is important to discuss the material—perhaps retell or summarize—and utilize it in some format.

Advice for Parents

◆ Try to read *to* and *with* your child every day. You can do shared reading in a number of ways: "You read this paragraph, I'll read the next." You can read together in unison with your child—with you as the lead reader running your finger under the words. You can try a three-step technique: First, you read a portion of the text ranging from a sentence or two to a paragraph. Read at a normal rate while moving your finger smoothly under the words as your child watches. Then you read the same sentences or paragraph together as you continue to point to the words. Finally, your child reads aloud again the same sentence or passage alone with you pronouncing any of the words your child stumbles on.

◆ Encourage your child to read to a younger child.

◆ When you listen to your child read, don't correct or make him or her stop to sound out every single word. Prompt your child to use different "cueing strategies." For example, pass over words in a sentence that he or she isn't sure of and read to the end of the sentence. Then see if your child can go back and figure out the unfamiliar words. Prompt with questions like, "Does that make sense?" "Did that sound right to you?" "What other word beginning with that sound would make sense here?"

◆ Consider purchasing or borrowing another set of books for your ADHD child to keep at home, so he or she has a copy at home and at school.

◆ It is all right and often helpful for your child to use a bookmark to keep his or her place, or to block the page partially by placing a piece of cardboard or index card over part of the page.

◆ Use books on tape. Check out books on tape from your local library. If your child is receiving special education services due to reading disabilities, he or she is entitled to a service of being provided books on tape through Recordings for the Blind and Dyslexic (phone 800–221-4792 or 609–452-0606). Contact them directly or ask your local chapter of the Learning Disabilities Association (LDA) for information on how you can apply for this service. LDA National Headquarters can be reached at 412–341-1515.

◆ Increase the motivation to read. Readers of all ages will improve their reading if allowed to choose material they are interested in. Struggling readers are easily intimidated by lengthy chapter books with few illustrations. There are wonderful options: picture books that are interesting and appropriate for older children, joke and riddle books, magazines, reference books with color pictures and small reading passages, sheet music with lyrics of favorite songs, and poetry.

55. WHY IS WRITING SUCH A STRUGGLE?

It is very common for children with ADHD to be verbal and knowl-edgeable but unable to communicate what they know on paper. They are generally weak in written language because the process in-volves the integration of numerous skills, many of which are their specific areas of weakness. Writing requires:

◆ **Pre-planning:** Being able to generate, plan, and organize ideas. This stage of the writing process is often the most neglected and the most difficult, especially for those who experience difficulties with written expression. When given a written assignment, students with ADHD often get stuck at this stage. They don't know what to write about, how to organize and begin, or how to focus on a topic that will be motivating to write about.

◆ **Language expression:** Being able to express thoughts and tran-scribe them in complete, descriptive sentences, with proper sen-tence and paragraph structure, as well as logical flow and sequence of ideas from start to closure.

◆ **Spelling:** People with attentional difficulties are often inatten-tive to visual detail, and don't notice and recall the letters and se-quence of words. They are often not visually aware of patterns in words and tend to be careless in their writing and spelling. Those who also have learning disabilities are typically weak in spelling due to auditory-sequential memory deficits (causing great difficulty learning letter/sound associations and hearing/remembering and writing those sounds in the correct order). Others may have deficits in visual-sequential memory, causing them difficulty recalling the way a word looks, and getting it down in the correct order/sequence. They consequently misspell common, high-frequency words such as *said, they, because,* and so forth that can't be sounded out phonetically.

◆ **Editing:** Individuals with ADHD have significant difficulty at this stage of the writing process. They are typically inattentive to this boring detail work of finding and correcting errors. It is very common to find lack of capitalization, punctuation, and complete sentences, along with numerous spelling errors in their written products.

◆ **Physical task of writing and organization:** It is very common for those with ADHD and/or learning disabilities to have signifi-cant difficulty copying from the board or book onto paper. They have trouble writing neatly on or within the given lines, and spacing/organizing their writing on the page. Many reverse or invert letters (b/d, p/q, n/u) and form letters in strange, awkward ways. Fine-motor skills (those skills requiring small muscle movements, such as holding a pencil properly and writing) are often weak. Written work is often messy and immature looking.

◆ **Speed of written output:** Remember that ADHD is a *production disorder* causing inconsistent, variability of work performance. The nature of ADHD means trouble being able to "show what they know." It is very common for those with ADHD to rush through their writing, making for illegible work with many careless errors. It is equally common for others with ADHD to write excruciatingly *SLOW*. Even though they know the answers, and can verbally express their thoughts and ideas with high skill and detail, it is very frustrating because they are unable to put more than a few words or sentences down on paper!

56. Strategies to Help with Pre-writing

The following are some *pre-writing* techniques designed to stimulate the production of ideas, and focus on a topic to write about. These strategies are very helpful for structuring and organizing as well as motivating to write:

♦ **Brainstorming:** These sessions are very short and focused (no more than 3–5 minutes). Given a general theme or topic, students call out whatever comes to mind related to that topic while someone records all responses.

♦ **Quickwrites:** Students are given a few minutes (no more than 3–4) to write down everything they can think of related to a given topic. You are also modeling the same uninterrupted writing along with your students at this time.

♦ **Writing topic folders:** Have students maintain a list or folder of possible writing topics that they can refer to. Include hobbies, places they have visited, jobs they have done, personal interests, interesting/colorful family members, neighbors, friends, pets, favorite restaurant, favorite sport, and so forth.

♦ **Personal collage writing folder:** Have students make a personal collage writing folder by using words and pictures cut out from magazines, newspapers, and travel brochures, and laminating the folder when done. Students should include things they like, places they have visited, hobbies, favorite foods, cars, etc.

♦ **Reference books:** Pass out reference books to groups of students to look through for ideas of writing topics (vehicles, antique cars, deserts, horses, motorcycles, fashion, mammals, oceans, boats, baseball, mysteries of nature, etc.).

♦ **Writing prompts:** Provide a stimulus such as a poem, story, picture, song, or news item to prompt writing. Keep a file of pictures from magazines, old calendars, postcards, etc., as stimuli for writing activities.

♦ **Vocabulary lists:** Have students generate a vocabulary list of words related to a theme or topic. For example, everyone might supply a word related to: nature, climate, archaeology, words that make me shiver, words that make me hungry, soft words, angry words, and so forth.

◆ **Self-talk:** Teach students to self-talk through the planning stage of their writing: "Who am I writing for? Why am I writing this? What do I know? What does my reader need to know?"

◆ **Telling personal stories:** In cooperative groups have students orally respond to prompts by telling personal stories. ("Tell about a time you or someone you knew got lost.") After the oral telling and sharing of stories in small, cooperative groups, students write a rough draft or outline of the story they told.

◆ Encourage the use of a tape recorder to first verbalize what the child wants to say. Then it is easier to go back and transcribe onto paper.

◆ Parents can help their child focus on a writing topic by talking with their child about experiences shared. Look through family picture albums together and ask leading questions that may expand their thoughts and language.

◆ **Graphic organizers:** One of the most effective ways to help students generate, formulate, and organize their thoughts is through training and practice using graphic organizers. For students with written language difficulties, use of a graphic organizer of some sort is a critical intervention in helping them plan before they begin to actually write.

- *Clustering:* Write the main idea in a box or rectangle in the center of the page; surround the main idea box with bubbles containing all of the supporting ideas.

- *Writing frames:* Students fill in blanks from a framed outline.

- *Mind mapping:* A circle is drawn in the center of a page. The topic is written inside the center circle; on lines stemming from the circle are related ideas. (This technique is also called webbing, and the graphic is called a web.)

- *Diagrams:* Venn Diagrams, for example, are graphics of overlapping circles used to show comparison between two or three items, topics, characters, or books.

- *Compare/Contrast charts:* This is another way of depicting similarities and differences.

- *Story maps:* These are used in planning the critical elements to be included when writing a story (setting, characters, problem, action, resolution).

Provide Models

◆ Students who have difficulty with writing need many models of good writing presented orally and visually.

◆ Read examples of written works that demonstrate the skill you are emphasizing (e.g., expanded, descriptive sentences; well-developed paragraphs; use of metaphors/similes).

◆ Teach and display steps of the writing process (pre-writing, composing, responding, revising, editing, publishing).

◆ Post the alphabet (print and cursive) for reference.

◆ Provide many examples and display samples of pre-writing graphic organizers.

◆ Stop students after a few minutes of writing and ask for student volunteers to share what they have written so far.

◆ Make lists and charts of certain vocabulary or parts of speech, and display for reference (e.g., lists of adjectives, adverbs, transition words, etc.).

◆ Provide models of papers containing introduction, body, conclusion.

◆ Provide models and displays of capitalization/punctuation rules and samples.

◆ Teach and post charts of abbreviations and contractions.

◆ Model how to write. Using large chart paper have students watch as you go through the process of picking your topic, thinking out loud, and demonstrating how you structure and write: a friendly letter, a descriptive paragraph, a persuasive paper, a 'how to' procedural paper (or whatever writing format you are teaching at the time).

◆ See *How to Reach & Teach All Students in the Inclusive Classroom* by Sandra Rief and Julie Heimburge (The Center for Applied Research in Education, 1996) for more detailed, extensive strategies.

57. Multisensory Spelling Activities and Choices

Student-Directed

◆ Dip clean paintbrush in water and write words on tabletop or chalkboard.

◆ Pair movement with practicing spelling words (clap to each letter, bounce ball, yo-yo). Get creative!

◆ Tap out the sounds or syllables in words.

◆ Sing spelling words to common tunes/melodies.

◆ Write word in air while sounding it out.

◆ Make a word search on graph paper using all of the words in your spelling list. Include an answer sheet.

◆ In your neatest handwriting, write out each of your words five times.

◆ Make a set of flash cards. Study each of your words with a partner (or your parent). Leave out the words that you missed. Restudy them.

◆ At home say your spelling words into a tape recorder. Spell them correctly into the recorder. Listen to yourself. Bring the tape to school.

◆ Write the words by syllables in different colored markers.

◆ Write words in a flat tray or box of either sand or salt using one or two fingers.

◆ Write words in glue or liquid starch on pieces of cardboard. Then sprinkle any powdery material, glitter, colored sand, yarn, beans, dry macaroni, sequins, etc., to create textured, three-dimensional spelling words. (Substances such as sand, salt, and glitter are good to use for students who benefit from tracing the words with their fingers. **Note:** The act of tracing with your fingers on a texture helps make a sensory imprint on the brain that increases memory and retention.)

◆ Pair with another student and write words on each other's back with your fingers.

◆ While sitting on the carpet, practice writing the words directly on the carpet with two fingers using large muscle movements.

◆ Practice writing words on individual chalkboards (or dry-erase boards) with colored chalk (or colored dry-erase pens).

◆ Fingerpaint words using shaving cream on tabletops; or pudding, whipped cream, or frosting on paper plates.

◆ Make a rebus using some of your words. Use syllables and pictures to get your idea across clearly.

◆ Make a word picture with your spelling words. Lightly draw with pencil a basic shape. In thin black marker, write your words in small lettering around your basic outlined shape. Now erase your pencil marks and your words will form the shape!

◆ Give each letter of the alphabet a value; (such as a = 1, b = 2, c = 3, d = 4, e = 5, etc.). Then find the value of your words. Example: The value of the word *spelling* is $19 + 16 + 5 + 12 + 12 + 9 + 14 + 7 =$ _____ .

◆ Find letters in magazines or newspapers. Glue down each letter on a paper to form your spelling words with a variety of printed letters.

◆ On your computer, write each of your words in different fonts and sizes. If you have a color printer, change the color of the words.

◆ Make up word skeletons for your words. Give them to a partner, who must figure out the words. Example: _ _ s _ r _ _ m c _ t for the word **instrument.** You may need to give a clue if your partner is stumped. Check that your partner has spelled the words correctly.

◆ Place the words on your list in alphabetical order.

◆ Write the words using some kind of alphabet manipulative such as magnetic letters, alphabet cereal, letter tiles.

◆ Write out each of your words. Circle the silent letters and underline the vowels.

◆ Study with a partner. Write your words on a dry-erase board. Have your partner write down how many words you got correct..

◆ Write your words using the "rainbow technique" of tracing over each of the words at least three different times in different colored pencils, crayons, chalk, or markers.

◆ Find as many little words within words as possible (words in sequence only). Examples: **incredulous** (in, red, us); **lieutenant:** (lie, tenant, ten, ant).

Teacher-Directed

◆ Introduce words on the overhead projector. As a class, ask students to look at the configuration, little words within the word, and any mnemonic clues that would be helpful in remembering to spell the word. Write the word in syllables in different colored pens. Discuss meaning and use in context.

◆ When modeling and guiding students in sounding out a word in print, cover up part of the word while demonstrating how to sound out one syllable at a time. Point to the individual sounds as you model decoding the word. Then slide your hand or finger rapidly under the letters as you blend the sounds to quickly say the whole word.

◆ Have readily available several resources for student access such as: dictionaries, electronic spell-checkers (Franklin Speller®), lists of commonly used words, etc.

◆ Use commercial games that teach and reinforce spelling (e.g., Scrabble™, Boggle™, Hangman). **Note:** When playing games in which correct spelling is not a requirement, extra bonus points can be awarded for words that *are* spelled correctly to add the incentive for spelling accuracy.

◆ Have students develop their own personal lists, word banks, word cards attached to a ring, notebooks, card files, etc., for spelling words they wish to keep and practice. This is particularly useful when these personal spelling words are selected from misspelled words from the student's own written products.

◆ Teach students to look for patterns in words. Teach word families.

◆ Provide additional systematic phonetic training to students who are deficient in this skill and are poor spellers. Many uppergrade students have not had the benefit of sufficient, teacher-directed phonics instruction. Therefore, a number of our children are totally unaware of some letter/sound associations in our language and how to sound out words effectively to spell. They may be able to decode and read adequately, identifying words from sight and context; but if they can't recall what a word looks like in print, often they have no efficient strategies for spelling. **Note:** Programs such as *Project Read—Phonology* (Greene & Enfield, Language Circle, Bloomington, MN [612–884-4880]), *Developing Independent Readers* (Cynthia Conway Waring, Center for Applied Research in Education, 1995), *Spelling Smart: A Ready-to-Use Activities Program for Students with Spelling Difficulties* (Cynthia Stowe, Center for Applied Research in Education, 1996), *Simply Phonics* (Sandra Rief, EBSCO Curriculum Materials, [800–633-8623]) are recommended.

◆ In addition to teaching words with different phonetic spelling patterns, teach words from high-frequency word lists. Make it a grade-level priority to teach and reinforce spelling a certain number of words from a list of high-frequency vocabulary words.

◆ Teach students to write rough drafts using every other line. When they are writing, they can circle, put a question mark, or write "sp" above any words they think are probably spelled wrong. This helps them to self-monitor. Then they can apply strategies for checking the spelling of those words.

◆ Color-code tricky letters (silent letters) in hard-to-spell words.

◆ For a more extensive list of additional strategies and spelling techniques, see *How to Reach & Teach All Students in the Inclusive Classroom* by Sandra Rief & Julie Heimburge (The Center for Applied Research in Education, 1996).

58. HELP WITH EDITING STRATEGIES AND OTHER TIPS

◆ Teach students the skills of proofreading and editing. One method is by making transparencies of unedited work of anonymous students or teacher samples of writing that is lacking in capitalization, punctuation, etc.; and editing as a group.

◆ Teach students to respond to their own writing. "My best sentence is _____." "A simile or metaphor I used was _____."

◆ Teach students to self-talk through the editing/revising stage of their writing: "Does everything make sense? Did I include all of my ideas? Do I need to insert, delete, or move ideas?"

◆ Use peer editing. Have students work with a partner to read their work to each other. The partner listens and reads along as the author reads. The peer-editing partner tells what he or she liked best. Then the editor questions the author about anything that doesn't make sense, suggests where more information is needed for clarification, and helps edit when he or she hears/sees run-on or incomplete sentences.

◆ Conduct teacher-student writing conferences. At that time the teacher provides feedback, the student reflects on his or her own work, and both share what they like about the piece of writing. The student self-evaluates improvement and skills to target for continued improvement. "My writing has improved in: _____ (sentence structure, paragraphing, fluency, creativity, organization, capitalization, punctuation, spelling). I plan to work on _____."

◆ Provide students more time to write in class and more direct, supportive feedback.

◆ Parents should provide positive, supportive feedback without being too critical of their child's writing—particularly creative writing.

◆ Teach students parts of speech and have them practice locating nouns, verbs, adverbs, etc., in their text. For example: "List 10 verbs or action words you find in the chapter." "Find 5 adjectives."

◆ Have students do a search for parts of speech and record in notebooks, or keep class charts of examples.

◆ Provide direct instruction and guided practice in the skills of mechanics (punctuation and capitalization).

◆ Display models and standards for acceptable written work.

◆ Display models of proper headings, spacing, and organization of written work.

◆ Provide alphabet strips/charts for individual students.

◆ Teach editing symbols and provide a reference chart (e.g., insert, delete, capitalize, new paragraph).

◆ Teach sentence expansion and combining of sentences. Given a short 2- to 3-word sentence, practice expanding with detail and description to the simple sentence frame by adding: "where?" "how?" "when?" "why?"

◆ Parents should encourage their child to self-edit by circling words he or she thinks were possibly misspelled, and then checking the spelling of those words together later.

◆ Purchase an electronic spell-check device (such as Franklin Speller®) for easier editing. These are useful tools for school as well as home use.

◆ Encourage writing on the computer, which makes editing and revising so much easier. Teach how to use the tools and options (thesaurus, spell-check, cut and paste) on a word-processing program.

59. How to Help with Handwriting, Written Organization, and Legibility

◆ Use real-life situations (job applications, filling out checks) to stress the need for legible writing.

◆ Stress how studies have proven that teachers tend to give students the benefit of the doubt and grade higher if their papers look good as opposed to being sloppy or hard to read; how neatness and legibility reflect attitude and caring about your work, and make a very important impression.

◆ Avoid the pressures of speed.

◆ Set realistic, mutually agreed-upon expectations for neatness.

◆ If student writes too heavy or too light, change the pencil type, use pencil grips, try a mechanical pencil.

◆ Often small-lined paper is better than large-lined paper for students who struggle with fine motor control.

◆ Teach placing of index finger between words (finger spacing) to help students who run their words together without spacing.

◆ Use special paper with vertical lines to help space letters and words appropriately.

◆ Provide a strip of alphabet letters (manuscript or cursive) for a reference on their desk or to place in the Homework Supply Kit.

◆ If the student's paper is frequently sliding around, try a clipboard.

◆ Make sure there is always a sufficient supply of sharpened pencils and erasers on or in the desk.

◆ Use writing warm-ups: physically stretching, wiggling fingers. Try doing the warm-ups to a song, rhyme, chant, or rap.

◆ Make an "ooze bag" by placing some hair gel in a zip-lock baggie. With permanent marker write each letter for practice on the outside of the bag. The student traces the letter, which is an interesting texture with the gel inside of the bag (especially when gel or ooze bag is refrigerated).

◆ Using the gel bag, color-code the strokes of a letter on the outside of the bag. The first phase of the stroke can be one color (purple), the second phase can be another color (yellow). Arrows can be drawn indicating the directions of the letter formation, as well.

◆ Practice correct letter formation by tracing sandpaper letters, or letters written on other textures.

◆ Many upper-grade students haven't mastered how to form cursive letters, so they struggle with formation or speed. Provide guided practice for students in need by modeling on the overhead projector in color while talking through the steps.

◆ Use a parent volunteer or aide to work one-to-one with upper-grade students who need help mastering cursive formation. Use tactile-kinesthetic techniques of tracing in sand or salt trays, on the carpet, or other textures with two fingers. Sometimes the adult needs to gently place his or her hand over the student's writing hand to guide in the formation. Parents should try this same technique at home.

◆ Parents can provide a lot of practice at home, particularly when their child is first learning how to print or write in cursive. Parents should ask you which letters have been taught in class and request a model of how you teach those letters. Parents observe how their son or daughter is forming letters and gently correct before learned the wrong way.

◆ Provide prompts for correct letter formation/directionality by placing dots indicating where to begin and arrows indicating in which direction to write the strokes of the letter(s).

◆ Allow for frequent practice and corrective feedback using short trace-and-copy activities.

◆ For upper-grade students who struggle significantly with cursive, permit them to print.

◆ Encourage appropriate sitting, posture, and anchoring of paper when writing.

◆ Alternate the size of the paper or lines.

◆ For motivation, add *variety*—paper size, paper shape, texture of paper, colored paper, fancy stationery, different writing instruments.

◆ Use computer paper for rough-draft copies. Students write either on the green lines or white lines only, so editing can be easily done in the space above.

◆ For variety, have students write on individual chalkboards with chalk, or on dry-erase boards with colored pens.

◆ Allow students to sometimes show their work by providing them with a blank transparency and requiring them to do their neatest writing in color to be shared with the class on the overhead.

◆ Teach standards of acceptable work in your classroom, whatever those standards may be (e.g., writing on one side of paper only, rough-draft papers written on every other line, math papers with two- to three-line spaces between problems, heading on upper right section of paper).

◆ Use a computer and encourage final drafts to be typed for upper grade students, providing assistance as needed.

◆ Parents can encourage and motivate their child to write by buying a diary or journal (especially for use during summer vacation to write about their summer activities), and buying special stationery and stamps to write to friends and relatives.

◆ Parents can display the work the child is proud of or mount and save it in albums or portfolios.

60. STRATEGIES FOR BYPASSING WRITING DIFFICULTIES

◆ Substitute non-written projects for written assignments such as oral reports.

◆ Give students options and choices that don't require writing; rather, draw on individual strengths. Examples are hands-on project-oriented assignments of: investigating, building, drawing, constructing, creating, making, doing, simulating, experimenting, researching, telling, singing, dancing, and so on.

◆ Provide worksheets with extra space.

◆ Enlarge the space for doing written work (math papers, tests, etc.).

◆ Stress accuracy, not volume.

◆ Follow written exams with oral exams and average the grades for those students. *(See Checklist 50 on Assessment/Testing: Modifications and Adaptations for other testing accommodations.)*

◆ Allow oral responses for assignments/tests when appropriate.

◆ Permit student to dictate his or her responses and have someone else transcribe for the student.

◆ Permit student to print if cursive is a struggle.

◆ Do not assign a large quantity of written work.

◆ Provide in-class time to get started on assignments.

◆ Assign reasonable amounts of homework. If parents and student report that an inordinate amount of time is spent on homework most evenings, be willing to make adjustments.

◆ Allow students to use a tape recorder to record thoughts, rough drafts, responses to questions, etc.

◆ Provide access to a computer and motivating writing programs with a variety of fonts and graphics. Examples are: *Student Writing Center* (published by the Learning Company) and *Write Out Loud* (a word processor program with auditory feedback to increase self-monitoring, published by the Don Johnston Company). Both are available through Educational Resources (800-624-2926).

◆ Provide note-taking assistance. Assign a buddy to take notes, share, and compare.

◆ Provide NCR paper or carbon paper for the note-taker to use. Students (including those with ADHD) should still be taking their own notes in the classroom, but be allowed to *supplement* their own notes with the more detailed and organized copies from a note-taker.

◆ Make photocopies of teacher notes or of designated students who take neat, organized notes to give to those students who can't copy from the board easily.

◆ Teach proper keyboarding/typing skills and provide practice to increase skills.

◆ Teach word processing skills including the use of editing options (e.g., cut and paste) and various format options.

◆ Provide assistance for typing/printing final drafts of papers.

◆ Encourage parents to invest in a word processor or a computer with printer for the home.

◆ Accept modified homework with reduced amounts of writing.

◆ Help students to get started writing by sitting with them and talking or prompting through the first few sentences.

◆ Have the student dictate while an adult writes the first few sentences to get the student started.

◆ *See other writing checklists in this book for additional strategies.*

61. MATH DIFFICULTIES AND INTERVENTIONS

Many children with ADHD and/or learning disabilities are quite strong in mathematical reasoning and math aptitude, particularly in areas such as geometry. This is because many individuals with ADHD and/or LD are highly skilled in spatial learning. However, it is very common for them to do poorly in skills requiring *sequential learning* (i.e., algebra/step-by-step equations). Math computation is often a struggle because of difficulties many of these students have with *copying and organization* of math problems. They often have significant *difficulty aligning numbers, writing within the minimal amount of given space on the page, remembering the directionality of which number gets carried up when regrouping,* and so forth. They are frequently inattentive to processing signs like add, subtract, multiplication, and divide; and don't notice when the signs change.

Some have significant *weaknesses in their memory skills* (particularly for abstract symbols such as number combinations). No matter how hard they try, they struggle in their memory and retention of basic math facts. Fortunately, there are a number of ways that teachers and parents can help. These students should be provided with supports and accommodations to help them bypass these disabilities so that they can be successful with their classroom math.

◆ Provide many kinds of manipulatives, as well as number lines, to help visualize and work out problems.

◆ Allow and encourage use of calculators. Have students use calculators to check their work.

◆ Give students a choice of computing with a calculator, paper/pencil, or mentally.

◆ Allow extra time on math tests so students aren't rushed to make careless errors.

◆ Avoid the anxiety of timed tests and drills (especially those posted for all students in the class to see); and/or extend the amount of time permitted for certain students as "passing."

◆ Encourage students to write and solve their computation problems on graph paper rather than notebook paper (to help with number alignment). Experiment with graph paper of varying square/grid sizes.

◆ Allow students to write and solve their problems on notebook paper held sideways (with lines running vertically rather than horizontally). This makes it much easier for students who have difficulty aligning numbers, and it reduces careless errors.

◆ Reduce the number of problems assigned (half-page, evens only, odds only).

◆ Provide immediate feedback whenever possible. Go over homework assignments the next day, allowing students to comfortably ask questions and work any problems that they didn't understand together as a class.

◆ Encourage students to come to you for help when needed (before, during, or after class). Don't allow students to remain confused without providing any necessary reteaching and/or tutorial assistance.

◆ Reduce the amount of copying required by photocopying the page or writing out the problems on paper for certain students.

◆ Remove individual pages from consumable workbooks. Give one page at a time instead of the whole cumbersome workbook.

◆ Teach TOUCH MATH™ (by Innovative Learning Concepts, Colorado Springs, CO [800-888-9191]). This is an excellent supplementary technique and highly recommended for children with ADHD and/or learning disabilities. Through the use of touch points strategically placed on numerals 1–9, students learn to rapidly visualize and accurately compute without having to pull up their fingers. This is a very useful bypass strategy and technique for students who struggle with learning basic facts.

◆ Color-dot the ones (units) column to remind students the direction of where to begin computation.

◆ Color-highlight processing signs for students who are inattentive to change in operational signs on a page. For example, color addition signs yellow, subtraction signs pink, and so forth.

◆ Provide a large work space on tests. If necessary, rewrite test items on other paper with lots of room for computation.

◆ Provide models of sample problems.

◆ Grade by number of correct problems over the number assigned (which could be different for students receiving modified homework/classwork).

◆ Teach steps needed for solving math problems. List steps clearly.

◆ Teach strategies for solving word problems (e.g., reading a few times, finding clue words, drawing pictures).

◆ Teach key words that indicate the process. For example, the words *product, times, doubled, tripled* all indicate multiplication. The words *average, quotient, equal parts, sharing, divisible by* all indicate division.

◆ Teach and model a variety of problem-solving strategies (examples: looking for a pattern, constructing a table, making an organized list, acting it out, using objects, drawing a picture, working backwards, making a model, eliminating possibilities, guessing and checking).

◆ Let students use their own methods for solving problems (e.g., mental, pictorial, fingers, manipulatives, paper/pencil). Always build in time during the lesson for students to share how they solved the problem, and emphasize that there are a variety of ways, not just one method.

◆ Provide many opportunities for students to make up their own word/thought problems to share with the class, and do as a group whenever possible within the context of the classroom activities. For example, when planning a class party or field trip, the students can work in teams deciding how many cars/drivers are needed, how many bottles of soda need to be bought, how many dozens of cookies are to be baked, and so forth.

◆ Give as many opportunities as possible at home and school for using math in context and real-life situations. Have children frequently utilize estimation skills and determine reasonable, ballpark answers.

◆ Use math portfolios/assessment. Have students keep a journal of their thinking, reasoning, questions, and understanding of math concepts. Have students write their understanding about mathematical concepts before and after the unit is taught.

◆ Encourage keeping a card file of specific math skills, concepts, rules, and algorithms taught, along with specific examples of each on the card for reference.

◆ Provide a chart of multiplication facts/tables for student reference.

◆ Use computer games for drill and practice.

◆ Pair students to practice and quiz each other on skills taught.

◆ Motivate the practicing of skills through the use of board games, card games, and other class games. Try using as many games as possible that don't have a heavy emphasis on speed of recall, or the type of competition that will discourage struggling students from even trying.

◆ When testing long division or multiplication problems that involve using several digits and regrouping, give problems with numbers for which most all students know the math facts. Example: **6274 × 52 =** _____ . Most students know the times tables 5s and 2s. This way they are tested on their understanding of the process, and aren't penalized because they have poor memory skills.

◆ For students who haven't mastered multiplication facts, try using mnemonic devices to help. There are a variety of rhymes, raps, and songs to help students memorize the multiplication tables.

◆ Since there is not enough time during a school day for the needed daily practice of math drill and rote memorization, parents should try to spend at least 5 minutes a day practicing at home in a variety of formats. They should do so in a fun, relaxed manner—without pressure or tension.

◆ Keep tools such as number lines and multiplication tables/charts handy at homework time.

◆ Many children with ADHD and/or learning disabilities are not proficient with functional math skills (measurement, time concepts, counting money/change). Parents should give as much practice as possible at home, as these are critical skills that teachers often don't have enough time to teach until mastery. Parents should include their child and let him or her help parents with cooking/baking, constructing, sewing, gardening, home improvements, etc., that involve measurement and other functional math skills.

◆ Use mnemonics such as DEAD MONSTERS SMELL BADLY or DEAR MISS SALLY BROWN for learning the steps of long division (divide, multiply, subtract, bring down).

◆ First give students a blank multiplication chart and have them fill in the ones they know. Look for patterns and shortcuts. First the row of zeros, ones, and tens are easily identified and eliminated from the list of multiplication facts that must be memorized. When students are able to visualize the commutative property of multiplication (e.g., $3 \times 7 = 7 \times 3$), it helps reduce the stress and feeling that there are so many facts to learn that it is overwhelming.

◆ Teach the different "finger tricks" available for learning $\times 6$, $\times 7$, $\times 8$, and $\times 9$ tables.

◆ Have students practice one sequence of multiples at a time ($\times 3$'s) in a variety of formats until mastery. Then continue to review with high frequency as they move on to the next.

◆ Some mnemonic programs are available that use picture associations and clever stories to help master multiplication facts, as well. One such program is *Time Tables the Fun Way: A Picture Method of Learning the Multiplication Facts* (Key Publishers, Inc., Sandy, UT [800–585-6059]).

◆ Another wonderful program for teaching math through creative associations and mnemonics is *Semple Math* (Stevenson Learning Skills, Inc., 800-343-1211). The math section of the book *How to Reach & Teach All Students in the Inclusive Classroom,* by Sandra Rief and Julie Heimburge, contains a comprehensive list of "Survival Math" activities that involve students in the discovery and use of mathematics in the "real world." *(See Checklist 74 on Recommended Resources and Organizations for additional information.)*

☑ Other Important Checklists for Parents and Teachers

This final section addresses some very important information for parents and educators. The checklist on the necessity of a team approach focuses on how any intervention for children with ADD/ADHD requires the collaboration and partnership of the home and school (as well as professionals in the community). The Student Study Team process is what is being used in many schools for identifying needs of students experiencing difficulties (academic, behavioral, social/emotional), and developing a plan of action to address those needs.

For those students requiring evaluation and a school intervention plan for their success, a child may be eligible for extra school services and support through an IEP or through 504. It is important that parents and teachers understand what is an IEP (Individualized Education Plan) as well as what is 504 (Section 504 of the Rehabilitation Act).

It is very common for individuals with attention deficit disorders to have difficulty remembering and retaining information. Two of the checklists address strategies for building and strengthening memory skills, and the accommodations that parents and teachers can use to help circumvent memory weaknesses.

It is also common for children and adolescents with ADHD to be immature and lacking social skills competency, and to have the tendency to be over-reactive, easily stressed, and provoked to anger. Some of the checklists in this section address social skills issues and strategies, and how to use relaxation, guided imagery, and visualization techniques to better cope and gain self-control. When children experience frustration, rejection, and a high degree of negative feedback, it affects their self-esteem. Strategies for building self-esteem are the topic of one of the checklists in this section.

There are special concerns regarding the very young child with ADHD and teenagers with ADHD. This section includes a checklist on preschool/kindergarten issues and strategies, as well as adolescent issues and strategies. The recommendations and strategies are for parents and teachers of children/teens of these age brackets.

For teachers and parents to really know what motivates and interests their children, or what their learning preferences are, it is very helpful to ASK them. This information is very valuable for teachers trying to utilize their students' strengths and interests—by taking the time to question/interview them, it helps build a more positive relationship. The Student Learning Style/Interest Interview contains a number of interview questions that a teacher may use to gain insight into his or her students.

The final checklist contains a number of resources for parents and teachers. There are books, materials, and programs for more information in organization/study skills, behavior management/discipline, self-esteem, math, reading, writing, spelling, vocabulary, and other topics of interest to educators. This checklist also includes several recommended books, videotapes, audiotapes, and other resources on ADD/ADHD as well as national organizations of support and information about attention deficit disorders and other special needs.

62. THE NECESSITY OF A TEAM APPROACH

The success of children/teens with ADHD is dependent upon a *team effort* in a number of situations.

The Diagnostic Process

◆ The school-based gathering of information/data from classroom teachers, school nurse, other school personnel directly working with the student or observing the child's functioning in various school settings

◆ The multidisciplinary assessment (IEP) team that may conduct a more formal evaluation of the student (i.e., special education teacher/resource specialist, school psychologist, speech/language therapist, school nurse)

◆ An evaluation team outside of school that often involves a medical doctor working collaboratively with other professionals (i.e., child psychologist) in the diagnostic process

◆ Through interview and filling of questionnaire forms, a great deal of parent input is required to make the diagnosis: supplying the child's medical (prenatal through current) history, school history, the family history, describing the child's behaviors (and onset of behaviors), and so forth

◆ *See Checklist 11 on Making the Diagnosis: What Is a Comprehensive Evaluation for ADHD? for more information.*

The Treatment Plan

◆ The most effective approach in treating ADHD is also multimodal, involving a number of interventions from a variety of different professionals and service providers. *(See Checklist 13 on A Comprehensive Treatment Program for ADHD.)*

◆ Treatments outside of school may include individual counseling for the ADHD child/teen, counseling for his or her parents, or family counseling. Often it involves a combination, with counseling of various types as needed at different times in the child's life.

◆ School interventions are generally provided through a variety of school personnel and other resources that may include: classroom teachers, school counselors, the school nurse, special education teachers, administrators, tutorial service providers, instructional aides, guidance aides, peer tutors, cross-age tutors, and parent or community volunteers.

◆ Medical intervention can be provided by different medical doctors (i.e., pediatricians, family practitioners, child psychiatrists, neurologists).

◆ Involving the child/teen in activities that build upon his or her interests and strengths, develop other skill areas, and provide an emotional and/or physical outlet are very important. This may require the involvement of coaches, trainers, instructors, youth group leaders, scout leaders, mentors, and others working with the child/teen in extracurricular activities.

◆ Sometimes the parents find other treatments to address specific needs of their child (i.e., social skills classes, private academic tutoring).

◆ The involvement of the school's Student Study Team for ongoing monitoring and updating of the intervention plan is very important.

◆ Parent support groups, parenting classes, and other interventions geared specifically to aiding parents of children/teens with ADHD also involves a variety of people—with different perspectives and areas of expertise sharing with parents.

◆ It is critical in the diagnostic process as well as *any* treatment and intervention provided that there be close communication among all parties: the home, school, physician, and other service providers in the community.

◆ Most students with ADHD require close monitoring between the home and school to be successful. Teachers need to keep parents well-informed about work assignments, upcoming tests and projects, how the student is performing and keeping up with daily work, as well as behavior and other issues. Parents need to communicate with teachers how the child/teen is functioning at home, the stress level, and other issues. They need to stay on top of monitoring that homework is being done, and following through with any home/school plans (i.e., to aid and reinforce behavior, work production and organization skills).

◆ Inclusive schools that have a "collaborative" model for servicing special education students (with special educators working closely with classroom teachers) are often quite successful in meeting the needs of students with ADHD. Even if the student with ADHD is not a special education student, the collaboration between general and special education can help students who are having difficulty either directly or indirectly.

◆ Any child/teen taking medication requires close monitoring, especially at the trial stages where the proper medication and dosage are being determined by the physician. It is imperative that teachers observe students on medication and report directly to the parent, physician, or school nurse; and that they complete in a timely manner any rating or observation forms that are given to them by the school nurse or doctor to fill out. The school nurse often is the liaison among the parents, classroom teachers, and physician—keeping in close communication with all parties.

◆ Teachers who team-teach different subject areas, plan and team as a grade level, or team for special projects and/or disciplinary purposes often report much greater job satisfaction. In addition, the students benefit from the opportunity to have more than one teacher, especially when teachers are able to enthusiastically share their areas of interest, strength, and expertise with students.

◆ Finally, the child/teen must be included in the team effort. Older students must learn what ADHD is and is not, and why teachers, parents, and other service providers are using the various interventions. If they are taking medication, they need to understand what it does and does not do. The older child/adolescent needs to take an active role in his or her treatment. Self-monitoring skills need to be taught, and students have to learn how to advocate for themselves in an effective manner. Adolescents, in particular, need to assume more ownership in the decision making regarding their treatment and intervention.

63. ACCOMMODATIONS FOR MEMORY DIFFICULTIES

It is very characteristic of children with ADHD to do poorly in school because **they forget** to do their assignments, and/or **forget** to turn in those assignments to the teacher—even when they have done them! Because their attention was not engaged throughout the instruction, children with ADHD **don't remember** a lot of what may have been presented by the teacher. Retention of information and recall of skills learned is erratic and inconsistent. In addition to building memory strategies, these children typically need accommodations for their memory weaknesses and should be allowed to use tools to bypass those weaknesses.

These children need an adult to monitor on a high-frequency basis that long-term assignments (projects, book reports, etc.) are being worked on systematically. This is one of the biggest academic difficulties for those with ADHD.

◆ Use a big white board (dry-erase board) and colored markers for the home to write down all projects and progress on the stages of the project.

◆ Use a monthly calendar at home and school to enter all activities and projects due.

◆ Use things-to-do lists and checklists on a daily basis at home and school.

◆ Require that students write down all assignments (preferably on an assignment calendar that is kept in the same place consistently).

◆ Teach, model, and expect that all assignments are recorded, and monitor that students have done so. This often requires monitoring by way of teacher initialing assignment calendar, or student partners check each other and initial each other's assignment calendar.

◆ Provide simple, written instructions and reminders of what they need to do.

◆ Greatly increase positive feedback and reinforcement (rewards) for remembering.

◆ Have the child paraphrase instructions or information to be remembered—with you checking for their understanding and recall.

◆ Remember to use COLOR and PICTURES to help them remember.

◆ After directions are given, have student tell someone (a partner, person next to them, teacher) what they are to do.

◆ Increase the amount of practice and review in a variety of formats.

◆ **Allow use of tools and aids** such as multiplication charts and tables, and spell-check devices (such as Franklin Speller®).

◆ Encourage use of electronic organizers.

◆ Avoid timed tests. Give extra time for recalling and responding.

64. STRATEGIES FOR AIDING MEMORY SKILLS

Difficulties with memory and retention of information is very common for individuals with ADHD. It is hard for them to remember when their attention is erratic. In addition, there are many people with ADHD who also have coexisting learning disabilities in the area of auditory and/or visual short-term sequential memory. This makes it very difficult to memorize, especially non-meaningful symbols (i.e., sequence of letters in a word, numerals, and basic math facts).

♦ To build memory we have to help create meaningful links and associations between bits of information. Teach a variety of **mnemonic (memory) devices and strategies** like the following:

– *How to make associations* (visually, conceptually, or auditorily to help memorize). Look for ways the items go together (i.e., sound alike, look alike) to help remember.

– *How to link* a series of events, terms, or facts together through a silly story. The key is creating a nonsense story using vivid mental images and linking one to the next to the next to recall the series of key words or items to memorize.

– *How to pair* unfamiliar, new terminology with similar sounding, familiar words.

– *How to draw and visualize ridiculous pictures* that create a vivid image. Any way to activate the IMAGINATION aids memory greatly.

♦ Make all associations, silly stories, linking, and pairing techniques with as much VIVID IMAGERY, ABSURDITY, COLOR, EXAGGERATION, EMOTION, and ACTION as possible.

♦ Teach and practice visualizing with huge size, lots of color, and motion.

♦ Use acronyms (D.E.A.R. = Drop everything and read); DEAD MONSTERS SMELL BADLY or DAD, MOM, SISTER, BROTHER to recall the steps for long division: Divide, Multiply, Subtract, Bring Down).

♦ Use melody and rhythm to help memorize a series or sequence. There are raps, rhymes, and songs that help in learning multiplication tables and other information (such as days of week, months of year, presidents of U.S.)

◆ Teach and practice attaching information to be memorized to a familiar melody.

◆ Teach and practice how to categorize and chunk information into small bits to memorize.

◆ Use **RCRC:** Memorize chunks of information by **reading, covering** the information and saying verbally **(reciting),** and **checking** self.

◆ Activate prior knowledge and experience to make connections—critical for memory and retention.

◆ Motivation aids memory. Discuss the benefits of memorizing the information (e.g., knowing math facts makes learning all mathematical concepts much easier).

◆ Use frequent review and practice.

◆ Have students repeat instructions given by teacher back to the teacher before beginning the task.

◆ After instruction have students *list all they remember in whatever order as fast as they can.* **Note:** This act of listing or writing what they just learned greatly increases recall and retention.

65. BUILDING SELF-ESTEEM

In spite of the many challenges that individuals with ADHD face, they are so often blessed with at least average intelligence, many talents, and a great deal of potential. We need to help them to develop their skills and areas of interest, which will be their source of self-esteem and motivation in life.

We need to provide every opportunity at home and school for our children to develop their areas of strength and to showcase those strengths—especially to their peers. Parents and teachers need to do whatever they can to help nurture the talents of our children/students—whatever they may be (musical, artistic, dramatic, verbal, athletic, mechanical, technical/scientific, mathematical).

How Teachers Can Help Promote Self-Esteem in Students

◆ Provide an atmosphere of acceptance when ideas are being generated.

◆ Write students personal, positive notes to place on their desks, attach to their work before it is returned to them, or mail home.

◆ Send special messages and notes to students recognizing their efforts and behaviors with which you are pleased.

◆ Find the humor in situations, and try to bring fun and laughter into the classroom as much as possible.

◆ Incorporate literature into the curriculum that helps students express and understand feelings and emotions, that ties in thematically with a variety of topics such as: caring and determination, belonging and acceptance, rejection and taunting, handicaps, etc.

◆ Call one parent each night to report positive things about his or her child's efforts.

◆ Use questioning techniques and sharing methods that allow all students to have the opportunity to be heard and share with equity.

◆ Teach students how to make positive statements, compliments, and both recognize and use esteem-building language. Enforce in the classroom that "in here we only say positive things about ourselves and others, and no put-downs or negative comments to or about others are acceptable."

◆ Discuss negative comments and how those words make us feel. Name those negative comments (i.e., "put-downs," "zingers") and use a cue word/signal to remind students not to use esteem-hurting language.

◆ Schedule brief 5- or 10-minute conferences with each student as frequently as possible throughout each grading period/school year.

◆ Teach about and talk about learning styles and multiple intelligences, and address these at every opportunity.

◆ Many teachers have students applaud their peers' accomplishments, positive behavior, and so forth.

◆ Help students recognize their strengths and competencies. Keep a record or profile of what students do well.

◆ Designate students as "class experts" on certain topics or with specific skills that they shine in or have a special interest in. Be sure to target lower-achieving students as "class experts" in an area of their strength/interest.

◆ Provide many activities and opportunities for students to showcase their strengths, perform or teach others a skill they do well, share about their hobbies, interests, and so forth.

◆ Create a class book on "OUR STRENGTHS" with each student having his or her page. Each student can provide pictures, write about his or her strengths, and/or list positive character traits.

◆ Buddy up a child with low self-esteem with a younger child as a cross-age tutor to that younger child. Cross-age tutoring and upper-/lower-grade buddy systems are a wonderful way to boost self-esteem of all children.

◆ Model how to use positive self-talk, especially to illustrate how to think positively and not give up when frustrated.

◆ Point out students' errors in a way that is not demeaning and respects their efforts. On written work, take care not to mark up students' papers (especially with red ink!). It is often helpful and respectful to indicate errors in the margins, or on self-stick notes when possible.

◆ Many elementary classrooms have their own class pet and their own patch/area of school garden to care for, which helps students to feel good about themselves and more connected to their class and school.

◆ Schools should provide many kinds of interest clubs, support groups, and programs that will enable students to grow in self-confidence and self-esteem. Besides the intervention of support services, school tutorials, etc., tutorial programs under a school/community partnership can provide students with role models as well as academic help.

◆ Mentoring programs and clubs/interest groups are very beneficial for students. Besides developing skills in an area of interest, they are effective for building positive relationships and social skills.

◆ Community service is an important way to help our children. Through the act of reaching out into the community, providing a needed service and making personal connections with others, we enhance our students' self-esteem.

How Parents Can Help Build the Self-Esteem of Their Children

◆ Many of the above recommendations to teachers are appropriate in the home, as well.

◆ Give your son or daughter reasonable, developmentally appropriate responsibilities. This is important for developing self-confidence.

◆ When you correct your child, take care to avoid sarcasm, humiliation, or criticism of his or her character or intelligence.

◆ Let your children know as often as possible how much you appreciate them for who they are.

◆ Communicate your unconditional love and unwavering belief in your child.

◆ Display and save your child's projects or work that he or she is proud of. Maintain a portfolio collection of those projects, or take photos of them to keep as a memory.

◆ It is very important to instill in children a sense of obligation and responsibility for helping others. Try to make the effort as a family to get involved in volunteering in some community service. There are numerous avenues for doing so (e.g., through churches/synagogues, schools, hospitals, park districts, scouts). Any opportunity we provide to involve our children in service projects will be of value to the community and society. The additional benefit is that most people gain in self-esteem, feeling very positively about themselves when they experience the act of giving to others.

66. Preschool/Kindergarten Issues and Strategies

◆ Most children with ADHD aren't diagnosed until first grade or higher. However, those exhibiting significant difficulties with hyperactivity, impulsivity, and attention are often identified in kindergarten, preschool, and even earlier. With very young children it is harder to distinguish the line between what is "normal" rambunctious, active, uninhibited early childhood behavior, and what may be abnormal (maladaptive and inconsistent with the child's developmental level).

◆ There are children with ADHD diagnosed under the age of five and receiving various treatments (including medication) with success. However, most children enter preschool and kindergarten programs without a diagnosis or a label. Teachers and parents use all of their skills and put forth their best effort to manage the behaviors as well as they can.

◆ Many children—not just those with ADHD—have difficulty adjusting to a classroom environment, the hours away from home, the structure and expectations of their preschool/kindergarten teacher, and relating to the other children. Sometimes it just takes time to make the adjustment and feel comfortable in the new environment. It is often the case that some of the behaviors that were problematic at the beginning of the year diminish and are no longer an issue, once the children have learned the routine and structure, bonded with their teacher, and matured somewhat.

◆ For children with ADHD the preschool/kindergarten teacher will often notice that the behaviors continue to remain problematic and excessive in comparison to the other children. It is appropriate to share concerns with parents and support staff, and to put into place strategies and interventions to address the needs of the child.

◆ Most all of the techniques and interventions recommended throughout this book are applicable and effective for children in this age bracket as well.

◆ Often children with ADHD display other developmental difficulties (i.e., speech/language problems, gross and/or fine motor skills). Parents or the school team will want to have the child screened for possible visual or hearing deficits and perhaps be evaluated for these other concerns (e.g., by a speech/language therapist, adapted PE teacher, occupational therapist).

◆ Early intervention is always helpful for children with special needs. Some children qualify for special early childhood programs designed for students displaying developmental delays or considered at-risk.

◆ Other young children may not developmentally be ready for a formal preschool or kindergarten program, and will benefit most from waiting another year before entering into such programs. They have many years ahead of them to be "in school." Placing a child in a situation that is too demanding and frustrating for him or her may be damaging. Parents may wish to spend time at the preschool or kindergarten observing their child in comparison with the other children. They should keep an open mind and listen to teacher input in making decisions as to where their child will experience success.

◆ The same principles of parenting, effective behavior management, and problem prevention applies to young children as to older children. Parents will need to provide the necessary structure and manage the environmental factors to help their child be successful. They will need to anticipate potential problems and plan accordingly. For example, parents of highly active young children will need to take great care to "childproof" the home for safety.

◆ Parents can seek help from specialists in learning how to cope with and manage their young child's challenging behaviors and more difficult temperament. There are many resources available to help parents learn how to do so.

◆ Early childhood teachers who have effective, positive programs have many of the same characteristics as successful teachers in upper grades. These effective preschool and kindergarten teachers:

- Provide a classroom environment that is loving, nurturing, comfortable, and safe

- Are generous with hugs, smiles, praise, and affection

- Maintain close contact and involvement with the parents

- Are specific, firm, and clear in their expectations

- Provide structure, consistency, and follow-through

- Establish a predictable routine and schedule

- Offer children choices
- Are flexible, kind, and tolerant
- Teach with a great deal of music, movement, and hands-on activities
- Use individualized discipline and behavior management
- Allow the children time and opportunity to explore and make discoveries
- Teach, model, and practice all behavioral expectations
- Use positive reinforcement with very high frequency
- Teach through fun, exciting curriculum and activities
- Are well-planned and prepared
- Create a room environment that takes into account different learning styles
- Adapt activities and provide for the needs of all students (whatever their developmental level may be)
- Have a clear awareness that children's self-esteem and feeling good about themselves is of utmost importance
- Respect each child's individuality

◆ In kindergarten, everything—every behavioral expectation and social skill—has to be taught. You need to explain and model each desired behavior and practice until all students know precisely what is expected from them. This includes how and where to: line up, walk in line, stand in line, move to groups, move to stations or learning centers, sit on the rug, sit at the table; as well as how to get your attention, use "indoor" and "outdoor" voices, and so forth.

◆ You need to role play and practice those expectations. Examples: "Show me what to do when you have something you want to say." "Who wants to show us how we get our lunch boxes and line up for lunch?"

◆ When possible, you will use literature that has manners and appropriate behavior as a theme. Teach behavioral expectations and social skills through the use of puppets, music, games, visual displays, role-play, etc.

◆ *Behavior-management techniques* in kindergarten are similar to those in the primary elementary grades. You may need to use:

- *Time-outs:* a system of removing disruptive students briefly from the group's activity. You need to clearly communicate your expectations and consequences. The child should know what he or she did inappropriately that resulted in the time-out. In most circumstances time-out or time-away will take place in a designated spot or area of the classroom, more removed from the center of activity. The child will be sent there for a short amount of time—always welcomed back to the group when he or she is ready. "We are glad you are ready to join us again. Welcome back!"

- In some cases the child's behavior is so out-of-control that it will require the intervention of other school personnel coming to the classroom and trying to redirect and calm the child—or remove the child from the classroom.

- *Quiet space:* Sometimes children with ADHD are on sensory overload or are fatigued. It is important to allow the child some limited choices, and to be given time and space to settle, re-group, and get away from some of the over-stimulation. Children should be given a chance to move away from the group when they need to do so. You may ask: "Do you need some time? Do you need to move to a different area? Is there a better place for you to do your work?" You may try redirecting to a quieter, calmer area by whispering to the child, "Go to the pillow area and read a book."

- *Diversionary tactics:* The perceptive preschool/kindergarten teacher will watch for signs of children beginning to get restless, agitated, or behave inappropriately; and effectively divert their attention and redirect behavior.

- Most young children love to be the teacher's helper. They can be given a task to do such as: wiping down tables, putting up chairs, passing out papers. It is important to find out what the child likes to do—identifying what is meaningful and motivating. Some children don't care at all about stickers or other tangible reinforcers, but would be highly motivated to be able to earn the chance to play with bubbles, ride a trike, or care for the class pet.

- *Positive attention:* As with older children, the best way to manage is through watching for positive behaviors, and recognizing children for what they are doing right. The most reinforcing way to teach appropriate behavior is through specific praise, smiles, hugs, and so forth. Many teachers have students applaud each other for individual accomplishments: "Let's give a big round of applause to . . . " (Children clap finger-to-finger in a large circular movement.) "Let's give ourselves a pat on the back." (Children reach over and pat themselves on the back.) "Let's give the silent cheer for . . . "

- *Checking for specific behaviors:* "Are you using your inside voice?" "Are your eyes watching?"

- *Behavior modification and reward systems:* Early childhood teachers may use various systems of monitoring individual children's behavior and rewarding/positively reinforcing those one or two specific behaviors. Some may use charts broken into brief time segments, with the child able to earn a sticker, star, smiley face, or stamp for positive behavior during that time frame. Some work towards other goals and reinforcers.

◆ *Learning styles environment:* Preschool/kindergarten classrooms are colorful, warm, and comfortable. Rooms often have carpet areas and beanbag chairs or other big, soft chairs for areas of comfort. There are often sand tables, rice tables, water tables, playhouses, computers, library areas, musical instruments, clearly identified centers with hands-on manipulatives and activities, listening posts/centers, easels, and a wealth of early literacy materials/activities. The room is well-organized, with areas well-defined. Children know the structure and routine of using materials and engaging in each of the specific activities. Materials are well-labeled (pictures/words).

◆ The kindergarten curriculum is rich in oral language—with children exposed to a lot of rhyme and verse, patterned literature, and fun, interesting stories.

◆ These classrooms should be inviting and child-centered, with children's work displayed freely. There are many puzzles, blocks of different kinds, and a variety of textures/materials to feel and manipulate. It should be an environment that is filled with love, affection, and respect. Move around and give personal attention to your children. Position yourself to make direct eye contact with children and provide one-to-one assistance.

◆ Music and movement are embedded in all aspects of the curriculum throughout the day. Use some kind of routine to signal transitions and help students through the change of activities by utilizing music, chants, songs, and motions. Combine music with movement for exercise, body awareness and coordination, following directions, and relaxation. Fingerplays, poetry, rhymes, and marches are generally used routinely.

♦ Use special props and motivators such as: a magic wand, "special binoculars" to see children engaged in appropriate behavior, puppets or stuffed animals for special cues and communication with children.

67. ADOLESCENT ISSUES AND STRATEGIES

As children with ADHD move to the adolescent years, some tend to "outgrow" many of the symptoms, and a number of the issues that were of concern when they were younger no longer appear to be problematic. However, **for most** adolescents with ADHD, the symptoms continue to persist to varying degrees. In fact, for many ADHD adolescents and pre-adolescents, these years can be the most difficult and stressful for them and their family.

Characteristics of hyperactivity and impulsivity may diminish or manifest themselves differently as the child matures. Hyperactivity generally looks different in adolescents than it does in younger children. It is very rare to see a junior high or high school student with ADHD running around a classroom or falling out of his or her chair frequently. Instead, these signs of hyperactivity look more like restlessness, fidgetiness, antsiness in older students. Impulsivity in teens can be more problematic during these years than it was when they were younger. Impulsive behaviors in adolescence can involve participation in high-risk activities that may pose a danger to the adolescent or others (i.e., traffic violations, accidents, sexual promiscuity, and conduct that results in conflict with school authorities, parents, and/or law enforcement).

◆ Some children with ADHD who were able to cope adequately in the elementary school grades may find themselves unable to do so with the high demands and work load of middle and secondary school.

◆ Many parents aren't aware that their children continue to need treatment or are in need of different kinds of treatment as they experience difficulty (academic, social, emotional) in middle school and high school. Many teens are in great need of support from mental health professionals. Depression is common for adolescents with ADHD. There is also a high rate of serious behavioral problems— oppositional/defiant, conduct disorders—and learning problems among teens with ADHD. It is very important to reassess the adolescent's needs and implement whatever interventions may be necessary (i.e., academic assistance, medical treatment, counseling) at this time in his or her development.

◆ Issues that tend to be problematic for middle school and secondary school students negatively affecting their academic performance often include: poor organization/study skills, time-management, test-taking, and note-taking skills. Study-skill classes that teach these useful strategies, monitoring of student progress on long-range projects, as well as computer classes, keyboard training, teaching students how to access information (i.e., in the library system, on the Internet), are all very helpful interventions.

◆ Students of this age still benefit from incentive systems, contracts, and home/school monitoring plans.

◆ Older children need to understand about ADHD, the nature of the disorder, and how they can best manage to deal with the symptoms. There are some excellent resources on ADHD geared to the older child/adolescent. Parents and doctors need to take the time to explain and educate the preadolescent/adolescent about ADHD. It is very important to acknowledge their feelings, and solicit their input in decision making, monitoring, and management.

◆ As students with ADHD enter the middle school and high school grades, they will need to advocate for themselves—understand their needs and learn how to approach teachers respectfully with requests for accommodations. Parents still need to take an active role in their child's education and maintain communication with teachers. However, it is also appropriate for students to speak directly with their teachers. Students with ADHD can politely explain to their teachers what makes it easier or harder to learn in the classroom, and the kind of supports/accommodations that help them, such as preferential seating.

◆ One of the advantages in middle and secondary school is the availability of more options in scheduling. Sometimes the best intervention is a change of classes or teachers. Other times, rescheduling a class with the same teacher but at a more optimal time of day makes a difference.

◆ Parents of adolescents with ADHD often need to be vigilant in monitoring their son's or daughter's progress. They can request updates from teachers at any time. Many middle and secondary schools send home computerized progress reports halfway through the grading period. Parents may request this feedback on a more frequent basis and most teachers are willing to provide it. At this level many teachers keep students' daily grades and points on the computer, and are able to print out updated grades without much inconvenience.

◆ Teens and pre-teens with ADHD, besides having specific difficulties related to their ADHD, must also cope with all the normal stresses and anxieties of other kids this age. This includes: the changes and transitions to a new school, dealing with several teachers—each with his or her own teaching style, expectations and requirements; the enormous social and peer pressures; need to be accepted and "fit in"; physical changes of adolescence, and so forth.

◆ Students of middle school and high school age often complain about school being boring, and they don't see the connection between what is being taught in school and their own lives. Instruction at this level must be meaningful, challenging, and relevant—eliciting active participation and student involvement. The curriculum and schedule at this level need to provide for options, variety, choices, and balance.

◆ We must continue to do whatever is possible to motivate our adolescent students, engaging their interest and tapping into their strengths.

◆ Teachers in middle and secondary schools typically have little training about ADHD, learning disabilities, or other special needs. It is important that they are able to receive staff development/training that is informative, relevant, and helps them to understand/empathize with their students who are struggling with learning and/or attention difficulties.

◆ Adolescents have a strong sense of justice and fair play. Protection of their image and being treated with respect are of utmost importance. They need to feel safe and comfortable in their classroom environment, knowing that they will be treated with dignity and not deliberately criticized or humiliated in front of their peers.

◆ It often happens that when we have children with maturing bodies who look "grown up," we place unrealistic expectations upon them. Adolescents with ADHD may appear mature physically, but are often far less mature socially and emotionally than peers their own age.

◆ Adolescents have a critical need for structure and frequent monitoring both at home and school (even as they complain and resist). There is often a greater need for guidance and open channels of communication than ever before. This is especially true with all of the outside pressures and influences to which our children are exposed.

◆ These are years when it is very difficult for parents and teachers to find that proper balance: how to teach our children to assume responsibility for their own learning and behavioral choices, and how to intervene as we guide and support them to success.

◆ It is helpful when there is an adult at school who is willing to be a case manager (officially or unofficially)—someone who will be able to monitor progress, advise, and intervene in school situations. For students on IEPs, the special education teacher (e.g., resource specialist) is often that case manager. Sometimes it is a school counselor, one of the classroom teachers, a coach, or an aide working at the school. Some schools use upper classmen as peer counselors or mentors, although they wouldn't serve the same function as an adult case manager.

◆ It is important to realize that the bulk of strategies and interventions for ADHD (i.e., instructional, environmental, organizational, behavioral) that are effective in the home and school for younger children are still effective and recommended for older children/adolescents, as well.

68. Relaxation, Guided Imagery, and Visualization Techniques

Children with ADD/ADHD are often in a state of stress in school. It is therapeutic to teach them strategies (at home, school, or in private therapy) to help them calm down and relax. Hyperactive/impulsive students, in particular, gain the most from learning techniques that relax their minds and bodies, recognize their internal feelings, and release inner tension. These strategies empower children with a feeling of peace and self-control.

There are a variety of techniques that have proven effective in helping us to slow down, and to improve focus and awareness. One book, in particular, is a gold mine of wonderful ideas, step-by-step exercises, and activities for teachers and parents to help children achieve this sense of relaxation and well-being. This wonderful book, *Centerplay: Focusing Your Child's Energy* (Fireside, 1984), was written by Holly Young Huth, a relaxation consultant and teacher specializing in early childhood education.

◆ *Fun and laughter:* Laughter is one of the best ways to release stress and feel good. The chemicals released in the body through laughter reduce pain and tension. So, there is probably no substitute for finding ways to have fun and to laugh with our children.

◆ *Breathing techniques:* Many of us know the positive effects of controlled breathing through our training in Lamaze or other natural childbirth classes. Controlled, conscious breathing has the benefit of relaxing muscles and reducing stress. Many believe it is useful in the management, perhaps cure, of some physical ailments and disease.

- Help students learn to take conscious, deep breaths to relax. Show them how to inhale deeply (preferably through the nose, but through the mouth is fine) and *slowly* exhale through the mouth.

- Teach children to isolate different body parts and relax them with each slow breath they exhale. For example, while lying on the floor, instruct them to tighten or squeeze their toes on the left foot, then relax with a deep breath. Now tighten their left knee and upper leg . . . then relax and breathe. Proceed in this fashion to the right side of the lower body, to the abdomen and upper body, each arm, hand/fingers, chest, neck, jaws, and face.

– It is particularly helpful for children to recognize that when they are nervous, stressed and angry, they should feel the tightening of certain body parts. If they can recognize when fists clench, jaws tighten, and stomachs harden, they have the power over their bodies to relax and gain control. They can begin to breathe deeply and "send" their breaths consciously to relax body parts. By sending the breaths to their hand, the child can silently prompt him- or herself to relax the hand (until the fist is released and fingers are loose). Teach children that when their bodies are relaxed, they are better able to think and plan.

– Help guide students to visualize that with each breath they take in, their body becomes filled slowly with a soothing color, aroma, sound, light, warmth, or other pleasant, comfortable feeling.

– Ask students to think of a color that makes them feel very comfortable, peaceful, and relaxed. Then have them practice—with closed eyes—breathing in that color and "sending" it (blowing it) throughout the body. If a child, for example, chooses "turquoise," guide him or her to visualize the turquoise going down his or her throat, into the neck and chest, down to the stomach, and so on until the child is filled with the beautiful, peaceful, wonderful turquoise . . . and is relaxed and in control.

◆ *Yoga and slow movement exercises:* Various yoga postures and slow movement games and exercises are fun and helpful for teaching children to relax, use controlled movements, and increase their creative imagination and imagery skills. Some movements and postures shared in *Centerplay* include: scaling through space; climbing a pyramid; carrying a fragile gift to someone; being a scarecrow, rag-doll, popped balloon, among many others.

◆ *Visualization and guided imagery:* The ability to visualize with colorful, vivid images, rich imagination and detailed action are natural skills of childhood. These same skills have been found to be very useful in empowering people to overcome obstacles in their lives, improve memory, enhance learning, and to be healing—physically, mentally, and emotionally. Imagery is helpful in developing focus and concentration, calming, coping with stress/anxiety, and increasing positive study skills, social skills and creative expression

- There are specialists who train individuals in these techniques, and who use visualization/guided imagery as part of their therapy in treatment of different health, social, behavioral, and emotional problems.

- There are also books and resources that can be purchased utilizing these techniques for self-help and management. One of these resources is *Imagery for Kids—Discovering Your Special Place,* an audiotape combining gentle music and a guided journey, developed and presented by Dr. Charlotte Reznick, Educational Psychologist (310-393-2416).

- Teach students to visualize themselves in situations where they are achieving and being successful. Once students have had practice with guided visualization, encourage them to use the techniques of deep breathing and visualizing themselves doing what they want to do. For example, prior to taking a test, they can visualize themselves in detail working diligently taking the test. Encourage them to see themselves being persistent and reading each item carefully, being relaxed and not getting nervous or excited, and being confident with their answers. Have students picture themselves finishing the test, going back and checking for careless errors. In addition, playing the theme song from the movie *Rocky* or another motivational song can help build confidence.

◆ *Use music.* Music can be very helpful for relaxation, as a previsualization activity, to soothe away worries and distractions, and bring a sense of inner peace.

- Music also stimulates the brain in other ways—besides relaxation. Many people find that they are better able to focus, and are more productive and motivated when listening to the radio or some of their favorite music.

- Many teachers find that playing cassettes/CDs of classical music, Baroque, soothing environmental sounds, and instrumental arrangements is very effective in the classroom. Different forms of music have been found to be effective in increasing the ability to focus and concentrate, calm, soothe and relax, and to enhance learning, creativity, and critical-thinking skills.

- Research has found that instrumental musical arrangements at 60 beats per minute has therapeutic effects. Gary Lamb creates music (at 60 beats per minute) that is widely used in different settings (classrooms, pain clinics, hospitals). Some of the music is recommended for use when teaching handwriting, art, creative writing, and to play during math testing, science labs, computer labs, homework time, silent reading, and so forth. For more information about Gary Lamb's music, call 800-772-7701.

– Musical therapy is being used in different settings, and research supports that listening to various rhythmic patterns has calming and focusing effects. *Calming Rhythms* developed by REI Institute, Inc. is another audiocassette designed for this purpose (800-659-6644).

69. SOCIAL-SKILLS ISSUES AND STRATEGIES

For whatever reason, many students are lacking social-skill compe-tency. Children and teens with ADD/ADHD in particular tend to be deficient in social-skill awareness and application. These skills need to be explicitly and directly taught, modeled, and practiced in order to be developed.

◆ There are a number of weaknesses common among children/ teens with ADHD that negatively affect their interactions with oth-ers and social acceptance. They often exhibit poor problem-solving skills (easily provoked to fighting, arguing, name calling, and inappropriate means of resolving conflicts). Children/teens with ADHD are often unaware of their own behaviors that others find annoying or intrusive. They are often inattentive to verbal and non-verbal or visual cues. Their difficulty controlling noise/activity level and emotions interferes with the situation/activity they may be engaged in; and they frequently display poor communication skills (listening to others, taking turns, making eye contact).

◆ Within the classroom there is no better place and structure for teaching and practicing appropriate social skills than in the context of cooperative learning groups. All teachers should have training in cooperative learning—which is *not* just group work, but a well-structured format and vehicle for teaching throughout the school day. Cooperative learning has been well researched and found to be effective in increasing: student achievement, retention of mate-rial, motivation, positive/supportive relationships, critical-thinking skills, positive attitudes, student acceptance, and the ability to view from other people's perspective.

◆ Some elementary schools provide social-skill training through various lessons and units taught by the classroom teacher to the whole class, or in sessions facilitated and presented by the coun-selor (either in the classroom or small-group sessions outside of the classroom). There are some excellent programs and social-skill cur-riculum on the market from which to choose.

◆ Some elementary schools have schoolwide social-skills pro-grams that involve selecting one topic or behavior each month (i.e., responsibility, courtesy, listening skills, friendship). All teachers spend time at the beginning of the month discussing that topic/skill with their students. All adults on campus wear a badge that has the social-skill topic/word of the month printed on the badge. Staff members are given a certain amount of "I Got Caught" tickets that they are to distribute to any student they happen to observe on campus exhibiting the targeted social-skill behavior of the month (being respectful, being courteous, being a good friend, being helpful). Students who receive tickets write their names on them and place the ticket inside the school box/jar designated for that purpose. Once a week there is a raffle—with prizes going to students whose names are drawn from the school box/jar.

◆ Some middle schools are teaching social skills through their P.E. programs. The specific social skill (i.e., encouragement, giving/accepting compliments, manners, sportsmanship, responsibility) is taught in 3- or 4-week units. Skills are discussed in terms of what it would sound like and look like to display those particular skills, as well as the rationale for using the skill. For example, *encouragement* might look like: thumbs up, pat on back, smile, high five. It might sound like: "Nice try," "You can do it." Then, through a number of entertaining and motivating cooperative games and activities, the skills are practiced and reinforced. Students receive positive reinforcement in a variety of ways for exhibiting those skills. Students are responsible for processing and evaluating how well they and their group performed regarding use of the specific social skill.

◆ You can be very helpful in increasing student awareness of appropriate skills by modeling, giving positive attention to, and reinforcing displays of politeness, good manners, and the appropriate way to say and do things in classroom settings and out-of-classroom settings. You should try to provide corrective feedback in a manner that is nonjudgmental or embarrassing, but focuses on teaching positive social skills.

◆ You can help children weak in social skills by carefully pairing them with positive role models, and assigning them to groups that will be more supportive.

◆ Sometimes you will need to try facilitating friendships for certain students who tend to be socially isolated.

◆ In any context or format that social skills are being taught, it is important to explain the need/rationale for learning the skill. This can be done through discussion and reinforced by visual displays (posters, photos). Teaching the skill requires modeling of the skill, rehearsing or role-playing, and having students look for and observe the skill being displayed in different settings. The students need to have a great deal of opportunity to practice the skill and receive prompting and coaching in when to do so. Corrective feedback and positive reinforcement are also necessary in the process of learning these skills.

◆ Various systems for positively reinforcing use of social skills may include contracts (home/school) and positive reinforcers (social, activity, material, privileges) contingent upon display of targeted social skills.

◆ Photographs of students engaged in appropriate behavior are powerful reinforcers of good social skills. Take photos of groups or individuals engaged in cooperative behavior and display them in a prominent place. It is also effective to take photos of groups role-playing the proper social skill. These serve as a visual reminder when students move into their cooperative learning groups.

◆ Take a photo of the student with ADHD sitting properly at his or her desk engaged in appropriate behavior. Tape to the desk as an individual reminder and visual cue.

◆ Some social skills that schools may wish to focus on teaching and positively reinforcing include:

✔ How to accept feedback

✔ How to listen to others without interrupting

✔ How to disagree

✔ How to give and receive praise/compliments

✔ How to participate in a conversation without dominating it

✔ How to enter into a conversation/activity with others

✔ How to share and take turns

✔ How to ask for help

✔ How to play a game and accept losing appropriately

✔ How to apologize

✔ How to use appropriate tone of voice and volume for a setting/ situation

✔ General manners—using respectful, polite verbal and body language

◆ Parents need to focus on teaching their child appropriate social skills, as well. Besides directly teaching, modeling, and setting up situations that enable the child to practice those skills, parents may wish to provide their child with specific social-skills training outside of school. In some communities there are centers and clinics specializing in ADHD, which offer different kinds of training to children/teens with ADHD and to their families. Other specialists in the community also offer social-skills training sessions. It is recommended that parents investigate about such services that may be available in their community.

◆ Social-skills groups designed specifically for children/teens with ADHD teach skills through modeling, role-playing, rehearsing, and opportunities in structured activities to practice applying the skills. They are given feedback and positive reinforcement. Any social skill taught should be one that is able to be generalized to other settings—with the hope of becoming internalized and part of the child/teen's repertoire of appropriate skills/behaviors that they will then use in their interactions with other people.

◆ Parents will be asked to reinforce those skills being taught at home, and often teachers are informed and asked to positively reinforce those targeted social skills when observed at school.

◆ Parents may try bringing to their child's attention the inappropriateness of some of their social behaviors at a time when it is a more "teachable moment." When emotions are not running high and it is a calm time (not in the midst of a conflict), parents may wish to discuss with the child why other children get angry with them, and they are having trouble keeping their friends. Perhaps practice or role-play problem areas at these times (i.e., showing sportsmanship and appropriate ways to lose a game). Depending on the child and how sensitive he or she is, parents may wish to videotape different scenarios (i.e., role-play) to use for teaching their child social skills when they feel the time is right for doing so.

70. The Student Study Team (SST) Process

◆ Many schools utilize a very effective process for identifying students in need of assistance/intervention. It involves bringing together on a regular basis (i.e., once a week for 1–2 hours) a multidisciplinary team of professionals serving the school site.

◆ There are different names for this team process depending on the school district. Some include: Child Study Team, Pupil Study Team, Consultation Team, Pupil Personnel Team, School-Based Support Team, Student Study Team. Throughout this book the school "team" process will be referred to as SST (or Student Study Team).

◆ Depending on the support personnel available at the school site, the members of the team vary. Generally, it includes: the school psychologist, the school counselor, a special education teacher (resource specialist), the school nurse, administrator, and classroom teacher. The speech/language teacher and adapted P.E. teacher are other members of the team, who may not be in attendance at all team meetings, but are often in attendance when the team is discussing a student with issues involving speech/language or motor skill development. Some schools have social workers and other specialists with various areas of expertise who are able to join the team.

◆ Parents may or may not be in attendance at Student Study Team meetings. This depends on the school/district protocol. Some schools prefer to meet initially without parents—generally for efficiency purposes—to be able to discuss more students within the designated amount of time. (When parents are in attendance, it is harder to keep to a tight time schedule.) These schools will inform parents prior to meeting, as well as immediately after, regarding any plan of action, and then will invite parents to attend a follow-up meeting.

◆ Many schools request that parents attend the SST meeting. Parent input is extremely important and helpful in the problem-solving/strategy-planning process. Generally, parents appreciate being invited to SST meetings, whether they are able to attend (i.e., due to work schedules/availability) or not. In any case, whether meetings are held with or without parents, it is necessary to inform parents when the SST meeting will be taking place, as well as the outcome of the meeting (which will involve some written plan of action).

◆ Teachers should follow through on preliminary steps prior to the SST meeting. (Examples: implement various interventions and document effectiveness, communicate with previous teachers, review the cumulative records and student data, collect work samples, share concerns and action taken with appropriate SST members at the informal level, establish communication with parents—notifying them of observations, concerns, attempts to assist.) With pre-referral steps taken, then the SST meeting is more productive. The team is in a position to recommend "next step" interventions.

◆ Teachers will be asked to complete a referral form prior to meeting. *(See Checklist 48 on Typical Teacher Referral Forms.)* The facilitator of the meeting generally makes copies of the referral form to distribute to team members either before or at the time of the meeting.

◆ At SST meetings, the team typically examines records—looks at the student's past report cards, assessment data, portfolio of work collected (if available), current work samples and assessments, attendance record, health records/vision and hearing screenings, etc. Members of the team share their observations of the student in different settings. Any strategies and interventions that have been implemented (and how successful they have/have not been) will be discussed. The teacher will share about the student's performance, observed areas of strength and weakness, and may be asked to identify what he or she has learned to be effective in motivating and reinforcing the student.

◆ Parents will be asked to share their perceptions of the child's functioning at home and school, areas of strength, areas of difficulty, needs, and so forth. If behaviors are exhibited at school that are of concern, parents will be asked if any of these behaviors are observed outside of school. Any information that parents are willing to supply can assist in determining an appropriate plan of action for the child. Parents may be asked what they have found to be effective in motivating and reinforcing their child.

◆ At the team meeting someone will be a designated recorder (generally everyone is taking their own notes in addition to the teacher referral form each person receives). A plan of action—indicating at least a few interventions—will be written during the meeting. Each member of the team, including parents, will receive a copy of the plan. Often the plan will include a follow-up date to examine the effectiveness of the strategies and interventions designated in the plan. Either a follow-up SST meeting (i.e., scheduled in a specified number of weeks), or a less formal follow-up among the teacher, parents, and one or two members of the team is appropriate.

◆ If the student exhibits the symptoms of ADHD, this SST meeting is often the perfect forum to discuss the possibility. The preliminaries have already been in effect. The teacher has been trying a number of strategies appropriate for students exhibiting difficulties with attention, impulsivity, high activity level, disorganization, etc. Other staff members have informally observed the student, as they have been alerted by the teacher. If it appears that the student may have ADHD, this can be discussed with the parent at the time of the SST meeting. Parents can be provided with resources and information, if they are interested.

◆ *See Checklist 11 on Making the Diagnosis: What Is a Comprehensive Evaluation for ADHD?, Checklist 12 on What Parents Should Expect from the School in the Diagnostic Process, Checklist 30 on Pursuing an Evaluation for Your Child, and Checklist 47 on If You Suspect Your Student Has ADHD.*

◆ One of the recommendations in the plan of action for students coming through SST may be to initiate screening, or formal psycho-educational assessment. *(See Checklist 71 on What Is an IEP?)*

◆ Some SST meetings are follow-up meetings on students who have previously been referred and discussed through the team.

◆ Many schools reserve a few minutes at the end of SST meetings to share names of other students who have come to their attention (by teachers communicating their concerns with them at the informal level). It can be decided at that time to schedule specific students for future SST meetings.

NOTE:

In most districts the SST process is NOT a function of special education. It is part of the *general* education process for identifying students in need, planning appropriately for those students, and using a team approach to problem-solving and strategizing appropriate interventions.

◆ A proactive team encourages this identification process at the school site. Often schools must react to "crisis" situations and prioritize the referrals on certain students exhibiting significant needs. However, the early identification of student needs and potential problems should also be a high priority. Many teachers mistakenly believe that they are to refer to the SST team only those students who may be special education candidates; or be hesitant to refer a student because his or her needs are not so severe as other students. Teachers should bring to the attention of SST members, students who exhibit any number of difficulties—not just those difficulties that are academic in nature, or which appear to warrant special education services. Teachers should alert SST members about students who exhibit health, behavior, attendance, academic, communication, social, and emotional difficulties. These are all appropriate reasons for referring students for intervention.

71. What Is an IEP?

◆ IEP stands for "Individualized Education Plan." This is a written statement for every child with a disability that is developed, reviewed, and revised in accordance with the IDEA.

◆ In spring, 1997, the U.S. Congress reauthorized the Individuals with Disabilities Education Act (IDEA). This important legislation has been providing children with disabilities the access to a free appropriate public education for over twenty years.

◆ On June 4, 1997, President Clinton signed into law Public Law 105-17, the Individuals with Disabilities Education Act Amendments of 1997, which made substantial changes to the IDEA. These amendments will, hopefully, lead to improvements in the implementation of IDEA—strengthening the federal effort to provide every child with a "world-class" education.

◆ IDEA guarantees all students with disabilities ages 3 to 21—no matter how severe the disability—the right to a free appropriate public education. This means special education and related services, at no cost to parents.

◆ When a student is referred for evaluation due to a suspected disability, and a process of formal evaluation is initiated to determine eligibility for special education services, this is known as the IEP process. After completion of assessment, an IEP meeting is held—at which time parents, professionals involved in the assessment, classroom teachers, and other key parties come together to discuss results, determine eligibility, and plan for the student's needs.

NOTE:

Not all students who display the characteristics of ADD/ADHD will require special education assessment or services. If the student is achieving in the classroom and the ADHD behaviors/symptoms are not significantly interfering with his or her ability to learn and function successfully, there is certainly no need to pursue the route of special education. Many students with ADHD will be able to perform and achieve at a successful level when appropriate teaching strategies, environmental/organizational modifications, and other general education interventions are employed. This is, indeed, our goal.

◆ However, there are many students who will continue to have significant difficulty functioning and achieving, in spite of numerous interventions. These students should be tested, and any services they may qualify for should be provided.

◆ Special education referrals may come directly from teachers or parents. The referral process begins a legal timeline during which a designated case manager: prepares paperwork, informs parents of legal rights, obtains parental permission in writing, and contacts all involved members of the assessment team who then each conduct their evaluations, write their individual reports, and meet with parents in an IEP meeting.

◆ To receive special education services, a student must proceed through the IEP process which involves several specific steps, procedures, and timelines. The child will receive a psycho-educational evaluation by qualified professionals of the multidisciplinary team (IEP team). The student will be assessed based upon the areas of suspected disability.

◆ A psycho-educational evaluation often includes: observations, examination of school records and history; health/developmental history from parents; vision and hearing screenings; academic, cognitive, social/emotional/adaptive assessment, perceptual-motor testing; and—depending on other indicators and needs displayed by student—speech/language, motor skills, etc.

◆ To qualify for special education services, there are various categories under which a child may qualify (deaf/blind, language or speech disorder, severe orthopedic impairment/physical disability, autism, visual impairment, hearing impairment, specific learning disability, mental disability/retardation, multi-handicapped [multiple disabilities], other health impairment, developmental delay [for children ages 3–5]). Some states have a category of emotional behavioral disability (EBD); others don't have a specific behavioral disability, just the serious emotional or social-emotional disability (SED) category.

◆ Notice that ADHD is not a specific category (a separate handicapping condition) under IDEA. Many children with ADHD have been and will continue to be served under IDEA, receiving special education services because they qualify under one of the other disability categories that exists along with their ADHD. Children with ADHD are most commonly able to qualify under the category of SLD (specific learning disabilities), EBD, or SED.

◆ The U.S. Department of Education issued a Policy Clarification Memorandum in September, 1991, which confirmed that children whose "ADD is a chronic or acute health problem that results in limited alertness which adversely affects educational performance" could qualify for special education and related services under IDEA based solely on their ADHD.

◆ Children with ADD/ADHD, therefore, may also be able to qualify for special education under the category of OHI (other health impaired). Now that the Amendments of 1997 have been signed into law, the new regulations that will be written to implement IDEA will hopefully clarify some of the ambiguity and special education guidelines regarding ADHD.

◆ Under IDEA there are very specific procedures and requirements that school districts must follow relating to notification, evaluation, due process rights, the components of the IEP and development of the plan, as well as the range of services that need to be provided to qualifying students.

◆ IDEA sets clear eligibility criteria under each category that school districts follow in determining if a child qualifies for special education or related services. To determine need for special education services, the child must fit one of the classification criteria as having a disability, and that disability must be significantly impacting the child's ability to learn or function. This is an IEP team decision based upon the data collected, assessment, and the input of parents, educators, and other team members.

◆ At all stages, parents are an integral part of the IEP process and team. They are notified and receive a copy of the referral. They must sign permission to allow any testing on their child and agree to the assessment plan. Parents are invited to the IEP meeting, and schools will generally do their best to accommodate parents in setting up this important meeting.

◆ Parents are encouraged to provide input and recommendations in planning for their child at the IEP meeting (i.e., establishing appropriate goals and objectives, need for modifications/adaptations, opinions on placement options). The plan does not go into effect until parents sign the IEP and agree to the plan.

◆ The IEP is reviewed annually (with classroom teacher, special educators, parents, administrator, and other service providers) to review the student's progress on goals/objectives of the IEP, and determine whether the student continues to need special education services. Then a new IEP is written for another year indicating how the child is currently functioning, continued needs, and updated goals and objectives. For annual reviews, formal standardized testing is not required.

◆ An IEP meeting can be set up (initiated by parent or school) at any time to review the plan and make changes, perhaps adding or dropping services, changing the placement, etc. In all cases, parents must agree and sign their permission for any changes in the plan, services rendered, or placement.

◆ Students receiving special education are re-evaluated by the team every three years (triennial review). This is the time that they receive an updated, more comprehensive evaluation from the school. Again, parents sign permission and agree to the assessment plan for the 3-year reviews.

◆ The IEP contains certain required information:

– A written statement of the child's present levels of educational performance (including strengths and weaknesses), as well as demonstrated needs, and how the child's disability affects his or her involvement and progress in the general curriculum

– Measurable annual goals and short-term objectives related to meeting the child's needs that result from the disability

– Special education, related services, supplementary aids/services, and program modifications or supports to be provided to meet the special needs of the child

– Any modifications needed for the student to participate in districtwide or state assessments and, if the child will not participate in general assessment, explaining why the assessment is not appropriate and how the child will be assessed

– The projected date that services are to begin and expected duration, frequency, or length of time that these services will be provided for

– Explanation of the extent (if any) to which the child will not participate in the regular class and activities

– Beginning at age 14, transition service needs focusing on the child's course of study

– The dates by and methods used for measuring the child's progress toward annual goals

◆ Some related services children may have included on their IEP are: assistive technology, transportation, occupational therapy, physical therapy, speech/language therapy, etc.

◆ It is important to understand that under IDEA children are guaranteed the right to being educated in the "least restrictive environment." This means that whenever possible, children should be able to participate in activities and be educated with their non-handicapped peers.

◆ Many schools have a very successful "inclusive model" of serving their special education students. Classroom teachers have had some degree of training regarding the special needs of students, and appropriate strategies and techniques that are effective in meeting those needs. There is sufficient support to the student and teacher through collaboration with special education (as well as through schoolwide interventions and support programs) to enable the child to be mainstreamed and served in an inclusive environment. Most children with mild to moderate disabilities can be effectively served with an inclusive model.

◆ Inclusive education does not mean that the special education child must only be served throughout the day within the classroom. Pull-out services for small-group instruction is still very appropriate and effective for many students.

◆ School districts must provide for a continuum or range of service options from full inclusion, to some pull-out, to special day classes for those students whose needs are best served in a special education class for the majority of the school day. A very small population of disabled students will require even more restrictive educational settings (i.e., residential placements) to meet their severe needs.

◆ Whenever there is a dispute or disagreement between parents and the school regarding a child's special education plan or program, there are various avenues for resolving the differences. Disagreement may arise over the evaluation, the goals, services, placement, or other issues. In most cases, these issues can be worked out in a regular meeting format by sharing concerns and utilizing a cooperative team approach.

◆ Parents have a right to request a due-process hearing. However, it is recommended to use a *mediation process* as the next step for resolving disputes. Mediation is often highly effective in settling differences between the school district and parents. It is a collaborative, problem-solving approach that can resolve conflicts without the need for litigation. Mediation is beneficial to both parties as it is non-adversarial in nature, focuses on the child's needs, and is cost effective.

◆ Parents may file a formal complaint if they believe the school district is violating their rights regarding the laws and regulations pertaining to students with disabilities (i.e., evaluation, IEP process, provision of services/implementation of the agreed-upon plan). Parental rights and processes for requesting mediation or a due-process hearing, filing disagreements, appealing decisions, etc., is available in writing through every school district. If you don't have a copy of your legal rights, request one from the school or district special education department.

72. WHAT IS 504?

Section 504 of the Rehabilitation Act (P.L. 93-112) is a federal civil rights law that prohibits discrimination against people with disabilities. Section 504 is enforced by the Office of Civil Rights. Even though there isn't funding for providing services required under 504, the Office of Civil Rights (OCR) can withhold federal funds to any programs or agencies (i.e., school districts) that do not comply.

◆ Students with ADHD who may not be eligible for services under IDEA (because they do not meet eligibility criteria for special education) are often able to receive support and intervention under Section 504.

◆ Many children/adolescents with ADHD would be considered as having a disability under the definition of "handicapped person" in the Section 504 regulations. This definition is "anyone with a physical or mental impairment that substantially limits one or more major 'life activities' (including: walking, breathing, speaking and/or hearing, seeing, *learning* [author's emphasis], performing manual tasks, and caring for oneself").

◆ Many children/teens with attention deficit disorders may fit the definition of "handicapped," depending on how severe/disabling their disorder.

◆ If the ADD/ADHD *does not* significantly impact or limit their learning or major life functioning, they would not be considered eligible under Section 504.

◆ If their ADD/ADHD *does* significantly limit their learning or functioning, the child/adolescent would be eligible for services and support. This typically means developing a plan of appropriate interventions within the general education program, designed to accommodate some of the student's special needs. The implementation of the plan is primarily the responsibility of the general education school staff.

◆ Students who do qualify for special education services under IDEA are also protected under Section 504.

◆ On September 16, 1991, when the U.S. Department of Education and Office for Civil Rights issued a joint policy memo, it was clearly established that children with attention deficit disorders are protected under the law. They may be eligible for services, accommodations, and supports under the IDEA category of "other health impaired" or a different disability category (if they have a coexisting disorder such as specific learning disabilities or behavior/emotional disorder); as well as under Section 504 of the Rehabilitation Act of 1973.

◆ According to the memo, "The child's education must be provided in the regular education classroom unless it is demonstrated that education in the regular environment with the use of supplementary aides and services cannot be achieved satisfactorily."

◆ The memo lists some specific classroom adaptations and accommodations that might be appropriate:

✔ Providing a structured learning environment

✔ Repeating and simplifying instructions

✔ Supplementing verbal instruction with visual instructions

✔ Using behavioral management techniques

✔ Adjusting class schedules

✔ Alternative testing formats

✔ Using tape recorders, computer-aided instruction, and other audio-visual equipment

✔ Using modified texts

✔ Tailoring assignments

◆ Also suggested were other modifications and provisions of service including: consultation, reducing class size, use of one-on-one tutorials, classroom aides and note takers, use of a services coordinator to oversee implementation of special programs and services, and possible modification of nonacademic times such as lunchroom, recess, and physical education.

◆ There are many of the same protections under Section 504 as mandated under the IDEA. Section 504 provides the right to: a free appropriate public education, placement in the least restrictive environment, a nondiscriminatory evaluation by the school district, procedural due process, the opportunity to participate in extracurricular and non-academic activities, and a 504 Individual Educational Plan (described later).

◆ Students found to be ineligible for special education under IDEA are not automatically covered under 504. Section 504 requires evaluation by a team (often the Student Study Team serves as the 504 team). The team needs to determine eligibility. Parents may request that their child be evaluated. The diagnostic team determines a student's eligibility for services (under IDEA or Section 504).

◆ Similar to IDEA, under Section 504 the school has a meeting with parents to discuss eligibility. If found eligible under 504, they will develop a written individualized 504 plan, and be required to monitor and review the plan and continued need for services at least annually. Children with disabilities must also receive special consideration prior to expulsion or suspensions of more than ten consecutive days.

◆ The 504 Individual Educational Plan is different from an IEP. It is much simpler, and it falls under the responsibility of general education, not special education. The 504 team (often this is the SST along with parents and classroom teachers) meets to develop a plan. A 504 plan generally lists and summarizes interventions and accommodations that are decided upon at the meeting as being the most important for the success of the student. Reasonable and appropriate interventions and modifications are agreed upon. These are typically classroom interventions that the classroom teacher is responsible for providing. However, other interventions can also be included in the plan involving other school support personnel and services.

◆ The eligibility criteria for Section 504 are broader than the eligibility criteria under the Individuals with Disabilities Education Act (IDEA); and services are less clearly defined. It does not include a list of eligible handicaps.

◆ School personnel must be informed about the law and their own personal responsibility and potential liability if they do not comply with any plans (504s or IEPs) that are active on any of their students.

◆ School districts have the responsibility of providing ongoing training to their classroom teachers about children with disabilities and effective strategies and interventions for meeting their needs.

◆ Classroom teachers need training in order to develop the skills necessary for teaching students with disabilities in inclusive settings. They need to understand the rationale and be willing and conscientious in making the necessary adaptations, modifications, and accommodations for their students with special needs.

◆ School personnel need to be aware that when students are on plans governed by legal mandates (i.e., IEPs, 504s), their compliance with what is written into the plan is *not optional.* They are required under the law to make those provisions and carry out the plan. If they refuse to do so, they are opening themselves up to personal liability.

◆ Parents may request a copy of their district's 504 plan.

◆ Parents seeking service for their children may ask the school to consider whether or not their son or daughter may be eligible for any accommodations or supports under 504 if not under IDEA.

◆ Parents may file a complaint with the Office of Civil Rights if they believe their district is violating their child's rights under Section 504.

73. Student Learning Style/Interest Interview

When teachers are trying to learn more about their students' learning-style preferences, interests, and motivators, one of the best ways to find out is to *ask* them. The following are some sample questions teachers may wish to ask students in a one-to-one interview. It is very rewarding to find the time to meet with students, talk with them, and get their input (as to how they learn best and what they enjoy doing in and out of school). A great deal of information can be learned in this interview format, and students typically appreciate their teacher's interest in learning more about them as unique individuals.

◆ Think back over the past few years of school. Whose class did you feel most comfortable in? Tell me a little about your favorite classes—ones you felt successful in. What did you particularly like about those classes or teachers?

◆ What are some of the best school projects you remember doing? Is there any project you did or activity that you participated in which you are especially proud of?

◆ Do you prefer working in a classroom that is warmer or cooler in temperature?

◆ When you are trying to concentrate in class or read silently, do you need the room to be completely quiet? Do you mind some amount of noise and activity during these times when you are trying to concentrate, study, or read silently? Would it help to have some music in the background or would it bother you? (**Note:** More questions may be asked regarding music preferences/dislikes.)

◆ I want you to imagine that you can set up the perfect classroom any way you want. Think about it and tell me or draw for me how you would like the classroom to be arranged. Would you like the tables or desks in rows? Tables in clusters? Tell me (show me) where you want the teacher to be, and where would be your choice of seating in this room.

◆ Do you like to do school projects alone, or would you prefer to work with others?

◆ If you had to study for a social studies test, would you prefer to study alone? With a friend? Small group? With a parent or teacher helping you?

◆ In your classroom, if you had a study carrel (private office area or partition) available, would you choose to do your seat work in it if some other students in your class were also using them?

◆ When do you feel you are able to do your best work and concentrate best: in the morning before recess? after recess but before lunch? after lunch in the afternoon?

◆ Do you usually get hungry and start wishing you could have a snack during the school day? What time of day do you usually start getting hungry?

◆ If your teacher assigned a big project, giving you choices of how to do it, would you prefer to:

   – Make an oral presentation in front of the class?

   – Tape-record something?

   – Act it out/drama?

   – Build something? (e.g., from clay or wood)

   – Draw something?

   – Write something/type it or have someone else type it?

◆ Do you think you are good at building things? Taking things apart and putting them back together?

◆ Do you like listening to stories?

◆ Are you good at learning words to songs?

◆ Do you like to: read? write stories? do math? do science experiments? do art projects? sing? dance? play any sports—which ones?

◆ What school subjects and activities do you usually do best in? What do you like about those subjects/activities?

◆ What are the subjects/activities that you usually have the hardest time doing at school? What don't you like about those subjects/activities?

◆ What kind of school assignments do you dread, or hate having to do?

◆ Tell me what you think you are really good at. What do you think you are not so good at?

◆ Do you ever feel you cannot concentrate in class and have problems paying attention? What kinds of things distract you?

◆ How is it easier for you to learn: when someone explains something carefully to you or when someone shows you?

◆ If you have to give directions to somewhere or instructions for how to do something, is it easier for you to explain and tell that person or is it easier for you to draw a map or write it down for them?

◆ When do you concentrate best and prefer to do your homework: soon after you get home from school? have a break (play first) after getting home from school, but do it before dinner? do it after dinner?

◆ What are your favorite things to do at home?

◆ If you had the chance, what would you love to learn to do? For example, if you could take special lessons or have someone work with you to teach you, what would you really want to learn how to do?

◆ At home, where do you usually do your homework? If you had your choice, in what place in the house would you like to do your homework/study?

◆ Pretend that your parents would build you or buy whatever you needed in your home for a good study space. What would it look like and have in it?

◆ Do you like to be alone or with someone else around you when studying/doing homework? Do you need it to be real quiet? Do you like having some music or background noise when studying?

◆ At school (in this classroom) name five people you prefer to work with in partner activities. Don't name your best friends; give me names of students with whom you can productively get work done well.

◆ If you were to work towards earning a special privilege, activity, or other reward at school, name some things you would like to be able to earn.

◆ What do you think is important for your teacher to know about you?

◆ If you were promised a trip to Hawaii with your family and also $10,000 for spending money only if you got an A on a very difficult test (for example, a social studies test covering four chapters, with lots of information and stuff to memorize and learn):

- How would you want your teacher to teach it to you? Tell me exactly what you would like your teacher to do in class so that you can learn the information.

- How would you go about memorizing all the information you were taught?

- How would you need to study at home? What kind of help would you want your parents to give you? Do you want to study alone? With someone? Tell me as much as you can.

NOTE:

Teachers choosing to interview students will need to record responses either in direct notes, on a tape recorder, or a combination of both.

74. RECOMMENDED RESOURCES AND ORGANIZATIONS

Books, Materials, and Programs Recommended for Teaching and Motivating

Organization and Study Skills

Archer, Anita and Gleason, Mary. *Skills for School Success* (grades 3–6) (N. Billerica, MA: Curriculum Associates, Inc., 1989; 800-225-0248).

Custer, S., McKean, K., Meyers, C., Murphy, D., Olesen, S., and Smoak, S. *SMARTS: A Study Skills Resource Guide* (Longmont, CO: Sopris West, Inc., 1990).

Schumm, Jeanne Shay and Radencich, Marguerite. *School Power—Strategies for Succeeding in School* (Minneapolis, MN: Free Spirit Publishing, 1992).

Spizman, Robyn and Garber, Marianne. *Helping Kids Get Organized* (Carthage, IL: Good Apple, 1995).

Behavior Management and Discipline

Canter, Lee and Canter, Marlene. *Succeeding with Difficult Students* (Santa Monica, CA: Lee Cantor & Associates, 1993).

Garber, Stephen, Garber, Marianne, and Spizman, Robyn. *Good Behavior— Over 1,200 Sensible Solutions to Your Child's Problems from Birth to Age 12* (New York: St. Martin's Paperbacks, 1987).

Rhode, Ginger, Jenson, William R., and Reavis, H. Kenton. *The Tough Kid Book (Practical Classroom Management Strategies)* (Longmont, CO: Sopris West, 1995).

Rhode, Ginger, Jenson, William R., and Reavis, H. Kenton. *The Tough Kid Tool Box* (Longmont, CO: Sopris West, 1995).

Sprick, Randall S. *Discipline in the Secondary Classroom: A Problem-by-Problem Survival Guide* (West Nyack, NY: The Center for Applied Research in Education, 1985).

Reading, Writing, Spelling, and Vocabulary

Bornstein, Scott J. *Memory Techniques for Vocabulary Mastery* (Canoga Park, CA: Bornstein Memory Improvement Programs, 1988).

Bridges to Reading (Developed by Parents' Educational Resource Center, underwritten by the Charles and Helen Schwab Foundation, P.O. Box 389, Brisbane, CA 94005-0389; 800-471-9545). A comprehensive kit full of step-by-step strategies to identify, understand, and address your child's reading problem.

Greene, Victoria E. and Enfield, Mary Lee. *Project Read—Language Circle* (Bloomington, MN: Language Circle Enterprise, P.O. Box 20631, Bloomington, MN 55420; 612-884-4880). Highly recommended multisensory program for teaching phonology, comprehension, and written expression.

Levine, Michael. *The Kid's Address Book: Over 3,000 Addresses of Celebrities, Athletes, Entertainers, and More . . .* (New York: Perigee Books, 1997).

Rief, Sandra. *Simply Phonics—Quick & Easy* (Birmingham, AL: EBSCO Curriculum Materials,1993; 800-633-8623).

Rief, Sandra and Heimburge, Julie. *How to Reach & Teach All Students in the Inclusive Classroom* (West Nyack, NY: The Center for Applied Research in Education, 1996). Contains numerous lessons, strategies and ready-to-use language arts activities as well as math and other curricular areas especially for grades 3–8.

Routman, Regie. *Invitations—Changing as Teachers and Learners K-12* (Portsmouth, NH: Heinemann, 1991).

The Stevenson Program (Stevenson Learning Skills, Inc., 8 Commonwealth Ave., Attleboro Falls, MA 02763-1014; 800-343-1211). An effective alternative approach for teaching reading and writing—based upon imagery, mnemonics, and multisensory techniques.

Stowe, Cynthia. *Spelling Smart! A Ready-to-Use Activities Program for Students with Spelling Difficulties* (West Nyack, NY: The Center for Applied Research in Education, 1995).

Walker, Rena M. *Accelerating Literacy Handbook* (San Diego, CA: Walker Enterprises, 1995).

Waring, Cynthia Conway. *Developing Independent Readers: Strategy-Oriented Reading Activities for Learners with Special Needs* (West Nyack, NY: The Center for Applied Research in Education, 1995).

Math

Baretta-Lorton, Robert. *Patterns & Connections in Mathematics* (Saratoga, CA: Center for Innovation in Education, 1993).

Burns, Marilyn. *About Teaching Mathematics* (Sausalito, CA: Math Solutions Publications, 1992).

Rodriguez, Dave and Judy. *Times Tables the Easy Way—A Picture Method of Learning the Multiplication Tables* (Sandy, Utah: Key Publishers, Inc., 1994).

Semple, Janice L. *Semple Math* (Stevenson Learning Skills, Inc., 8 Commonwealth Ave., Attleboro Falls, MA 02763-1014; 800-343-1211). Teaches math facts, computation, place value, regrouping, numeral formation, etc., through a creative approach of imagery, association, and memory clues.

TouchMath (Innovative Learning Concepts, 6760 Corporate Dr., Colorado Springs, CO 80919-1999; 800-888-9191). Teaches basic math skills through a technique of touching and visualizing points strategically placed on numerals.

Self-Esteem

Borda, Michele. *Esteem Builders: K-8 Self-Esteem Curriculum for Improving Student Achievement, Behavior and School Climate* (Rolling Hills Estates, CA: Jalmar Press, 1989).

Brooks, Robert. *The Self-Esteem Teacher* (Circle Pines, MN: American Guidance Service, 1991).

Other Recommended Books for Educators

Flynn, Kris. *Graphic Organizers . . . Helping Children Think Visually* (Cypress, GA: Creative Teaching Press, Inc., 1995).

Forte, Imogene and Schurr, Sandra. *The Definitive Middle School Guide* (Nashville, TN: Incentive Publications, 1993).

Gibbs, Jeanne. *Tribes—A New Way of Learning Together* (Santa Rosa, CA: Center Source Publications, 1994).

Huth, Holly Young. *Centerplay: Focusing Your Child's Energy* (New York: Simon & Schuster, 1984). Recommended for parents as well as teachers for teaching relaxation, visualization, and guided imagery.

Books about ADD/ADHD and other Related Issues

Barkley, Russell A. *Taking Charge of ADHD—The Complete, Authoritative Guide for Parents* (New York: Guilford Press, 1995).

Bender, William N. *Understanding ADHD: A Practical Guide for Teachers and Parents* (Upper Saddle River, NJ: Prentice Hall, 1997).

CH.A.D.D. *ADD and Adolescence: Strategies for Success from CH.A.D.D.* (Plantation, FL: CH.A.D.D. National, 1996).

Coleman, Wendy S. *Attention Deficit Disorders, Hyperactivity & Associated Disorders* (Madison, WI: Calliope Books, 1993).

Dendy, Chris A. Zeigler. *Teenagers with ADD—A Parents' Guide* (Bethesda, MD: Woodbine House, 1995).

DuPaul, George and Stoner, Gary. *ADHD in the Schools: Assessment and Intervention Strategies* (New York: Guilford Press, 1994).

Flick, Grad L. *Power Parenting for ADD/ADHD: A Parent's Guide for Managing Difficult Behaviors* (West Nyack, NY: The Center for Applied Research in Education, 1996).

Fowler, Mary C. *Maybe You Know My Kid: A Parent's Guide to Identifying, Understanding and Helping Your Child with Attention Deficit Disorder* (New York: Carol Publishing Group, 1990).

Garber, Stephen, Garber, Marianne, and Spizman, Robyn F. *Is Your Child Hyperactive? Inattentive? Impulsive? Distractible?—Helping the ADD/Hyperactive Child* (New York: Villard Books, 1990).

Goldstein, Sam and Goldstein, Michael. *Hyperactivity: Why Won't My Child Pay Attention?* (New York: John Wiley & Sons, 1992).

Goldstein, Sam and Mather, N. *Overcoming Underachieving: An Action Guide for Parents of Children with School Problems.* (New York: Wiley Interscience Press, 1998).

Gordon, Michael and McClure, F. Daniel. *The Down & Dirty Guide to Adult ADD* (GSI Publications, Inc., P.O. Box 746, DeWitt, NY 13214).

Hallowell, Edward. *When You Worry About the Child You Love—Emotional and Learning Problems in Children* (New York: Simon & Schuster, 1996).

Hallowell, Edward and Ratey, John. *Driven to Distraction* (New York: Pantheon Books, 1994).

Hartmann, Thom. *Attention Deficit Disorder: A Different Perception* (Grass Valley, CA: Underwood Books, 1993).

Ingersoll, Barbara and Goldstein, Sam. *Attention Deficit Disorder and Learning Disabilities: Realities, Myths, and Controversial Treatments* (New York: Doubleday, 1993).

Ingersoll, Barbara and Goldstein, Sam. *Lonely, Sad and Angry: A Parent's Guide to Depression in Children and Adolescents* (New York: Doubleday, 1995).

Johnson, Dorothy Davies. *I Can't Sit Still: Educating and Affirming Inattentive and Hyperactive Children* (Santa Cruz, CA: ETR Associates, 1992).

Jones, Claire. *Sourcebook for Children with Attention Deficit Disorder—A Management Guide for Early Childhood Professionals and Parents* (Tucson, AZ: Communication Skill Builders, 1991).

Katz, Mark. *On Playing a Poor Hand Well—Insights from the Lives of Those Who Have Overcome Childhood Risks and Adversities* (New York: W. W. Norton & Co., 1997).

Kilcarr, Patrick and Quinn, Patricia. *Voices From Fatherhood: Fathers, Sons, and ADHD* (New York: Brunner/Mazel, Inc., 1997).

Latham, Peter S. & Latham, Patricia. *Documentation and the Law (For Professionals Concerned with ADD/LD and Those They Serve)* (Washington, DC: JKL Communications, 1996).

Levine, Mel. *All Kinds of Minds* (Cambridge, MA: Educators Publishing Service, 1993).

Levine, Mel. *Keeping a Head in School: A Student's Guide About Learning Abilities and Learning Disorders* (Cambridge, MA: Educators Publishing Service, 1994).

McCarney, Stephen and Bauer, Angela. *The Parent's Guide: Solutions to Today's Most Common Behavior Problems in the Home* (Columbia, MO: Hawthorne Educational Services, 1989).

McEwan, Elaine. *Attention Deficit Disorder—A Guide for Parents & Educators* (Wheaton, IL: Harold Shaw Publishers, 1995).

Nadeau, Kathleen. *ADD in the Workplace* (New York: Brunner/Mazel, Inc., 1997).

Parker, Harvey. *The ADD Hyperactivity Handbook for Schools* (Plantation, FL: Impact Publications, 1993).

Parker, Harvey. *The ADD Hyperactivity Handbook for Parents, Teachers and Kids* (Plantation, FL: Impact Publications, 1988).

Pierangelo, Roger and Jacoby, Robert. *Parents' Complete Special Education Guide* (West Nyack, NY: The Center for Applied Research in Education, 1996).

Quinn, Patricia and Stern, Judith. *Putting on the Brakes: Young People's Guide to Understanding ADHD* (New York: Magination Press, 1991).

Rief, Sandra. *How to Reach and Teach ADD/ADHD Children* (West Nyack, NY: The Center for Applied Research in Education, 1993).

Rief, Sandra and Heimburge, Julie. *How to Reach & Teach All Students in the Inclusive Classroom* (West Nyack, NY: The Center for Applied Research in Education, 1996).

Shapiro, Edward and Cole, Christine. *Behavior Change in the Classroom: Self-Management Interventions* (New York: Guilford Press, 1994).

Silver, Larry B. *The Misunderstood Child: A Guide for Parents of Children with Learning Disabilities,* Second Edition (Blue Ridge Summit, PA: TAB Books, 1992).

Stern, Judith and Ben-Ami, Uzi. *Many Ways to Learn—Young People's Guide to Learning Disabilities* (New York: Magination Press, 1996).

Turecki, Stanley. *The Difficult Child* (New York: Bantam Books, 1989).

Videotapes

Barkley, Russell A. *ADHD: What Do We Know?* (35 min.) Guilford Press Video, 1992.

Barkley, Russell A. *ADHD: What Can We Do?* (37 min.) Guilford Press Video, 1992.

Barkley, Russell A. *ADHD in Adults* (36 min.) Guilford Press Video, 1994.

Barkley, Russell A. *Managing the Defiant Child.* Guilford Press Video, 1997.

Barkley, Russell A. *Understanding the Defiant Child.* Guilford Press Video, 1997.

Brooks, Robert. *Look What You've Done! (Learning Disabilities & Self-Esteem: Stories of Hope and Resilience)* The Learning Disabilities Project at WETA, Washington, DC, PBS Video, 1997. PBS Video, 1320 Braddock Place, Alexandria, VA 22314; 800-344-3337.

Computers & ADD/LD: How Computers and Multimedia Can Empower Those with Attention and Learning Differences. A.I. Media, P.O. Box 333, Chelsea, MI 48118.

Goldstein, Sam and Goldstein, Michael. *Why Won't My Child Pay Attention?* (76 min.) Salt Lake City, UT: Neurology, Learning and Behavior Center, 1989.

Goldstein, Sam and Goldstein, Michael. *Educating Inattentive Children* (120 min.) Salt Lake City, UT: Neurology, Learning and Behavior Center, 1990.

LaVoie, Richard. *How Difficult Can This Be?: The F.A.T. City Workshop,* PBS Video, 1989.

LaVoie, Richard. *Learning Disabilities and Social Skills: Last One Picked . . . First One Picked On,* PBS Video, 1994.

Office of Special Education & Rehabilitation Services. *Education of Children with Attention Deficit Disorder.* A kit for parents and educators including a video for parents—*Facing the Challenges of ADD;* a video for teachers—*One Child in Every Classroom;* and other written information. Division of Innovation & Development, Office of Special Education Programs, Office of Special Education & Rehabilitation Services, U.S. Dept. of Education, 1995.

Phelan, Thomas W. *1-2-3 Magic: Training Your Preschooler and Preteen to Do What You Want Them to Do!* (120 min.) Glen Ellyn, IL: Child Management, Inc., 800-442-4453.

Rief, Sandra. *ADHD: Inclusive Instruction & Collaborative Practices* (38 min.) Viewing effective strategies and interventions in general education classrooms. Port Chester, NY: National Professional Resources, Inc., 1995; 800-453-7461 or available through Educational Resource Specialists: 800-682-3528.

Rief, Sandra. *How to Help Your Child Succeed in School—Strategies & Guidance for Parents of Children with ADHD and/or Learning Disabilities* (56 min.) Viewing parents and school-age children demonstrating numerous strategies to help improve organization/study habits, homework, and academic skills in reading, writing, and math. San Diego, CA: Educational Resource Specialists, 1997; 800-682-3528.

Robin, Arthur and Weiss, Sharon. *Managing Oppositional Youth: Effective, Practical Strategies for Managing the Behavior of Hard to Manage Kids and Teens!* (45 min.) Specialty Press Videos, 1997. (Available through ADD Warehouse.)

Audiotapes

Lamb, Gary. Music compositions at 60 beats per minute. Available through Golden Gate Records, P.O. Box 4100, Santa Cruz, CA 95063; 800-772-7701.

Mills, Jerry. *Urgent Reply.* Cassettes and CDs of songs regarding living with ADD. Impulse Presentations, P.O. Box 572, Marquette, MI 49855; 906-228-5736.

Recommended Vendors for Resources on Attention Deficit Disorders

ADD WAREHOUSE
300 Northwest 70th Avenue, Suite 102
Plantation, FL 33317
800-233-9273

COUNCIL FOR EXCEPTIONAL CHILDREN RESOURCES
1920 Association Dr., Dept. K4092
Reston, VA 22091-1589
800-232-7323

EDUCATIONAL RESOURCE SPECIALISTS
P.O. Box 19207
San Diego, CA 92159
800-682-3528

FREE SPIRIT PUBLISHING
400 First Avenue North, Suite 616
Minneapolis, MN 55401-17300
800-735-7323

GUILFORD PUBLICATIONS, INC. (GUILFORD PRESS)
Dept. Y, 72 Spring Street
New York, NY 10012
800-365-7006

HAWTHORNE EDUCATIONAL SERVICES, INC.
800 Gray Oak Drive
Columbia, MO 65201
800-542-1673

THE MASTER TEACHING PLANNING CATALOG
Leadership Lane
P.O. Box 1207
Manhattan, KS 66502-0038
800-669-9633

NATIONAL PROFESSIONAL RESOURCES, INC.
25 South Regent Street
Port Chester, NY 10573
800-453-7461

PAUL BROOKES PUBLISHING CO.
P.O. Box 10624
Baltimore, MD 21285-0624
800-638-3775

PRENTICE HALL/CENTER FOR APPLIED RESEARCH IN EDUCATION
200 Old Tappan Road
Old Tappan, NJ 07675
800-922-0579

NOTE: In addition to these recommended resources on ADD/ADHD, there are other very high-quality materials on attention deficit disorders (books, publications, newsletters, articles, audio- and video-cassettes, diagnostic and intervention tools) that can be found in bookstores, websites, and catalogues of vendors specializing in this area.

National Organizations

AMERICAN OCCUPATIONAL THERAPY ASSOCIATION
1383 Piccard Drive
Rockville, MD 20852
800-729-2682

AMERICAN PSYCHOLOGICAL ASSOCIATION
1200 17th Street, N.W.
Washington, DC 20036
800-374-2721

AMERICAN SPEECH-LANGUAGE-HEARING ASSOCIATION
10801 Rockville Pike
Rockville, MD 20852
800-638-8255

CH.A.D.D. (CHILDREN AND ADULTS WITH ATTENTION DEFICIT DISORDERS)
499 NW 70th Avenue, Suite 308
Plantation, FL 33317
954-587-3700
http://www.chadd.org/

CH.A.D.D. is the largest national organization devoted to improving the lives of those with attention deficit disorders and those who care for them, and increasing awareness about ADD/ADHD. There are hundreds of local chapters throughout the United States. CH.A.D.D. is an excellent source of information and support, with regional conferences, an annual international conference, and two excellent publications— *Attention!* and *CHADDER Box.*

COUNCIL FOR EXCEPTIONAL CHILDREN
1920 Association Drive
Reston, VA 22091-1589
800-232-7323

COUNCIL FOR LEARNING DISABILITIES
P.O. Box 40303
Overland Park, KS 66204
913-492-8755

LEARNING DISABILITIES ASSOCIATION OF AMERICA (LDA)
4156 Library Road
Pittsburgh, PA 15234
412-341-1515

NATIONAL ADDA (NATIONAL ATTENTION DEFICIT DISORDER
   ASSOCIATION)
P.O. Box 972
Mentor, OH 44061
800-487-2282

ADDA is another national organization dedicated to helping those with attention deficit disorders, and providing up-to-date information, resources and support.

NATIONAL CENTER FOR LEARNING DISABILITIES
99 Park Avenue
New York, NY 10016
212-687-7211

NATIONAL INFORMATION CENTER FOR CHILDREN AND YOUTH WITH
   DISABILITIES
P.O. Box 1492
Washington, DC 20013-1492
800-999-5599

ORTON DYSLEXIA SOCIETY
Chester Bldg., Suite 382
8600 La Salle Road
Baltimore, MD 21204

TOURETTE SYNDROME ASSOCIATION
4240 Bell Blvd.
Bayside, NY 11361-2874
718-224-2999

Other Resources

RECORDINGS FOR THE BLIND & DYSLEXIC
20 Roszel Road
Princeton, NJ 08540
800-221-4792 (for ordering books on tape)

FRANKLIN LEARNING RESOURCES
122 Burrs Rd.
Mount Holly, NJ 08060
800-525-9673

(Franklin Learning Resources has a number of electronic aids from simple to sophisticated such as spell-checks, dictionaries, thesaurus that are very helpful for those with learning difficulties)

INTERACTIVE TEACHING NETWORK
The University of Georgia, College of Education
577 Aderhold Hall
Athens, GA 30602-7151
800-296-4770

(Producers of ADDNET Series—national teleconferences on ADD/ADHD presented by specialists and leaders in the field)

Index

Accidents, 10, 19, 63
Achievement tests, in diagnosis, 24
Activity reinforcers, 65, 112–113
Adapting learning materials, 153–157
  math materials, 153–154
  printed materials, 154
  reading materials, 155
Adderall, 37
Administrators
  effective, 35
  support for teachers, 45
Adolescents, 210–213
  monitoring, 212, 213
Adults, symptoms in, 5–6
Amytriptyline, 38
Anger control, 62, 108
Assessing learning styles, 236–239
Assessment factors, 140–142
Assignments
  modifying, 121, 132, 144, 185–186
  remembering, 197–198
Attention
  focusing, 124–125
  maintaining, 126–127, 131–133
Attention-getting strategies, 123–125

Barkley, Dr. Russell, 13, 19
Behavior rating scales, 23
Behavioral strategies, 54–56, 57–67
  for teachers, 94–96, 100–106
  young child, 205
Behaviors
  adolescent, 210
  hyperactive/impulsive, 62–64,
    107–111
  in public, 60–61

in younger children, 204–205
observation during assessment, 24
preventing problem, 57–59, 92–103
rating of, 23, 30–31
reinforcing, 57–59
Birth injuries, 14
Brain
  chemistry, 15
  deficiency of neurotransmitters,
    14
  glucose metabolism in, 15
  physiology, 4, 14–15
Breathing techniques, 214

Calendars, classroom, 117, 197
Causes, 8, 14–15
Characteristics
  effective preschool teachers, 206
  effective teachers, 33–34, 107
  emotionality, 10
  hyperactivity, 9
  impulsivity, 9–10
  inattention, 12–13
  of ADHD child, 3–4, 9–13
  positive traits, 21, 201–202
Charts, behavior, 114
Children and Adults with Attention
    Deficit Disorders (CH.A.D.D.),
    47–48, 87
Chores, 58, 80, 203
Civil Rights Office, 232–235
Classroom
  boundaries, 110
  challenging times, 104–106
  distractions, 97
  effective, 92–93, 100–103

Classroom *(cont.)*
  environment, 134–136
    preschool, 208
  furniture, 136
  nonverbal signals in, 102, 104,
    109, 128
  preventing behavior problems,
    100–103, 104–106, 107–111
  reading materials, 160
  rules, 100–101
  seating, 97, 101, 131, 134, 136
Color
  for attention, 123
  in presentations, 152
  to aid memory, 199
Communication
  during diagnosis, 195
  school/home, 35, 86, 88, 103,
    143
  with other teachers, 137, 144
Comprehension, *See* Reading
Computer, editing, 181
Computer, writing, 185
Computers, 154
  editing, 181
  writing, 185
Consequences, 55, 57–58, 95
Contracts, 96, 102, 114, 128
Cooperative learning, 218
Counseling, 108
  for parents, 47
  in adolescence, 210
  in treatment program, 28
Creativity, 5
Cure, 7, 8
Cursive writing, 183
Cylert, 37

Daydreaming, 12
Definitions, ADHD, 3–4
Delayed gratification, 10
Descriptions, ADHD, 3–4
Desiprimine, 38
Desk space, organizing, 115–116
Developmental disabilities,
  204–205
Dexedrine, 37

Diagnosis
  comprehensive evaluation,
    22–25
  history, 22
  of similar conditions, 16–17
  teacher's "don't" list, 139
  teacher's role, 137–139
  team approach, 194–195
Diagnostic and Statistical Manual
  (DSMIV), 22
Dietary causes, 15
Directions, giving, 79–80, 129–130,
  197–198
Disabilities
  and educational rights, 227–228,
    232
  definition, 232
Disorganization, 68–73
  See also Organization skills
Disputes with school district,
  230–231
Distractible students, 131–133
  earphones, 132, 135
  manipulatives, 110, 132
Documentation, school records, 23,
  26, 85

Editing, 180
Environment, classroom, 92–93,
  134–136
  See also Classroom
Environmental causes, 15
Evaluation
  assessment forms, 140–142
  initial, 22–25, 84–85
  process, 84–85, 88
  professionals, 25, 85
  school-based, 138–139
  team, 194–196
Extracurricular activities, 122

Fearlessness, 10
Feedback, *See* Positive reinforcement;
    Negative reinforcement
Feedback, immediate, 156
Feelings, expressing, 56, 63
Fidgetiness, 5, 9, 210

Focusing, 124–125, 128
  See also Attention
Following directions, 80

Girls, diagnosis in, 5, 13
Glucose metabolism, in brain,
  14–15
Goldstein, Sam, 15, 19
Grading, 146–147
  older students, 211–212
Graphic organizers, 168–169, 174
Guided imagery, 215–216

Handwriting, 182–186
  older students, 183
Heredity, 14
High-risk behavior, 5, 10
History, role in diagnosis, 22
Home environment, 52–53, 57–59
  modifying, 81–83
Homework
  and medication, 120
  assignments, 120–121
  projects, 121
  schedule, 70, 74
  space, 68, 81, 83
  supplies, 68–69, 73
  tips for teachers, 120–122
Humor, 214
Hyperactivity
  description, 9
  in class, 107–111
Hyperkinetic disorder, 6
Hyperthyroidism, 14

Identification of ADHD students, *See*
  Student Study Team
Imiprimine, 38
Impulsivity
  definition, 3
  description, 9–10
  in adolescents, 210
  in class, 107–111
Inattentiveness, description, 3
Inclusive classroom, 44, 233
Inconsistent performance, 4, 12,
  143

Individualized Education Program
  (IEP), 88–89, 194, 226–231
  and legislation, 226–231
  parental input, 228
  required information, 229
Individuals with Disabilities
  Education Act (IDEA), 226–228
Information release form, 26, 85,
  138
Ingersoll, Barbara D., 15
Initial evaluation
  decision to pursue, 84–85
  from teacher, 137–139
Instructions, giving, 79–80, 197–198
Intelligence, 5
  assessing, 24
Interest interview, 236–239
Interventions
  documenting, 137–138
  effectiveness of, 7–8
  for success in school, 18

Kindergarten strategies, 204–209

Language skills, 171–172, 180–181
Law, rights of child, 86, 226–227
Laziness, 143
Learning assessments, modifying,
  145–148
Learning styles, 193, 202, 208
  student interest interview,
  236–239
Lectures, modifying, 149–152
Legislation, 226–228, 232–235

Manipulatives
  for distractible students, 110, 132
  math, 187
Martial arts, 28
Material reinforcers, 66, 113–114
Materials, modifying, 153–157
Math difficulties, 187–191
Medical testing, in diagnosis, 24–25
Medication, 28, 37–39, 40–43
  adderall, 37
  amytriptyline, 38
  buproprion, 39

Medication *(cont.)*
  clonidine, 39
  combining, 39
  cylert, 37
  decision to medicate, 40
  desiprimine, 38
  dexedrine, 37
  fluoxetine (Prozac), 39
  imiprimine, 38
  nortriptyline, 39
  parents' role, 42–43
  rebound effect, 38
  ritalin, 37
  stimulants, 37
  strategies for remembering, 41
  teachers' role, 40–42
  too much, 39
  tricyclic antidepressants, 38
  trough effect, 41
Memory skills, 197–198, 199–200
  mnemonic devices, 199
  music, 200
Metacognitive strategies, 159
Minimal brain dysfunction, 6
Model, writing, 175
Multimodal treatment program, 28,
    194–196
Multiplication, 190–191
Music, 82, 97, 135, 208
  for memory, 200
  for relaxation, 216–217

Negative feedback, 52
Negativity, in classroom, 201–202
Neurobiology, 4, 14–15
Neurotransmitters, and medication,
    37–38
Note-taking, 185–186

Oppositional-defiant disorder,
    19–20
Organization skills, 6, 13, 68–73
  class work space, 115–116
  materials, 115–116
  tips for teachers, 118–119
Overhead projectors, 125, 151
Over-medication, 39
Overview of ADHD, 5–8

Parents
  and SST, 222–223
  as advocates, 86–89
  blaming, 47
  developing social skills, 221
  effective, 35–36, 54–59
  getting child organized, 68–73
  help with homework, 71–78
  home environment, 52–53,
      57–59
  input in IEP, 228
  issues summarized, 50–51
  managing medication, 42–43
  marital problems, 47
  preventing behavior problems in
      public, 60–61
  promoting self-esteem, 203
  reading strategies, 169–170
  resources for, 86, 240–249
  rights under IDEA, 230–231
  tips for giving directions, 79–80
  training and support, 29, 42–43,
      47–49
  role in diagnosis, 26
Performance, 4, 12
  inconsistent, 143
  tests, 25
Personality traits, positive, 21
Phonetics, 178–179
Physical activity, 64, 83
Physical exam, 24
Point system, classroom, 114
Portfolio assessment, 147
Positive feedback, *See* Positive
    reinforcement
Positive reinforcement, 54–56, 61, 63,
    65–67, 95
  classroom, 101, 108
  for on-task behavior, 128, 131
  of social skills, 220
  older students, 101
  young child, 207–208
Positive reinforcers, 112–114
Praise, 57, 58, 61, 65, 72, 79–80,
    94
  See also Positive reinforcement
Preschool issues, 204–209
Prevalence of disorder, ix, 5

Preventing behaviors
  classroom, 94–96, 100–103
  in public, 60–61
Problem-solving, 189
Professionals
  attitude of, 29
  support team, 34, 44–45
Prognosis, 6
Proofreading, 180
Proximity control, 95, 100
Public places, 60–61
Punishment, 52, 55
  See also Consequences

Questionnaires, 30–31
  student interests, 236–239
Quiet area, 82

Rating scales, 30–31
Reading
  comprehension, 165–169
  disabilities, 159–161
  pre-reading, 165
  silent, 159, 163
  vocabulary, 160, 163–165
Recordkeeping, 89, 137
Redirecting students, 95, 100, 102
  pre-school child, 206
Referral forms, 140–142
Rehabilitation Act, 232
Reinforcers, 65–67, 112–114
Relaxation, 214–215
Rentention, *See* Memory skills
Reports and projects, 70, 77
Research, 8, 14, 15
  what is known, 5–8
Response cost, 96, 109, 128
Restlessness, 9, 210
Rewards and consequences, 54–55
Ritalin, 37
Rules, and expectations, 54, 57, 60, 62
  classroom, 94

School meetings, 87, 88
School nurse, managing medication, 40
School projects, 70, 77

School
  administration, 35
  dropout rate, 19
  effective, 32
  evaluation team, 85
  involvement in diagnosis, 26–27
  records review for diagnosis, 23, 26, 85
  strategies for success, 19
  supportive staff, 36
  suspensions, 19
School-based evaluation, 27, 85, 88
Seatwork, keeping on-task, 128
Section 504, 232–235
Self-esteem, 52–53, 122, 201–203
Sex differences, 5
Side effects, medication, 37–39, 43
Signals, use in classroom, 102, 104, 109, 128–129, 131
Social development, 109, 218–221
Social reinforcers, 65, 112
Social skills, 192–193
Special education, 226–227
Spelling, 176–179
Sports, in treatment program, 28
SQ3R technique, 167–168
Storage, materials, 134
Strategies
  anger control, 62, 102
  classroom behaviors, 94–96, 100–106
  distractible students, 131–133
  editing, 180–181
  effective parenting, 35–36, 54–59
  effective schools, 32
  effective teaching, 33–34, 97–99
  getting attention, 123–125
  giving directions, 129–130
  handwriting, 182–184, 185–186
  keeping on-task, 128, 131–133
  lesson presentation, 149–152
  math skills, 187–188
  memory skills, 197–198, 199–200
  organizing, 68–73
  prewriting, 173–174
  reading comprehension, 165–169
  reading skills, 159–170
  relaxation, 62

Strategies *(cont.)*
  school success, 18
  spelling, 176–179
  testing, 145–148
  word recognition, 163–165, 178
Structure
  in classroom, 94, 107
  in home environment, 62, 81–83
  in lesson presentation, 150–151
Student Study Team (SST), 84–85,
    137–139, 222–225
  records, 223
Study buddies, 118, 120–121, 163
Study skills, older students, 211
Study tips, 76, 81–83
  See also Homework
Supervision, unstructured class
    time, 105–106
Supplies, storage, 134
Support
  CH.A.D.D., 87
  for parents, 47–49
  for teachers, 44–46, 107, 143
  groups, 47–48, 87, 195
  resources, 240–249
  team, 34, 44–45, 137, 143
Symptoms, 5, 9–11
  evaluating, 25
  similarities to other disorders,
    16–17
  See also Characteristics

Tape recorder, 153
Teachers
  and medication, 40–42
  behavior management, 94–111
  "don't" lists, 139, 143–144

  effective, 33–34, 94–99
  issues summarized, 90–91
  monitoring of medicated students,
    40–42, 196
  promoting self-esteem, 201–203
  questionnaires, 31
  role in diagnosis, 26
  support for, 44–46
  training for, 44, 212
Team approach
  IEP, 228–231
  SST, 222
  to treatment, 7, 194–196
Team teaching, 44, 196
Testing, 145–148
Time management, 69–70, 116–119
Time-out, 96, 207
Touchmath, 188
Treatment program
  medication, 37–43
  multimodal, 28, 194–196
  overview, 28
Types of ADHD, 3–4

Visual aids, 125–126, 152
Visualization, 214
Vocabulary, 160, 163–165
Volunteer work, 203

Word-attack skills, 163–165
Writing
  assignments, modifying, 185–186
  difficulties, 155–156, 185–186
  skills, 171–172

Yoga, 215